THE HISTORY OF
PROFESSIONAL
BASKETBALL
SINCE 1896

THE HISTORY OF
PROFESSIONAL
BASKETBALL
SINCE 1896

GLENN DICKEY

STEIN AND DAY/*Publishers*/New York

First published in 1982
Copyright © 1982 by Glenn Dickey
All rights reserved
Designed by Louis A. Ditizio
Printed in the United States of America
STEIN AND DAY/*Publishers*
Scarborough House
Briarcliff Manor, N.Y. 10510

Library of Congress Cataloging in Publication Data

Dickey, Glenn.
  The history of professional basketball.

  Bibliography: p.
  Includes index.
  1. Basketball—United States—History. I. Title.
GV885.7.D52   796.357′0973   81-40334
ISBN 0-8128-2823-2   AACR2

To Nancy and Scott,
whose love and encouragement
have always been
very important to me

Acknowledgments

With sadness, I acknowledge my debt to Bruce Hale, whose information and reminiscences of pro basketball in the '40s and '50s were invaluable. Bruce died before this book could reach print.

Publicity directors for NBA clubs have also been extremely helpful in providing information and pictures for me, as were Matt Winick, director of publicity for the NBA, and Lee Williams, of the Basketball Hall of Fame.

I have been fortunate enough to be able to talk to many former players and coaches, who gave me first-hand information on teams and players I had not seen. Alex Hannum, whose playing and coaching career spanned four decades of professional basketball, was especially helpful in providing anecdotes and insights.

I owe my love of pro basketball to my dad, who continued rooting for the Minneapolis Lakers even after we had moved from Minnesota to California. But it was my editor, Benton Arnovitz, who conceived this project.

My debt to Magic Johnson for the Introduction that follows is self-evident—but gratefully acknowledged nevertheless.

Contents

Magic Johnson, soaring for two points against Houston, was the catalyst with his ability and personality as the Los Angeles Lakers won a dramatic NBA championship. *(Los Angeles Lakers)*

Introduction

by EARVIN (MAGIC) JOHNSON

Professional basketball has been a part of my life almost as long as I can remember, first watching it, of course, and now playing it.

When I was a kid growing up in Michigan, I used to go to games with my family or friends. At that age, you always dream about being able to play pro ball, but I really had my doubts. There were such super players, and they had such super moves. I'd watch them and say, wow, how could they do that?

At this time, I seldom approached any of the players to try to talk to them. They were just so far removed from me. It was like they were in another world.

Later, when I was in high school, I talked to a lot of players. I especially remember talking to Kareem Abdul-Jabbar and Julius Erving, and George Gervin and I became good friends.

Since the games I saw were in Detroit, the Pistons were naturally a favorite team, but for some reason, I always liked Philadelphia, though I'm not sure why. It's just one of those things that kids do.

Of course, it might have been because Wilt Chamberlain was in Philadelphia when I first started watching games. Kids always pick up on a favorite player, and Wilt was mine. He was so much fun to watch, because he could do so many things.

It was the big guys I enjoyed watching the most. Those battles between Wilt and Bill Russell, for instance, were really something, and then, when Willis Reed came into the league, I really liked to watch him, too.

Of course, among the guards, I enjoyed seeing Oscar Robertson the most; he was the best I ever saw. We used to watch a lot of games on TV, and in those days, there were more regional games than national. We'd get a lot of Milwaukee contests when Oscar was playing there. I remember the Milwaukee-Chicago games especially, because it was Oscar going head-to-head against Jerry Sloan, and those were classic

But the game was played more down low then, so the big battles were between the centers. I think the game's changed somewhat since then because the players are quicker and you're seeing more big guards. However the game changes in the future, it's always going to be a big man's game.

I watched players at all positions because, when I was in high school, I played all positions—guard, forward, and center. It just depended on the team we were playing, and where my coach thought I could do the most good. I just did whatever he told me to, because it didn't really make any difference to me.

So, when I had to play center in the last game of the 1980 NBA championships, it wasn't like I wasn't comfortable there. Of course, this was the NBA, which made it a lot different from high school, believe me. But I enjoyed the challenge, and I just went out there and played. I wanted it to be fun, and it was.

By the time I got to college I was thinking seriously of the NBA, and after the first year I started thinking about turning pro after my sophomore season.

Then I put it out of my mind because I knew we had a good team and I didn't want to mess up the season because my mind wasn't on playing.

Though I didn't definitely decide that I would turn pro until just about a week before the deadline for submitting my name, winning the NCAA championship that year at Michigan State was a definite factor in my decision. That had been one of my goals, and I had reached it.

Another factor was the chance to play with Kareem. I think anybody would jump at that chance.

Plus, the city. I had never been to Los Angeles, and I really wanted a chance to live there. Most guys don't have any choice about where they're going to play. Sometimes they land with good teams in good cities, and sometimes they don't. I had the chance to be with a good team and a good city, and I took it.

That season was like a dream come true, winning the championship in my first year, and I'll never forget it. That story is in here, of course. This is the most complete book I've seen on professional basketball, and I'm happy to be in the book, along with the great stars of the past.

Preface

There are obviously different ways to approach the history of a sport. One that's been tried by others, for instance, is taking leagues season by season.

I preferred to work another way, to center my account around outstanding players, teams, and events. Thus, an individual chapter might involve a single season, such as the 1979-80 season in which Larry Bird and Magic Johnson were rookies, or a period of several years, which is true of the chapter on Wilt Chamberlain, who started his career setting scoring records on one coast and ended it with a record-setting championship team on the other coast.

Those who want to answer a question or settle a bet will find a statistical section at the back of the book.

THE HISTORY OF
PROFESSIONAL
BASKETBALL

Dr. James Naismith, the inventor of the game, holding the first basketball.
(Hall of Fame)

1. In the Beginning There Were Peach Baskets

Basketball is unique: the only truly American game. Even the Russians don't claim it. The English game of rounders may have influenced the invention of baseball, and rugby is clearly the forerunner of football, but there was never any game remotely resembling basketball until Dr. James Naismith invented it in the autumn of 1891 at Springfield, Massachusetts.

Basketball is different in another respect. Most games have evolved from simple beginnings, usually children kicking, hitting, or throwing a ball in the streets or on a playground. In contrast, basketball was invented on demand, to fill a specific need at a specific time in a specific place.

The place was a small Young Men's Christian Association (YMCA) school in Springfield which served as a training school for instructors, athletic directors, and YMCA secretaries. The curriculum required an hour of physical activity daily.

In the fall the students played football, and in the spring, baseball, but there was no winter sport. To satisfy the requirement, they performed calisthenics for an hour each day. Not surprisingly, they hated that.

Clearly, an alternative was needed, and Naismith, who had just become an instructor in the school's physical education department, was an obvious choice to develop it.

An amateur boxer in his youth and later a football player at the YMCA school, Naismith had abandoned his studies for the ministry because of his love of sports. Frequently, he had said that young men were more interested in competition than in merely achieving physical fitness. All right, then, said Dr. Luther Gulick, head of the physical education department: Develop a new game.

Naismith first thought of adapting an outdoor game, and he experimented with football, rugby, soccer, field hockey, lacrosse, and even water polo before deciding that none would work. He would have to invent a new sport.

His sport, he first decided, would have to be played with a ball, as most other team sports were. Players wouldn't be allowed to run with the ball, because he didn't want his sport to be as rough as football and rugby; if players couldn't run with the ball, it wouldn't be necessary to tackle them.

He also didn't want players throwing the ball with maximum force, so he decided they would have to aim at a target well over their heads. That, he reasoned, would force them to arch the ball. The good doctor obviously didn't foresee a Darryl Dawkins slam dunk.

Other decisions he made were based on what was available. He set the target at ten feet because that was the height of the balconies at each end of the gym, on which the targets would be placed. He used a soccer ball because the school had plenty of them. He asked the janitor for square boxes for the goals, but the janitor had none. Naismith was forced to substitute a pair of peach baskets. Hence, the name: basketball.

He set down 13 rules for the game and had his secretary type them and post them in the gym. These were the rules:

1) The ball may be thrown in any direction with one or both hands.

2) The ball may be batted in any direction with one or both hands (never with the fist).

3) A player cannot run with the ball. The player must throw it from the spot on which he catches it; allowance is to be made for a man who catches the ball when running at a good speed.

4) The ball must be held in or between the hands; the arms or body must not be used for holding it.

5) No shouldering, holding, pushing, tripping, or striking in any way the person of an opponent shall be allowed; the first infringement of this rule by any person shall count as a foul, the second shall disqualify him until the next goal is made; or, if there was evident intent to injure the person, for the whole of the game, no substitute shall be allowed.

6) A foul is striking at the ball with the fist, violation of Rules 3 or 4, or as described in Rule 5.

7) If either side makes three consecutive fouls, it shall count a goal for the opponents ("consecutive" means without the opponents in the meantime making a foul).

8) A goal shall be made when the ball is thrown or batted from the ground into the basket and stays there, providing those defending the goal do not touch or disturb the goal. If the ball rests on the edge and the opponent moves the basket, it shall count as a goal.

9) When the ball goes out of bounds, it shall be thrown into the field and played by the person first touching it. In case of a dispute, the umpire shall throw it straight into the field. The thrower-in is allowed five seconds. If he holds it longer, it shall go to the opponent. If any side persists in delaying the game, the umpire shall call a foul on them.

10) The umpire shall be judge of the men and shall note the fouls and notify the referee when three consecutive fouls have been made. He shall have power to disqualify men according to Rule 5.

11) The referee shall be judge of the ball and shall decide when the ball is in play,

in bounds, and to which side it belongs, and shall keep the time. He shall decide when a goal has been made, and keep account of the goals, with any other duties that are usually performed by a referee.

12) The time shall be two 15-minute halves, with 5 minutes' rest between.

13) The side making the most goals in that time shall be declared the winners. In case of a draw, the game may, by agreement of the captains, be continued until another goal is made.

There was one significant omission in Naismith's set of rules: the number of players to a team. Naismith didn't want to limit participation; he wanted a sport which all members of a gym class could play. Because his class numbered 18, the first basketball game was played with 9 players on a team.

The weakness in that concept was exposed when larger gym classes were exposed to the game. The nadir was reached when a Cornell class of 100 was split for its first game, 50 to a side; the ensuing action resembled a riot far more than a game.

So, in 1895, Naismith added a fourteenth rule: There would be five players to a team. The first known game matching five-man teams was played on January 16, 1896, between Chicago and Iowa, and the game has been played by five-man teams since.

The game was popular from the start. Members of Naismith's gym class went home for Christmas vacation and taught the game to friends and relatives, and it quickly spread to other schools and clubs. But because the game was new, it changed in many ways, and what evolved was considerably different from what Naismith originally planned.

Equipment changes were made almost immediately. Cylindrical baskets of heavy woven wire replaced the peach baskets a year after Naismith's game started; in another year, the modern basket with iron rim and cord basket was first used.

The ball size fluctuated for many years. A bigger ball was introduced in 1894, and the size of the ball kept growing until it eventually had to be reduced. Not until the 1930s was the size of the ball standardized.

Backboards were first used in 1895, mainly to prevent partisan fans from hanging out over the opposing team's basket, but they were optional. Those used were sometimes of wood, sometimes of wire. Not until the 1920s did wooden backboards become standard.

Naismith had only considered what we now call field goals, making no provisions for free throws, but by 1900, the rules had evolved to what has been standard since: two points for a field goal, one for a free throw.

But other rules were far different from those of the game now. After every basket, for instance, the referee threw up a jump ball at midcourt; not until 1937 was that eliminated from the rules, opening up the game immensely.

Until 1923, walking and double-dribbling were called fouls, instead of violations, which cause a team to lose possession. Until that year, too, one man on a team was designated to shoot all free throws. (Think what that could have done to Rick Barry's point totals if the rule hadn't been changed!)

Dribbling rules changed considerably before being standardized in the 1940s. Before 1916, a player wasn't permitted to shoot the ball after taking a dribble. Later, the pros allowed two-handed and interrupted dribbling for many years after it had been ruled illegal in amateur play.

Not until 1932 were rules adopted to prohibit offensive players staying more than three seconds in the "key" or lane, and to force the offensive team to get the ball past midcourt in ten seconds. And the controversial 24-second rule was not adopted by the pros for another two decades.

It was some time before courts were built specifically for basketball, so teams used whatever was available; Forrest (Phog) Allen, the legendary Kansas coach, remembered playing his first game on a court above a livery stable. Teams used armories for games, and thus often had to play on concrete floors. It was many years before wood floors became common.

Fans were a constant problem in those early days. Basketball has always been the most partisan of games because fans are much closer to the action than in football or baseball, and the rowdy, unsophisticated fans of the late nineteenth century and early twentieth were much more rabid than present-day fans.

In the Pennsylvania coal towns, for instance, there were reports that miners would heat nails with mining lamps and throw the nails at referees and opposing free-throw shooters. (Referees, in fact, sometimes carried revolvers for protection against fans.)

To protect both players and referees, courts were fully enclosed with chicken-wire netting (and, in at least one instance, a steel cage, thus leading to the term "cagers," which is still occasionally used to describe basketball players).

The wiring may have been a protection, but it was no treat for a player who dived for a loose ball and got caught in the wire. Sometimes it took a crowbar to get him out.

The game in those days more nearly resembled an indoor football scrimmage than the fast-flowing game it has become. Players wore as much protective equipment as they could—padded pants, knee guards, and elbow pads. Broken noses were common. A player was certain to be hammered when he took a shot, so he would try to shoot from the least vulnerable position, even underhanded. Certainly, no player would ever try a jump shot and thus expose himself to being hit while in the air.

It wasn't just players who got hammered, though; referees often got punched when they threw up a jump ball. It was no game for the faint of heart, but it is important to realize the context of the times in which the game was being played. Football was so brutal a sport at the time that there were campaigns to have it banned, and baseball was played much more aggressively than it is now.

The game was a slow one, too, dominated by defense. Teams would station a player, called a standing guard, at the foul line, to stop close-in shots. Sometimes, players would remain in the defensive end of the court for the whole game. As a result, games were low-scoring, with the winning team seldom getting more than 20 points.

Stalling was a common tactic, and teams even held the ball in the backcourt for long periods of time, since there was no rule prohibiting that.

(Only very basic strategy was used. A team would put its best layup shooter near the basket and then try to lure the standing guard away, so a layup could be shot. If that didn't work, another player would try a two-handed set shot. Many players, though, didn't shoot at all for the entire game.

Because the ball was often lopsided from wear, it was hard to control and there was no fancy dribbling. Indeed, one player, Dutch Wohlfarth, became famous as the "Blind Dribbler" simply because he didn't look at the ball as he was dribbling, a tactic other players never tried.

From our vantage point, able to watch the brilliant passing of Magic Johnson or the incredible mid-air moves of Julius Erving, it seems that basketball in that era must have been a dull game to watch and a tedious one to play. Yet its popularity was immediate and great.

That popularity posed a problem to the game's originators. Naismith and the YMCA officials had regarded the game as a more palatable form of exercise for gym classes; but it soon spread far beyond that. By 1895 some YMCA teams were even holding regional tournaments. The YMCA people simply couldn't reconcile the form the sport was taking—the all-out effort to win, the roughness of the game, the fan abuse—with the overall YMCA program.

And so, the YMCA moved to deemphasize the sport it had created, by discouraging the formation of teams and the holding of tournaments. It was too late. The sport was too popular. When the YMCA withdrew its support of teams, the teams stayed in business under other sponsorship.

That led, inevitably, to the start of the professional game. Without YMCA gyms, teams had to play their games elsewhere, usually in armories. Money was needed to rent these places, and that money was raised by charging admission. Any money that was left over went to the players, who became professionals.

Though there is a claim that a professional game was played as early as 1893 in Herkimer, N.Y., most historians feel that the first pro game was played in 1896 in Trenton, N.J. There was enough money from the gate receipts that night to pay each player $15, a fair sum in those days; Captain Fred Cooper got an extra dollar.

Soon enough, promoters came into the game, hiring players on a game-to-game basis, usually to play against a local team which would have some drawing power in the area. Often, the games were only part of the program, with a band playing for dancing both before and after the games. The slippery dance floor must have caused some problems for the players, but no doubt, those problems were minimized because the players usually weren't moving very fast, anyway.

The next logical step was the formation of professional leagues, and the first one, the National Basketball League, was organized in 1898, disbanding after the 1902-3 season.

Others quickly followed. The Philadelphia League began in 1903, becoming the Eastern League in 1909. The Central League started in Western Pennsylvania in 1906. The Hudson River League started in 1909, the New York State League in 1911, the Western Pennsylvania League in 1912, the Pennsylvania State League in 1914, the Inter-State League in 1915, the Metropolitan Basketball League in 1921 and, finally, the American Basketball League in 1925.

The best league team of that era was unquestionably the Troy (N.Y.) Trojans, who won two straight titles in the Hudson River League before it folded and then won three titles in the four years of the New York State League before it, too, folded. Player-coach Ed Wachter then took his team on tour, and the Trojans won 38 straight games.

Wachter was an innovator, which was one reason for his team's success. His team was apparently the first to use the bounce pass, for instance, and he also pioneered the use of the fast break. At that time, players on a team would all go for a rebound or loose ball. Wachter put his players in specific places, so a player who got the ball could pass to a teammate in scoring position.

Because all his players were good free-throw shooters, Wachter also campaigned for a new rule which would require a fouled player to take the free throw. But that rule wasn't adopted until 1923, too late to do him any good.

Conditions were not right, though, for a stable professional league and wouldn't be until the middle of the twentieth century. That wasn't surprising. Typically, there is a substantial time lag between the beginning of a sport and a stable pro league. Baseball, for instance, was invented in 1845, but it wasn't until 1876 that a lasting league, the National League, was formed. In football, there was a time lapse of a half-century between the start of organized games and the formation of the National Football League.

In basketball, the many pro leagues were very loose affairs. There were no binding player contracts, and players would jump back and forth between teams, playing for one team one week and another team the next; sometimes, they would be playing for two teams in the same league. And fan confidence in pro teams was minimal, because there was constant talk about fixed games, a recurrent problem which was to blow up in big scandals in college basketball in mid-century.

Some of the best teams of the era didn't even play in leagues, preferring to travel and play exhibitions. One such was the Buffalo Germans. It was first organized as a YMCA team in 1895, when the players were 14-year-olds. The team, with Al Heerdt and Eddie Miller as its stars, had a 792-86 record over two decades of play, once winning 111 straight.

The Germans' reputation was such that they attracted $500 guarantees for three-game series, traveling as far as Kansas. One of the teams they beat was the Carlisle Indians, with Jim Thorpe.

In 1931, having been apart for a decade, the Germans regrouped for one last exhibition game. Though the players on the team averaged 51 years in age, the Germans beat a much younger team from Tonawanda, N.Y., by one point.

Another successful independent team was the Oswego (N.Y.) Indians. In 1913, the Indians even beat the Germans three times in a four-game series, and their best stretch was yet to come: In 1914 and '15, they won 121 games and lost only six.

The best team in the first 25 years of the century, though, was unquestionably the Original Celtics, who deserve a chapter of their own. The next chapter will tell you why.

Nat Holman was the playmaker and biggest star of the Original Celtics, the first great team. *(Hall of Fame)*

2. The First Great Team

The Original Celtics hold a special place in basketball history. It's foolish to attempt to compare teams of that time with modern teams, whose players are taller, faster, and much better shooters, but no team has ever dominated an era as the Celtics did, nor had so much influence on the game.

The first thing to know about the Original Celtics is that they weren't. Original, that is. The first Celtics were the New York Celtics, organized in 1914. That Celtics team played together for three seasons, breaking up as the United States entered the First World War.

After the war had ended, New York promoter Jim Furey and his brother Tom wanted to reorganize the Celtics. Because Frank McCormack, founder of the New York Celtics, refused to give up his rights to the name, Furey retitled the team the Original Celtics. The two best players from the first Celtics team, John Whitty and Pete Barry, joined the new "Originals," along with Ernie Reich, Joe Trippe, Eddie White, and Mike Smolick.

The first Original Celtics team was good but not great. In the next year, though, Furey signed Swede Grimstead, a solid veteran, and young players Henry (Dutch) Dehnert and Johnny Beckman. Dehnert would become a solid pivotman, a good rebounder and defensive player; Beckman was very fast and the best free-throw shooter of his era.

The addition of those three players made the Celtics one of the two outstanding teams of the time. The other was the New York Whirlwinds, which had been organized by famed promoter Tex Rickard. The Whirlwinds had three of the best players in the game—Barney Sedran, Nat Holman, and Chris Leonard.

A matchup of the two teams seemed a natural, but it took some time to arrange because neither team liked even to acknowledge the other. Finally, in 1921, a three-game series was arranged, for the 71st Regiment Armory in New York.

A record crowd of 11,000 watched the first game, won by the Whirlwinds, 40-27. The next night, the Celtics came back to win, 26-24. The third game was never played. There was some talk that the owners could not rent the armory for the third game, though that seems unreasonable. Some thought the game was called off because it was feared the fans might riot, so heated was the competition; given the atmosphere of the time, that sounds like a sound reason for canceling the game.

There were also those who thought the game was called off because Holman and Leonard had already signed contracts with the Celtics. Whatever the timing of their signing, Holman and Leonard did play for the Celtics the next year, and that began the Celtics' period of true domination.

At that time there were many professional basketball teams, but they were all loosely organized. Team owners would sign players to individual game contracts, with the pay varying in relationship to the size of the crowd that could be expected. As they had from the beginning of pro basketball, players would jump from team to team, understandably going where the money was the best that night. In that framework, they seldom had a chance to develop the teamwork that's essential for the best basketball.

Furey, a far-seeing promoter, changed all that. Beginning with the 1922-23 season, he became the first owner to sign players to year-long contracts.

The money he paid was good, and he had many star players, so it was always a struggle to meet the payroll. For a time, barnstorming seemed the answer, because the Celtics could command impressive guarantees on the road.

In 1925, the new Madison Square Garden, seating 18,000 people, was opened. The Celtics used that for their home games and, with the games at the Garden and those on the road, were playing nearly every night.

But even that wasn't enough for Furey; in 1926, he was indicted for the embezzlement of $187,000 from the Arnold Constable clothing store. When he pleaded guilty to charges of grand larceny and forgery, he was sentenced to five years in Sing Sing. (He was released from jail in 1929.)

Furey's financial problems couldn't obscure the fact that he had put together a great team. The Celtics averaged about five wins out of every six games they played from 1922 until they finally broke up for good in 1936, and some years they did considerably better; in 1922-23, for instance, they won 193 and lost only 11.

Most of this record came on the road, too, under the most adverse conditions. The crowd was always against them, of course, and very often, the referees were, too; one night, Dehnert walked over to the opposing team's huddle and heard the ref assuring the players that he would call as many fouls as he could against the Celtics.

To try to overcome this problem, the Celtics tried both mental and physical intimidation. The first time a foul was called against a Celt, all five players would charge the ref, hoping that would make him think twice the next time he wanted to call a foul. And Horace (Horse) Haggerty, whose nickname gives a clue to his body build, was an especially menacing presence; at least once, Haggerty knocked a referee out with his solid right hand alone.

The composition of the team changed over the nearly two decades it played, but the most famous players of that team were probably Holman, Beckman, Dehnert, and Joe Lapchick.

ORIGINAL CELTICS

Johnny Beckman

Dutch Dehnert

Joe Lapchick

Nat Holman

Pete Barry

The Original Celtics revolutionized basketball and established plays that are still used today. *(Hall of Fame)*

Holman was an outstanding ballhandler and dribbler, and he was especially valuable when the Celtics had to stall away the closing minutes of a game. Lapchick, at 6'5", was a giant in that era, and a dominant player.

But it was less individual brilliance than great teamwork that made the Celtics so good. Because they played together so much, they could anticipate each other's moves. They had set plays for almost every situation, unlike most other teams, and their passing was remarkable.

A humorous incident involving Nat Holman and Horse Haggerty probably best illustrates how entrenched the habit of working together became for the Celtic players: After leaving the Celtics, Haggerty played one year for the Washington Palace Five, George Preston Marshall's team. Marshall was almost obsessed with the thought of beating the Celts, and his team seemed to have that accomplishment cinched in a game during Haggerty's year with the Palace Five.

With only a few seconds remaining, the Palace Five had a one-point lead and the ball out-of-bounds. Haggerty was passing the ball in. Holman suddenly cut for his basket and yelled "Horse!" Instinctively, Haggerty passed the ball to Nat, who laid it up for the winning basket!

In most of their games, the Celtics controlled the pace. They tried not to run up the score on a weaker team, partially because they didn't want to embarrass anybody but mostly because they realized that lopsided wins would destroy their box office appeal; fans liked to have some hope, however small, that the local team had a chance for an upset.

Occasionally, they would even play tie games—by design. When the score was tied at the end of the game, they would go to the promoter and ask for more money. If they got the money, they played an overtime period. If they didn't, they walked off the court.

One of the keys to their success was the way they worked off the center jump. In those days, of course, there was a jump ball at center court after every basket, as well as at the start of each quarter. With Lapchick jumping, the Celtics could control the tip, and they had several plays they worked off that.

More significant for basketball history, though, was the pivot play, which they discovered one night by accident. The Celtics were leading in a game against the Chattanooga Railites, but Johnny Beckman was upset because the Railites' standing guard was breaking up Celtic passes. As was the custom with many teams even into the 20's, the Railites used one player who never moved from around the defensive basket area, even when his team went up-court on offense.

Beckman called time to discuss what could be done, and Dutch Dehnert volunteered to play in front of the standing guard; the ball would then be passed to Dehnert, who could pass to another player.

As soon as they tried that, the Celtics discovered that a player could pass the ball to Dehnert, keep going and get a pass coming in—what we now call the give-and-go. Another time, the standing guard moved to try to take the ball from Dehnert on Dutch's right, so Dehnert simply pivoted to his left and went in for the basket. High-post centers have been doing that ever since.

Little things meant a lot to the Celtics. Holman, for instance, taught Dehnert to come forward to receive a pass, which made it virtually impossible for the defensive ...n to get the ball.

The Celtics were equally innovative on defense. At that time, teams simply played man-to-man defense; if an offensive man lost his defender, he was open for a shot. The Celtics were the first to use a switching man-to-man, so there was always a defender to pick up an open man.

That style, effective as it was, almost destroyed Lapchick when he first came to the club. Joe could not get used to the idea of switching, and he couldn't figure how the other Celtics did it. There seemed to be no signals and, as with everything else they did, the Celtics never practiced it—they never had the time. But Lapchick eventually caught on and became one of the Celtic stars.

One other thing is certain about the Celtics: They had to love the game. Barnstorming was hardly a pleasant way of life. They seldom even had time to wash their uniforms, and they would pull them out of the box, still sweaty and damp from the previous night, and put them back on. They faced hostile crowds and biased referees. They played in dance halls, armories, old barns.

The experience pulled them together, and they were as close off the court as on. Holman and Lapchick were probably the closest, and they remained friends years after they quit playing, when they were coaching rival college teams at CCNY and St. John's. When Holman finally got married at 49, Lapchick was his best man.

The Celtics' success and popularity boosted the popularity of professional basketball as a whole, and in 1925, the American Basketball League, the first attempt to go "big league," was formed, with George Preston Marshall the main instigator.

The league was the first to go beyond a regional concept, stretching from the Atlantic coast to Chicago, as did the two baseball leagues and the National Football League. Joe Carr was the league's first president; Carr was also acting as NFL president and as a minor-league baseball executive at the time.

Some big sports names were involved in the basketball league. George Halas of the Chicago Bears owned and coached the Chicago Bruins; Harry Heilmann, the great Detroit Tigers hitter, was the owner of the Brooklyn Arcadians. Allie Heerdt, who had played on the great Buffalo Germans team, was coaching a team of the same name in the ABL.

For the 1925-26 season, the league started with teams in Brooklyn, Washington, Cleveland, Rochester, Fort Wayne, Boston, Chicago, Detroit, and Buffalo. After the first half, Boston dropped out, leaving eight teams.

The Celtics refused to enter, reasoning that they could make more money barnstorming. The ABL clubs, hoping to capitalize on the Celtics' reputation, signed them up for exhibition games, but the Celtics embarrassed the league clubs by winning easily and with great regularity.

The season, a short one, was divided into two halves, with 16 games in the first half and 14 in the second. The Brooklyn Arcadians took the first-half championship with a 12-4 record, and the Cleveland Rosenblooms the second with a 13-1 mark.

In the playoffs, the Rosenblooms won three straight games to take the championship. The crowd for the first two games averaged about 10,000 (the last game drew only 2000 because Brooklyn was slumping and seemed to have no chance to win), which encouraged the owners. With or without the Celtics, pro basketball seemed to have a future.

The next year, the league dropped the Buffalo Germans and added the Philadelphia Warriors and Baltimore Orioles, again bringing the total up to nine teams.

In an attempt to force the Celtics to join the ABL, league officials prohibited exhibition games between league teams and the Celts, which removed the best and most logical opponents from the Celtics' schedule. The Celts still didn't join—at first. But when the Brooklyn team sank to the bottom of the standings with a 0-5 record, the Celtics finally agreed to replace Brooklyn.

It took the Celtics no time to establish their superiority. In the first half, they won 13 of the 16 games they played. Because they had started with the 0-5 Brooklyn record, they finished that half in fourth place at 13-8, but their percentage for the games they played was slightly higher than Cleveland's first place mark of 17-4.

The Celts were just hitting their stride. In the second half of the season, they won 19 of 21 games to take the league by four games. In the playoffs, they swept to three straight wins over Cleveland.

Ironically, they accomplished this without Beckman, who was often called the Babe Ruth of basketball at the time. At the start of the second half, Beckman was sold to Baltimore, where he became player-coach. The principal reason behind the sale was financial, because Beckman was the highest-paid player in the game, but it opened up a spot on the roster for young Davey Banks. Though Banks was weak defensively, he was an outstanding offensive player and worked well with Holman.

It was more of the same the next season. Winning 15 straight in December and January, the Celtics ran up a 40-9 record and won in the Eastern Division—the league had been divided into two divisions for the 1927-28 season—by a whopping 11 games. In the playoffs, they beat Philadelphia two straight games for the divisional title and then won three out of four from Western Division champion Fort Wayne for the league title.

In two years of league play, the Celtics had won 72 games and lost only 14. In the playoffs, they had won eight games, lost only one. That's domination.

But the Celtics' domination was ruining both them and the league. The essence of sports is competition, and it didn't require a genius to see that the Celtics were in a class by themselves, and that there was no real competition for the top in the ABL.

Even their own fans were beginning to tire of seeing the Celtics romp to win after win, and attendance was down at Madison Square Garden, as well as through the rest of the league.

That was critical for the Celtics because, with owner Jim Furey in prison, the players were running the team on a co-operative basis. To their dismay, they were learning that the amount of money they were getting that way was substantially less than Furey had been paying them in straight salaries.

So, economics did what the rest of the league could not: beat the Celtics. Before the next season, the team was disbanded, and players were distributed to other league teams.

Even then, the Celtics' influence was felt. Cleveland signed three ex-Celtics—Joe

Lapchick, Dutch Dehnert and Pete Barry—and won the first-half title with a 19-9 mark. (The league was back to one division, with eight teams.)

In the second half, Cleveland finished a game behind Fort Wayne, but in the playoffs, Cleveland swept four straight games, and the Celtic "alumni" had another championship.

Furey was out of prison before the start of the 1929-30 season and tried to put the Celtics back together, but the venture was doomed to failure from the start.

Because Lapchick, Dehnert, and Barry were still under contract to Cleveland, Furey could only put together about half of his old team, with Holman, Beckman, and Banks. However, Holman missed some games because he was already coaching CCNY. Worse, attendance was off for the Celtics' games, and Furey couldn't afford the $10,000 salaries he was paying to Holman and Beckman.

After ten games, half of them wins, the Celtics disbanded and their games were stricken from the standings. The league limped on with seven teams for the rest of that season and 1930-31, and then folded, the victim of the Depression as much as anything. It was re-formed for the 1933-34 season but as a regional, eastern league with no pretensions to major league status.

It wasn't the end yet for the Celtics. They hit the road again in 1930, barnstorming until 1936, when Lapchick quit to become head coach at St. John's.

But it wasn't the same. In the past, the Celtics had played for a guarantee of $400, and their actual cut often went higher; now, they were reduced to playing for $250. Hard as the travel had been before, it was even worse now; instead of train travel, they were going from town to town in an old jalopy.

The players were growing old, too. They were still winning about as often as they had in the past, but as often as not it was now on their basketball smarts and experience. They had to be conscious of pacing themselves and conserving energy against younger opponents.

Thus it was that they came up to their last game, against a collection of former college players in their first year of pro ball. The Celtics knew they couldn't run with the other team, so they planned to get ahead early and slow the game down. But the former collegians reversed the strategy; they took an early lead on the Celtics and toyed with them.

The rest of the basketball world had caught up. It was time to quit.

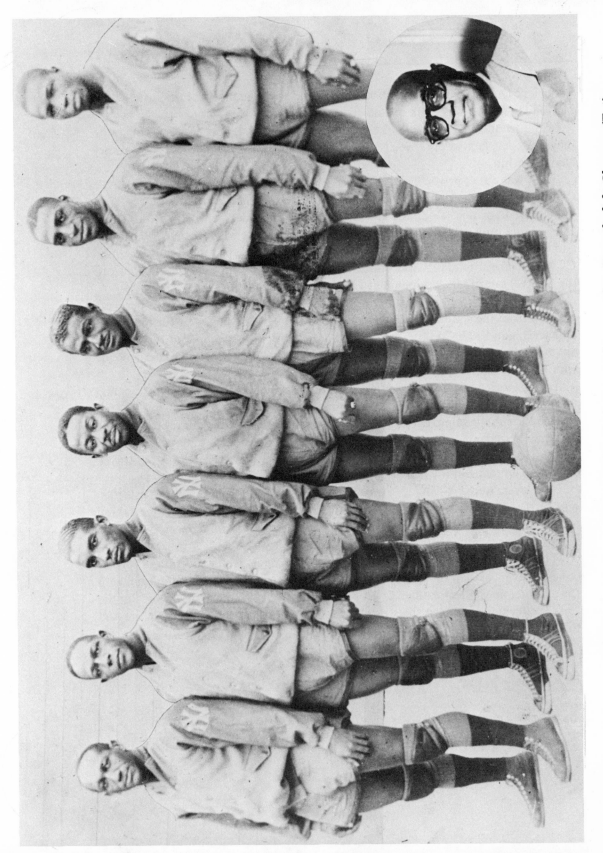

The New York Renaissance was a great black team in an era of segregation. From the left: Clarence (Fat)

3. Across the Color Line: Two Black Teams

In the 1920s and '30s, there was really only one team even comparable to the Original Celtics—the New York Rens. Indeed, by the mid-'30s, the Rens had succeeded the Celtics as the best team in basketball, but the Rens never really acquired the fame of the Celtics for one reason: It was an all-black team.

In recent years, basketball has become increasingly the black man's game. Black youngsters hone their skills on city playgrounds, looking at basketball as a way out of the ghetto, and the majority of pro stars are blacks.

It was far different in the '20s, when blacks were on the periphery in all sports. Organized leagues were generally whites-only, and so blacks formed separate teams and even leagues.

There were two strong black basketball teams, the Rens and the better-known Harlem Globetrotters. Both were independent, barnstorming teams, and the relative lack of structure in the basketball world worked to their advantage. In other sports, black teams were frozen out of competition with white teams, but in basketball, the Rens and Globetrotters often played against white teams. And by any standard, the best basketball of that era was played when the Rens and Celtics met in one of their many matchups.

Because the newspaper sports pages of the time reported chiefly on white sports, the Rens got little publicity. But the real basketball fans knew what they could do.

From the time the Rens split a six-game series with the Celtics in the 1926-27 season, a Celtics-Rens game was a very hot attraction. In New York, ticket prices went from the usual 75 cents to $1 for these games. Elsewhere, crowds were very big for those days, as high as 15,000 for games in Cleveland and Kansas City.

And the players acquired a lasting respect for each other. Celtics' center, Joe Lapchick, often said the best center he had ever played against was the Rens' John (Tarzan) Cooper.

The Rens—officially, the New York Renaissance, after the Renaissance Casino ballroom in Harlem, which served as the team's home court—were formed in 1922 by Bob Douglas. It was common in those days, of course, for a basketball team to play in a dance hall, but both the basketball and the music at the Renaissance Casino were decidedly uncommon; the Count Basie and Jimmy Lunsford bands were among those that played there.

Three early stars on the Rens were James (Pappy) Ricks, Clarence (Fat) Jenkins, and Eyre (Bruiser) Saitch. There was irony in the careers of the latter two players. Jenkins was an outstanding player in the Negro Baseball League, and Saitch was an excellent tennis player; neither could play against whites in his primary sport, but got the chance in basketball.

Later, as the prolonged series with the Celtics began, Douglas signed other excellent players—Bill Yancey, Cooper, and John (Casey) Holt. The Rens were on their way.

Like the Celtics, the Rens played together so long that they developed excellent teamwork. They prided themselves on always hitting the open man with their passes, but their real trademark was the fact that they seldom dribbled. Their theory was that, if one player was dribbling the ball and another cut to the basket, it would be harder for the dribbler to get the ball to the cutting man. Thus, even on a fast break, the ball would seldom touch the floor, being passed instead in a lightning-fast series.

Though the team was a good one in the '20s, it was in the next decade that the Rens achieved their peak. Starting in 1932, when Douglas signed the incongruously named (at 6'5") Wee Willie Smith, the Rens won 473 games and lost only 49 in four seasons; in one stretch, they won 88 straight.

By that time, it was clear they had passed the Celtics as basketball's best and in 1933, they won seven of eight from the Celts.

That great record was achieved despite conditions which were far worse than even the Celtics faced. Discrimination was the standard of the day, and ugly incidents were never far from the surface. In a game in Akron, Ohio, for instance, Smith got into a fight with a white player, and fans poured onto the floor to take the white's side in a brawl, until someone reached the light switch and turned off all the lights in the hall. The Rens had to be given a police escort out of town.

By that time, the Rens didn't have a home court, because the Depression had forced the closing of the Renaissance Casino. That meant the team was on the road for all its games, which posed great problems. Because they could seldom get served in restaurants or stay in hotels in towns in which they played, the Rens established headquarters in cities like Chicago and Indianapolis, and they would return to these cities after a game; sometimes, that meant traveling as much as 200 miles to a game, and then 200 miles back.

Douglas, who paid his players well, bought a $10,000 custom-made bus, so they could travel in some comfort; if necessary, they could even sleep in it.

Once, though, the bus broke down in Wisconsin and the players had to push it ten miles into the next town. Unable to get a hotel in the town, they waited in the railroad station until the next morning to catch a train to Chicago. Bone-weary, they lost the game in Chicago—and then had to escape through the back door because fans thought they had been paid to lose!

Adversity only toughened the Rens, though, and they prided themselves on their stamina; they would never call a timeout in a game, feeling this was a sign of weakness. Often, they would play to the point of exhaustion until the other team finally called time out.

In the great 1932-36 stretch, the Rens played with only seven players, and they were the same seven throughout—Cooper, Smith, Jenkins, Yancey, Holt, Ricks, and Saitch.

It was a very well-balanced team. Jenkins, often considered the fastest man in basketball, led the fast break. Smith and the 6'4" Cooper were strong rebounders and inside shooters. Jenkins, Saitch, and Yancey all shot well from outside.

Anyone who knew basketball realized that the Rens were the best team in the country, and in 1939 the Rens proved it in the first World Tournament.

The World Tournament was held in Chicago for ten years, starting in 1939. It was open to teams from leagues as well as to independent teams; in that first year, 11 teams entered. Because of its central location, it was easy for all teams to get to, and all the good teams played in it. In fact, teams from the National Basketball League— the closest thing to a major league at the time—used the tournament for recruiting, sometimes signing top players from independent teams.

The Rens were at the top of their game that year, having won 112 games and lost only seven. In the World Tournament, they beat the NBL champion Oshkosh All-Stars, 34-25, in the finals, to take the first tournament title.

Though the Rens played well until the late '40s, they never again quite reached the stature of the team of the '30s. They finally disbanded with a remarkable record of 2588 wins and only 529 losses over a period of more than a quarter-century.

Fittingly, they were voted into the Hall of Fame in 1963.

For the Rens, the World Tournament title was the icing on the cake, because they had been known as the best for some time. For the Harlem Globetrotters, the tournament was much more important. The Globetrotters finished third in the first tournament and won the second one, in 1940, beating the Chicago Bruins, 31-29. For the first time, fans realized just how good the 'Trotters really were.

Modern-day fans know the Globetrotters as basketball comedians, and their antics have drawn huge crowds, including a record 75,000 for an appearance in Berlin's Olympic Stadium in 1951. But the team was originally formed by Abe Saperstein in 1926 as a serious basketball team.

The team played first in the Savoy Ballroom in Chicago, but when the ballroom was turned into an ice rink, Saperstein decided to make it strictly a road team, playing wherever he could schedule a game.

He called the team the Harlem Globetrotters to (1) tell people the team was black, though none of the players actually came from Harlem or any other part of New York City; and (2) to let fans know the team had been around. Though Globetrotters

Abe Saperstein organized the Harlem Globetrotters, whose combination of basketball and comedy became an institution. *(Hall of Fame)*

was an exaggeration at the time, the team has certainly earned the right to that nickname many times over since then.

Saperstein took his team anywhere he could schedule a game, but scheduling was a problem. He suffered from an ironic problem: Because the 'Trotters had no big-name players, fans didn't realize how good they were—but other teams did and were reluctant to play them.

Out of desperation, Saperstein put in clowning routines to make the team more entertaining. The fans liked the act, and with the help of the publicity engendered by their win in the World Tournament, the Globetrotters started on their way to phenomenal success.

Since then the Globetrotters have played in more than 90 different countries, before royalty and popes. Serious basketball has long since taken a back seat to their routines, and nobody pays any attention to the score of the game. The Globetrotter "team" is actually a big operation with several units; at any given time, several teams with the 'Trotter name may be playing at different spots in the world.

Since the NBA has opened up to black players, the Globetrotters no longer get the top college players, either, and they are little more than a footnote in pro basketball history.

Still, the Globetrotters have had some outstanding players, who well deserve mention. Some, like Nat (Sweetwater) Clifton and Connie Hawkins, later went on to play in the National Basketball Association (NBA); and, of course, Wilt Chamberlain played one year with the Globetrotters before joining Philadelphia of the NBA—because Wilt had elected not to play his final college year.

The most famous of the Globetrotter players have probably been Reece (Goose) Tatum, Marques Haynes, and Meadowlark Lemon, all of whom would have been capable of holding their own in the NBA when they were in their playing prime.

Tatum and Haynes were particularly outstanding athletes. Tatum, though only 6′3″, had an incredible reach of 84 inches, and he had an unusually accurate hook shot. Haynes was the consummate dribbler and could keep the ball away from opponents for minutes at a time while assuming seemingly awkward positions—on his back, on his stomach, on his knees. Both Tatum and Haynes eventually formed their own touring teams.

And through their clowning—as much or more than their regular playing—the Globetrotters displayed that special agility and flexibility that NBA fans have since recognized as the trademark of the exceptional black players. Tatum did his moves for comic effect and Magic Johnson does his to produce points, but there is a striking similarity in their styles of play.

4. The War of the Leagues

The Original Celtics, the Rens, the first leagues, the American Basketball League . . . all made contributions to the eventual success of professional basketball. But it wasn't until after the Second World War that the foundations for a lasting league were finally laid.

It was boom time in the entertainment world in 1946, and professional sports was a big part of that. People were celebrating because the war was over. Many had more money than they'd ever had before. The Great Depression, the controls and rationing of wartime, were all just bad memories. They were eager to have fun, and to spend, spend, spend.

In baseball and football, attendance soared, and now pro basketball's time was coming, too.

Until then, basketball had been primarily a college game. The great names, except for those who'd been members of the Celtics, had been college players. The great tournaments were played by college teams. The doubleheaders which packed Madison Square Garden had matched college teams. Now, there were basketball people who felt it was time for the professional game to capitalize on this interest.

So, in 1946, two leagues went head-to-head in a market that previously had not been able to support even one pro league well. One of the leagues, the National Basketball League, had existed before. The other, the Basketball Association of America, was new. Out of this rivalry was to come the National Basketball Association, which represented maturity in pro basketball.

The National Basketball League (NBL) was only marginally a major league. Its base was regional, with almost all of its teams in the Midwest; then as now, there was more enthusiasm for basketball in the Midwest than in any other region.

The league was formed when two Akron corporations, Firestone and Goodyear, and General Electric of Fort Wayne decided to join pro basketball. The three corporations had fielded strong amateur teams in the Midwest Industrial Basketball Conference, and their teams joined with ten independent pro teams in the Midwest to form the NBL.

The first season, as is the norm when a new league is formed, was chaotic. League commissioner Hubert Johnson left the scheduling to the individual teams, so there was a great variance in the number of games played; Fort Wayne, for instance, played 20, and Buffalo played only nine.

Nor could teams agree on playing rules. The colleges had just eliminated the practice of having a center jump after every basket, but teams within the NBL were split on whether to eliminate that rule. As a result, it was left up to the home team to decide for each game whether the center jump would be used.

Because there was so little money in the game, players all had full-time jobs away from the court, playing only in their spare time. One such player, for example, was Johnny Wooden. An All-American at Purdue and later a great coach at UCLA, Wooden was coaching a high school team while playing for the Whiting (Indiana) team in the NBL.

In general, teams recruited veteran players from their areas. Though they also tried to lure recent college stars into the league, they had little success.

The star of the league in the first year of its operation was Leroy (Cowboy) Edwards, a 6'4" center for Oshkosh. Edwards had played one brilliant year at the University of Kentucky and then, the story goes, had demanded $3000 to return. He was told colleges did not pay their players (the cynical might add "openly"), so he dropped out of school and turned pro.

Edwards averaged a league-leading 16.2 points a game and had one incredible game in which he alone scored 30 points—this in a defensive-dominated era when winning teams often didn't score that many points. Edwards could shoot a hook shot with great accuracy with either hand.

Largely because of Edwards, Oshkosh won in the western division and had the best percentage in the league, .857 on 12 wins in 14 games; the Whiting team with Wooden finished only half a game back, at 12-3. In the eastern division, the two Akron teams battled for the top, with Firestone finishing a game ahead, 14-4, to 13-5 for Goodyear.

The top two teams in each division qualified for the playoffs. Goodyear upset Firestone in two straight games, 26-21 and 37-31, to qualify for the finals, but it was the western playoff which was the more interesting, because of Edwards and Wooden. In the individual duel, Wooden came out slightly ahead, scoring 17 and 16 points in two games while Edwards was getting 16 and 15, but Edwards' team, Oshkosh, beat Whiting twice, 40-33, and 41-38.

In the finals, Goodyear won the first game, 29-28, but Oshkosh came back, behind Edwards' 16 points, to win the second game, 39-31. In the third game, though, Edwards was held to nine points by Goodyear center Wes Bennett, and Goodyear won, 35-27.

Oshkosh won two more NBL titles in the next three years, but the best team in NBL history was probably the Fort Wayne Zollner Pistons, who won three straight titles in the mid-'40s and also three straight World Tournament championships; on both ends of the latter streak, the Pistons finished third in the tournament.

Fred Zollner, watching his beloved Pistons, was one of the early owners who made basketball a possibility. (*Detroit Pistons*)

Certainly, the Pistons were the most interesting team in the league, from the time they joined for the 1941-42 season (the earlier Fort Wayne team, representing General Electric, had dropped out after the opening season).

The team was sponsored by Fred Zollner, owner of the Zollner Machine Company in Fort Wayne, who also sponsored a world champion softball team in that period. Players were all on the company payroll—at inflated salaries—and at season's end, after expenses were deducted, they shared in the total gate receipts for the year, which usually meant a sizeable bonus.

The team played in a high school gym. The stands came right to courtside and had a railing around them. "We used to call that gym 'The Pit,'" remembered Bruce Hale, then marketing director for radio station KNBR in San Francisco but an NBL player in the mid-'40s. "Fans used to lean out over the railing and hit players over the head as they came by."

The players were just as rough as the fans. "I remember my first pro game, which was against Fort Wayne," said Hale. "The first time I came down the floor, Bobby McDermott, who was guarding me, grabbed me and threw me into the stands. I wondered, 'What in the world have I gotten into? This isn't for me.'

"But the next time I came down, I threw an elbow into McDermott's stomach as hard as I could, knocking him down. I was scared that the other players would come after me, but none of them did, and McDermott didn't bother me after that.

"I learned later that it was all part of the Fort Wayne strategy. Each player would rough up his man once early in the game, just so they could see if a player could be intimidated. They figured that, at worst, they'd give up five free throws and five points, but it was worth it if they could intimidate you."

McDermott was probably the best of the Piston players, with a two-handed set shot that he could hit from far out. "He'd take a couple of steps beyond midcourt," remembered Hale, "and let fly. He might miss a layup, but he was deadly with that set shot."

The league shrank from 13 teams to eight for its second season, but the worst was yet to come: During the war years, only four teams survived. But by the 1945-46 season the league was back up to eight teams, and there were some encouraging signs.

Most important was the fact that they were able to start getting some of the top college names, like Bob Davies, Jim Pollard, and Red Holzman. Davies was an especially intriguing player, as much for his personal qualities as his playing ability; he had such remarkable character that he was the model for Clair Bee's series of books on juvenile sports.

Davies was a brilliant collegian, an All-American for two years, Most Valuable Player on his Seton Hall team three years and captain for two. He led Seton Hall to a record 43 straight wins and was selected MVP in the 1942 College All-Star Game in Chicago. He led the Great Lakes Naval Training team to the service title in 1943; and 1945, he joined the Rochester Royals to start a ten-year career which eventually got him elected to the Hall of Fame.

Famed for his behind-the-back dribbling, Davies was the leading assist man in the league for six straight years and had 20 in a game, a more remarkable feat than modern fans might suspect. In those days, when statistics were less precise and shooting percentages were much lower, assists were much more difficult to get than they are now. A comparable figure today would probably be 33-35.

Davies made the All-League team seven times, was once the league's MVP, and three times led the Royals to a league title. Eventually, a wire service poll named him the sixth-best player of the first half-century.

It was the best player of the first half-century, George Mikan, who was most important to the success of pro basketball, however. In 1946, the Chicago Gears of the NBL were able to sign the 6'10" Mikan, who at DePaul had been the most famous collegian since Hank Luisetti. More than any other player, Mikan was to put the stamp of legitimacy on pro basketball.

Given that relatively few fans were coming out to see pro games, it seemed suicidal to start another league. But the men behind the Basketball Association of America (BAA) thought they had good, logical reasons for what they were doing.

There was a key difference between the two leagues, and one that would ultimately determine the course of pro basketball: The NBL owners had acquired their teams and then looked for a place to play; the BAA owners (with one exception) owned arenas and were looking for teams to fill them, between hockey games and ice shows. Pro basketball, though it hadn't done much yet, seemed to have that potential.

The idea behind the BAA apparently came from Max Kase, then the sports editor of the *New York Journal American.* Kase had promoted a 1944 pro basketball exhibition to raise money for war relief, and he had been impressed by the overflow crowd.

Earlier in his career, Kase had been a baseball writer in Boston, and he'd become friends with Walter Brown, president of the Boston Garden. He mentioned the possibility to Brown of forming a new pro basketball league. Nothing was done then, of course; it would have made no sense during the war.

By 1946 Brown was ready to move. By owning a team in the National Hockey League he had connections in New York, Chicago, Detroit, and Toronto. By owning an arena he had even more connections, and it was through the Arena Managers Association that he lined up the men who would own franchises in the BAA.

Maurice Podoloff, a short (five-foot) man who had much the shape of a basketball, was named commissioner because of his administrative experience as president of the American Hockey League. Kase was paid several thousand for his idea.

In the league for the first season were 11 teams:

The Boston Celtics were owned by Brown, who had chosen the name both because of its connection to the Original Celtics and because of the large Irish population in Boston.

The Chicago Stags were owned by Arthur Morse, the one exception to the rule of arena owners. Morse was a lawyer, but he had connections with the Norris family, which ran Chicago Stadium, so there would be no arena problem. (The Norris family also had an interest in the Olympia Stadium in Detroit.)

The Cleveland Rebels were owned by Al Sutphin, who also owned both the Cleveland arena and the Cleveland team in the American Hockey League.

The Detroit Falcons were owned by the Olympia owners.

The Pittsburgh Ironmen were owned by John Harris, who also possessed an arena in Pittsburgh as well as the Hornets of the American Hockey League.

The Philadelphia Warriors were owned by Pete Tyrell, who ran both the Philadelphia Arena and the Philadelphia Rockets of the AHL.

The Providence Steamrollers were owned by Lou Pieri, who had the Providence Reds of the AHL in addition to the arena.

The St. Louis Bombers were owned by Emory D. Jones, who also owned the St. Louis Arena and the AHL team in St. Louis.

The Toronto Huskies were owned by Maple Leaf Gardens, which also owned the Maple Leafs of the National Hockey League.

Ned Irish, owner of the New York Knickerbockers, insisted that pro basketball should go first class. *(Hall of Fame)*

The Washington Capitols were owned by Mike Uline, who owned the arena which bore his name, the largest in the District.

The New York Knickerbockers were owned by Ned Irish, who ran the very profitable Madison Square Garden in New York.

The New York franchise situation was an interesting one. Irish had been running college basketball doubleheaders in the Garden for years, and both the National Invitation Tournament (NIT) and the National Collegiate Athletic Association (NCAA) tournament were also held there. The previous season, Irish had had 29 total college dates, between doubleheaders and tournaments, and they had averaged a whopping 98 per cent of capacity!

The college games were played on the best dates, and Irish obviously wasn't going to change them to make room for pro basketball, a questionable attraction at this point. But he could see the potential of the pro game, and he didn't want somebody else owning the New York team. His solution was to buy the team but play it elsewhere; the first season, the Knicks played only six games in the Garden and the other 24 home games in the 69th Regiment Armory.

The new league had some definite assets. One was that they were new to pro basketball; the sport now had a generally unsavory reputation with much of the sporting public, and the BAA would not be burdened with that. Also, the BAA owners all had promotional experience and, presumably, knew what the public wanted.

But translating that experience into attendance proved more difficult than the owners had imagined, a problem common to all new leagues. Problems arose that the owners hadn't anticipated.

Originally, owners had agreed that they would try to present an entirely new face, by acquiring players who had just completed their collegiate careers. But as it turned out, the NBL actually got more of the top collegiate talent that first year, including the very important Mikan.

Some owners, most notably Irish of the Knicks, stuck with the idea of using players without pro experience. But others stocked their team with pro veterans, a strategy that proved more successful in the short run.

There was another split within the league; here again, Irish was a key man, usually disputing with a side led by Podoloff, the commissioner.

With the great revenues of Madison Square Garden behind him, Irish plowed money into his team and insisted that the league should always go first class, to project the right kind of image. He was willing to take sizeable losses at this point because he felt they would lead to long-range gains, and he was right.

Most of the league owners, though, weren't able to operate as Irish did. There is a pattern which applies to all new leagues. Owners start operations assuming they'll lose a certain amount of money that first year as they struggle to get their teams established. That amount is *always* less than they actually lose. Usually, about the middle of that first season, owners start seeing the red ink and immediately throw some big plans out the window.

And, of course, that's exactly what happened with the BAA. Crowds were minuscule, losses substantial. Most of the owners had to scrimp, cut corners, and put on questionable promotions just to stay alive, and Podoloff generally sympathized with that, in contrast to Irish's much more generous policy.

On the court, the Washington Capitols were the class of the league during the regular season. The Capitols were coached by a young man of 29 named Arnold (Red) Auerbach. In the years to come, Auerbach would become a pro legend; at that point, he was only a former high school coach in his first year with the pros.

Auerbach had a largely veteran team. Bob Feerick, a superb ballhandler, and hot-shooting Fred Scolari were the guards, John Mahnken, who had jumped from Rochester of the NBL, was at center. Johnny Norlander was at one forward and Bones McKinney at the other; McKinney was a rookie, but a 27-year-old one, his career having been interrupted by the war.

Because almost all the new owners were hockey-oriented, the BAA had an extensive playoff system. Playoffs are an excellent way to extend the season in those sports whose arena size limits crowd potential, and no sport has ever exploited that as well as hockey; the NHL for years played a lengthy season schedule just to qualify four teams out of six for the playoffs.

The playoff system was a strange one, though, pitting first-place teams in the two divisions against each other, as well as second-place teams against each other and third-place teams, too. That guaranteed that one division champion would not make it out of the first round. Surprisingly, it was Washington, upset by the Chicago Stags in six games.

The eventual playoff winner was Philadelphia, which had the surprise rookie of the season, Joe Fulks from small Murray State in Kentucky. Fulks was not a great athlete. He was slow, and a below-average defensive player. But how he could shoot! As a boy, he had sharpened his eye by throwing rocks into a tobacco can nailed at basket height on a woodshed, and he shocked both fans and other BAA players in that first memorable season.

Fulks was the first of the jump shooters; hence his nickname, Jumpin' Joe. "Other players thought he was crazy for shooting that way," said Hale.

Unlike today's jump shooters, Fulks shot with two hands, bringing the ball back up over his head. He would maneuver and maneuver inside until he got free to take a pass from a teammate, and when he got it, he knew what to do. "When he got the ball, he went up with it," says Howie Dallmar, then a teammate of Fulks on the Warriors and now a physical education instructor at Stanford. "Our offense was geared to getting him the ball—perhaps too much."

Joe Fulks was the first jump shooter and a scorer of electrifying proportions in the early days of the NBA.
(Hall of Fame)

Dallmar had a somewhat jaundiced view of Fulks. "Guys were always asking me how Hank Luisetti compared to Fulks," says Howie, "which made me mad right off. I told them it should be the other way around, because Hank was so much the better player, he was so far ahead of the game. There was really no comparison between Luisetti and anybody.

"Fulks overheard me saying that one time and got so mad at me, he wouldn't speak to me for two weeks. But then, I never could understand him anyway, with that Kentucky accent.

"But Fulks was in a class by himself with that jump shot. He wasn't a great jumper, but the novelty of it, plus the fact that he put it back over his head made him impossible to stop. And, he had a great touch."

The Warriors would set picks to free Fulks for his shots, and he would roll right or left to get them. Like all great shooters, he had great confidence; if a few shots didn't go in, he still kept shooting.

"Like all great shooters, he would go on streaks," says Dallmar. "It was common for him to have one or two bad quarters in a game, but then he'd have a couple of good ones when he'd score 12 to 15 points. Some nights, of course, he had four good quarters, and that was really something to see."

The most famous of those nights came on February 10, 1949, at the Philadelphia Arena against the Indianapolis Jets; he scored 63 points, a feat which astounded the basketball world in a way nothing else would until Wilt Chamberlain scored 100 in a game—interestingly enough, also for the Philadelphia Warriors.

A few notes will put that feat into perspective. At that time, whole teams often did not score 63 points in a game which was much slower and more defense-oriented than today's game.

Games were only 40 minutes long, not the 48 minutes now played; adjusted for playing time, Fulks' effort was the equivalent of 76 points in a game today.

Usually, when an individual scores a bundle of points, a lot of them come on free throws. Fulks, in contrast, got only nine points on free throws. His 27 field goals have been exceeded since only by Chamberlain, Rick Barry, David Thompson, and Elgin Baylor, all of whom accomplished that in 48-minute games.

Fulks' record lasted until November 8, 1959, when Baylor scored 64 for the Minneapolis Lakers against Boston. Even in today's high-scoring game, 63 points is still a great feat; Fulks is one of only ten players who've scored that many or more.

In his rookie season Fulks averaged 23.2 points a game, almost half again as many as Ed Sadowski, runner-up with an average of 16.5. In the playoffs Fulks was even more spectacular. He scored 37 points in the first game of the finals, 34 in the final series contest as the Warriors swept Chicago in four games.

Naturally enough, Fulks was a good draw around the league—though not always as good as everybody hoped. "I remember one night in Toronto," says Dallmar, "when we saw people lined up around the block to get tickets, and we were playing there that night. But we found out they were buying tickets for the hockey game the next night."

And Fulks was virtually the only good draw in the BAA. The NBL still had most of the best players, including Davies, McDermott, Holzman, Al Cervi, and Arnie Risen. Most of all, they had Mikan, playing his rookie season.

Mikan had been signed to a five-year contract by the Chicago Gears, supposedly for $12,000 a season, more than double what even the best players were getting at the time.

Before the season was a month old, though, he quit the team in a dispute over his salary. What had happened, according to teammate Hale, was that Mikan had an incentive contract.

"He was supposed to get $6000 guaranteed," said Hale, "but he had to earn the rest—$5 for a field goal, $3 for a free throw. He said that when he went to the free-throw line, all he could see were dollar signs."

(In a telephone conversation with the author, Mikan confirmed that his contract with the Gears was half guaranteed and half incentive, but would not speak of the details of the contract. "I've never talked about that publicly, and I'm not going to now," he said.)

Without Mikan, the Gears slipped below .500, and Gears' owner Maurice White could see what was happening. He finally agreed to pay big George the entire $12,000, without any conditions, and Mikan returned.

When he did, the Gears immediately improved. They won 17 of their last 23 to get into the playoffs; once in, they beat Oshkosh, Indianapolis, and Rochester to win the championship. That's the difference George made.

The Gears' success led owner White to think in big terms. He told fellow owners he wanted the NBL to be a truly major league. That was fine for him, in a metropolitan market; it wasn't acceptable for owners in towns like Oshkosh and Sheboygan, with their limited potential. The split was not unlike that in the BAA between Irish and his colleagues.

There is some question whether White quit the BAA at that point or was forced out; whatever, he decided to form his own league, the Professional Basketball League of America. He would fund all the teams, and stock them with players. He was Thinking Big, all right.

"He sent me around the country for a couple of months," said Hale, "investigating cities to see if they were big enough, if they had big enough arenas, if there was enough interest in basketball. It was quite an education for me.

"I came back and found that White wanted to have 24 teams in his league. I told him that if he cut that number in half, he'd be much better off.

"He told me, 'If that's the way you feel, take your hat and get the hell out of here.' I left, and I didn't see him for a couple of weeks.

"Then, he called me and told me the league was down to 16 teams. I told him again that he'd be better off if he'd cut *that* number in half. With the NBL and BAA going, plus the Eastern League and American League [minor leagues], there was terrific competition for players. There just wouldn't be enough for 16 teams.

"Finally, he cut back to 12. He broke up our team, of course, because we would have been much too strong for the new league. He made me player-coach of the St. Paul team.

"The league lasted a month. I remember we were in Tulsa for a game when a sportswriter asked me what I thought of the league folding; that was the first I had heard of it. Luckily, we had enough money to get back home. I heard that White lost $500,000 in that month, which was a lot of money in those days."

The good players from that league (who were almost entirely the old Gears) returned to the NBL, to be parceled out among the other teams. The new Minneapolis Lakers, who had already acquired Jim Pollard, a former Stanford All-American, got Mikan. Predictably, the Lakers won in their division and in the playoffs. And in the last year of the World Tournament, they won that, too, with Mikan scoring 40 points as the Lakers beat the Rens, 75-71, in the finals.

So, after two seasons of competition between the BAA and the NBL, it was obviously an impasse. The NBL was the stronger league, but that wasn't being translated into dollars because the league was saddled with small towns and small arenas. The BAA had the cities and the arenas—and the larger vision—but it lacked the players.

Clearly, something would have to be done to combine the advantages of each to form one league. Something was done: The BAA practiced cannibalism.

Bob Davies was a great shooter and ballhandler for Rochester, and also the inspiration for juvenile sports novels. *(NBA)*

5. Merger or Cannibalism?

The question was not whether there would be a merger, but when and how. During the summer of 1948, BAA commissioner Maurice Podoloff pursued ways of getting the two leagues together—with his league being the dominant force in a new grouping, of course.

Podoloff first tried to interest the Minneapolis Lakers in jumping to the BAA, because the Lakers were the best team in basketball. The Lakers, though, weren't interested.

Indianapolis and Fort Wayne were. Podoloff was able to convince Paul Walk, general manager of the Indianapolis Kautskys, and Carl Bennett, general manager of the Fort Wayne Pistons, that the future would be brighter for their teams in the BAA, with its larger arenas and more prestigious cities. Indianapolis and Fort Wayne jumped to the BAA.

For the NBL, worse was yet to come. The Lakers, not wanting to be stuck in a declining league, followed Indianapolis and Fort Wayne into the BAA. Soon, the Rochester Royals did, too, and the Royals were second only to the Lakers in pro basketball. Before the 1948-49 season had begun, the pro basketball war was effectively over, and the BAA had won.

There was more bad news for the NBL: The Toledo and Flint franchises folded, leaving only five teams, and commissioner Piggy Lambert resigned because of ill health, to be replaced by Doxie Moore.

The NBL struggled on for another season, adding four franchises, in Detroit, Denver, Hammond (Indiana), and Waterloo (Iowa); the Detroit franchise was shifted to Dayton (Ohio) after only 19 games, and a 2-17 record.

But it was only a death rattle. With its best teams and best players gone, the NBL was left only with minor league cities and, mostly, minor league players.

The BAA now was obviously *the* big league, a conclusion underscored by the fact that Ned Irish was more willing to schedule his Knicks into Madison Square Garden, because the players coming in were easier to promote. Indeed, one night, the Garden marquee read: George Mikan vs. Knicks.

As expected, the Lakers and Royals dominated the BAA as they had dominated the NBL. Surprisingly, though, the Royals finished a game ahead of the Lakers in the western division, with a 45-15 record to the Lakers' 44-16.

The Lakers and Royals were classic rivals; for six straight seasons, starting with the 1948-49 season, they finished 1-2 in their division. Three times the Lakers finished first; twice it was the Royals; once it was a tie, with Minneapolis winning a one-game playoff for the title. And before that, in their last season in the NBL when they were in separate divisions, each had won a divisional championship.

Moreover, it was a classic matchup in styles, the brawny Lakers against the clever Royals who depended on finesse. The strength of the Royals was in their backcourt, where they had Bob Davies and Bobby Wanzer, and Red Holzman coming off the bench. Davies was unparalleled as the middle man on the fast break, and many considered the Royals the most entertaining team in pro basketball.

The Royals also had an excellent center in Arnie Risen (6'9" and 200 pounds), who averaged 16.6 points a game in that first BAA season. But Risen, too, depended more on deftness than muscle, a technique that worked well against everybody but the Lakers and Mikan.

That was the rub for the Royals. Though the Royals could keep pace with the Lakers during the season, they couldn't match the Lakers' muscle in direct confrontations. Thus, they almost always lost in the playoffs; their one playoff-round victory over the Lakers came when Mikan broke a bone in his leg.

The pattern had been started in the last year of the NBL, when the Lakers had defeated the Royals in the playoff finals. (Of course, Mikan's Chicago Gears team had also beaten the Royals in the playoffs the previous year, his first as a pro.)

It was the same story in the first BAA season. Mikan had had an excellent season, averaging 28.3 points a game. He was even better in the playoffs, averaging 30.3 points in ten games as the Lakers defeated Chicago Rochester, and then Washington to win the championship. Remarkably, Mikan broke his wrist in the fourth game of the Washington series and played the last two games with a cast.

None of that was as important as what was happening off the court: Before the next season, the BAA fired the last shot of the basketball war, taking in four NBL franchises, Syracuse, Anderson, Sheboygan, and the Tri-Cities team, which represented two Illinois cities, Moline and Rockford, and Davenport, Iowa.

With that, the NBL officially expired.

Two other teams which had started the 1948-49 season in the NBL but had not finished it, Denver and Waterloo, were also brought into the expanded league.

Meanwhile, two BAA franchises were folding—Providence and the Indianapolis Jets. But the Jets were being replaced by the Indianapolis Olympians, consisting primarily of the national collegiate champion Kentucky team, which was turning pro as a unit.

The result of all these moves was a 17-team league which was retitled the National Basketball Association (NBA), thus combining the names of the two warring leagues.

The rapid expansion solved some legal problems; by taking in all the NBL teams that wanted to join the new league, the NBA could not be sued for violation of anti-trust laws.

But at the same time, it created enormous scheduling problems. The previous season, the BAA had played a tidy 60-game season with 12 teams. Tidy would be the last word that could be used to describe the NBA's first season. Because of travel difficulties, for instance, some teams played 62 games, some 64, some even 68.

But this was nothing compared to the weird circumstances which surrounded the Syracuse National team, one of the survivors of the NBL. The Nats were a good team and an interesting one, owned by Danny Biasone, the son of Italian immigrants and an owner who deserved the oft-misused description of sportsman.

"I think with every team, there's an attitude that descends from the owner," said Alex Hannum, a member of that team who later went on to coach the Nats and the Warriors before he went into the construction business in Santa Maria, Calif.

"Danny was just a great guy. He was great at analyzing what makes a sport go, and he was always looking for ways to improve it." (Biasone, in fact, is often given credit for the 24-second clock.) "He wasn't so much interested in making money as giving the people their money's worth.

"I can honestly say that in all my years of basketball I had the most fun playing and coaching with the Nats."

The Nats' style was set by player-coach Al Cervi, who had never gone to college; Cervi learned his basketball on the city playgrounds in Rochester. He had been an outstanding guard for the Rochester Royals, and his style—as player and coach—was strongly defense-oriented.

When the Royals had jumped to the BAA, Biasone had become annoyed with Rochester owner Lester Harrison, and Biasone had lured Cervi away to coach the Nats, who finished second in both the league season and the playoffs to the Anderson Packers in that final NBL season.

The unquestioned star of that Syracuse team was Dolph Schayes, a 6'7" forward from New York who went on to become a member of the Hall of Fame.

By present-day standards Schayes was an unlikely star. "He was slow," remembered Hannum, "and he couldn't jump. He never could dunk the ball."

But despite his lack of jumping ability, Schayes was an excellent rebounder (he averaged almost 11 rebounds a game for his career). And best of all, he was a scorer. He had a deadly two-handed set shot from outside, and he could drive to the basket if an opponent played him close to shut off his set shot. He was a master of the three-point play; his style got him to the free-throw line frequently, and he led the league in free throw accuracy three times, twice with percentages of .904. His career average of .843 from the line was second only to Bill Sharman's in NBA history when he retired.

Schayes was also a pivotal figure in the early days of the NBA. When he came out of NYU he was drafted by both the New York Knicks and the Nats. At the time, the BAA had a limit of $6000 that could be paid to a rookie, and Knicks' owner Ned Irish probably didn't feel that Schayes was good enough to break the rule for him. The Nats were willing to go higher—estimates vary from $500 to $1000—and so, Schayes signed with them.

Schayes himself felt his decision, though inspired by money, was the right one for him. "The Nats were a young team," he said, "and they needed a big man, so I got a chance to develop."

It turned out to be a bad decision for the Knicks, however, both from a playing and a financial standpoint. The Knicks would obviously have been a much stronger team with Schayes, and the presence of a star Jewish player would have meant many more dollars at the gate.

"We used to call him the absent-minded professor," remembered Hannum, "because his mind was always in a different world. But what a player he was, truly one of the first superstars."

Schayes, like all the Nats, worked hard to get a good shot, and he was a high-percentage shooter. But, though recognition came early to Schayes, that was not true of his team.

"We were like the ugly step-sister," laughed Hannum. "The big cities in the East didn't want us coming into their cities to play, not little old Syracuse."

Geographically, the Nats belonged in the Eastern Division, which is where they were put. But because of the reluctance of New York and Washington to schedule them, the Nats played only a home-and-home series (ten games) with the other five teams in the division. They won nine of the ten. All in all, the Nats won 51 of their 64 games that season and finished 13 games ahead of the second-place Knicks in the East.

The league in that first, chaotic season was split into three divisions, East, West, and Central. That created a lot of the playoff games that are so dear to owners' hearts, and the Nats swept through three rounds to get to the finals.

Once there, though, the Nats ran into the Lakers and, inevitably, bowed in six games. "One of the great frustrations of my career," said Hannum, who later played three years for Rochester, "was that I always seemed to be playing on teams that lost in six games to the Lakers."

It was obvious there would have to be some shakeouts after that first season if the NBA were ever to make any sense as a league, and before the next season, six teams folded.

Four of them were expected: Sheboygan, Waterloo, and Anderson were simply too small to compete with the metropolitan cities and their big arenas, and Denver was too far away in an era when airplane travel still was relatively rare.

Surprisingly, though, Chicago and St. Louis also folded, while smaller cities like Syracuse and Indianapolis—and the Tri-Cities grouping—survived.

Now, the NBA was down to 11 teams, a manageable size, and more uniform scheduling was possible. With fewer teams, it was also possible to have a greater concentration of name players, which was the key to the league's success. College sports can draw because of the loyalty of alumni who identify with the school. No pro league has that luxury. Pro sports draw because of strong teams and star players, and it's the players who are the more important in the early years of a league.

So it was very important in the first year of the NBA that the all-league team consisted of George Mikan, Jim Pollard, Alex Groza, Bob Davies, and Max Zaslofsky, all well-known players and, as a unit, unarguably the best team in history.

It was important that there were other name players in the league, including some like Schayes and Fulkes, who were making their reputations as pros, and others, like Easy Ed Macauley and Ralph Beard, who were illustrious college All-Americans.

It was important that an impressive group of collegians would be eligible for the draft, including Paul Arizin, Bob Cousy, Bill Sharman, Charlie Share, Don Lofgran, and Larry Foust.

And it was important that, for the first time, the pros were about to dip into the black player market. (At that time, of course, the accepted designation was Negro. To avoid confusion and multiple explanations, I will use the term black.)

The relationship of organized professional basketball to black players was a curious one. By 1949, there had been black players in professional football and Jackie Robinson had broken the color line in baseball. Yet, in basketball, the sport blacks play best, there had been none in the NBL, the BAA, or the NBA, in its first season. There had been black teams, of course, such as the New York Rens and the Harlem Globetrotters, but no individual players in the white leagues.

Oddly, this had little or nothing to do with racial bias of the owners themselves. There is no reason to believe that the NBA owners were either more or less prejudiced than the average person of that era.

The owners *were* concerned that white fans might not "identify" with black stars, a concern which still manifests itself today, as the percentage of black players in the league rises. Though they realized how good black players could be—there were, of course, many instances of black teams beating white teams in the past—there was no Branch Rickey among the owners, a man who could combine a desire to do the moral thing with the realization of the competitive edge he would gain.

And there was also, and perhaps most important, the special relationship owners had with the Harlem Globetrotters.

The 'Trotters, by the late '40s, were the most powerful basketball attraction going. In the BAA, owners had frequently brought the 'Trotters in for a preliminary game, knowing they could get more fans for that than they could for the regular BAA game.

Thus, the owners were not eager to jeopardize their relationship with Globetrotter promoter Abe Saperstein by signing black players, and Saperstein understandably was content to maintain his monopoly of the black market.

But the forces of history would soon change that. More and more blacks were playing college ball, and it was becoming evident to NBA owners that signing black stars would be more important to their success than Abe Saperstein's good will. So, in the fall of 1950, the first black players entered the NBA, Chuck Cooper with the Boston Celtics and Nat (Sweetwater) Clifton with the New York Knicks.

Cooper, the first to sign, had been a college star at Duquesne. Clifton had been a featured attraction with the Globetrotters and had actually purchased his contract so he could play in the NBA.

Neither became a star in the NBA. Clifton played eight seasons with the Knicks and averaged ten points a game for his career. Cooper played six seasons, averaging 6.7 points a game. Their significance lies in the fact that they were the first blacks, the ones who opened the door. In a very short time, the fact that blacks were playing pro basketball and in ever-increasing numbers would change the game dramatically.

But that was a long-run change. In the short run, at mid-century, the most important man in pro basketball was unquestionably the 6'10" giant who played center for the Minneapolis Lakers and made such an impression that coaches and players from that time casually refer to it as the Mikan Era.

6. The Immovable Object: George Mikan

George Mikan: Now, there was a force. He wasn't fast and he wasn't a great jumper, and there are those who insist he couldn't play in the faster game of the NBA today. Perhaps not, but in his time, he was *the* player. Nobody has ever dominated the game quite so completely as Big George. He set scoring records, his teams won title after title, he forced rules changes, and he made people in and out of the game think of basketball in an entirely different way.

There is one major difference between basketball and the other major team sports of football, baseball, hockey, and soccer: It is played vertically. In the other sports, the ball (or puck, in hockey) is advanced horizontally for the most part. In basketball, the goal is a vertical target, ten feet above the floor.

Given that, a taller player has a decided advantage over a shorter one, because he is closer to the target. Not only should it be easier for him to score, but he has a better chance to rebound a missed shot or to knock away an opponent's shot.

That seems obvious to us now. It wasn't so obvious before Mikan. In that era, tall players were called goons and freaks, and their height advantage was more than canceled out by their lack of co-ordination. Anybody over 6'5" was suspect.

The stars of the pro game had usually been the guards, clever ballhandlers, and shooters who could control the game, a line that stretched from Nat Holman through John Wooden to Bob Davies. Occasionally, there would be a hot-shooting forward, like Joe Fulks. Centers were there mostly to rebound, because the really big ones were generally too awkward to be effective shooters.

Mikan changed all that, because he proved that a big man could be co-ordinated, too. He was the first of the great big men, and he started a trend.

Now, everybody looks first for the big man in the middle, what Al McGuire calls the "aircraft carrier." NBA teams have proved that a championship can be won without an outstanding center, but when you talk dynasty, it always starts with the great center. An outstanding center brings the highest price graduating from college, and he continues to bring the highest price as a veteran pro.

As a result of the emphasis on the big man, there are a number of good ones around today. In Mikan's time, George stood alone. He owned the middle. In college, Bob Kurland of Oklahoma A&M had been roughly Mikan's equal, better defensively but not so strong offensively, but Kurland never turned pro, playing

George Mikan rewrote the record book and was voted the Player of the First Half Century. (Hall of Fame)

instead for the Phillips Oilers of the AAU league. Some people thought Don Otten of Bowling Green, even bigger than Mikan at 6'11" and 250, might be his equal, but Mikan ate Otten alive when their teams met in the National Invitational Tournament (NIT), and Otten was little more than a journeyman in seven NBA seasons.

Mikan was a force of Nature. Nothing seemed to stop him. Each of his legs was broken once. His right foot, the arch of his left foot, his right wrist, his nose, and a thumb were also broken at various times. Three of his fingers were broken. His nose was ripped open, and he had a total of 166 stitches during his career. He wasn't exempt in the playoffs, either. He broke a bone in his leg in one playoff game, but finished it; in another, he broke his wrist and played the final two games with a cast on his wrist.

George never complained. Even now, he says only, "It was pretty tough. Basketball's a rough game. You don't have the protection of equipment that you have in other sports, and there are big men coming at high speed hitting other big men."

Some players pad their scoring averages with meaningless points in runaway games, but Mikan was just the opposite: He got his points when they were needed most.

"The great thing about him," says Ray Meyer, his college coach, "was that if you won by 30 points, he'd probably get only ten or so, but if you won by two, he'd get 40 points."

Meyer remembers watching Mikan in a pro game in Chicago early in his career. "The score was tied and it was right near the end of the game," says Meyer. "I told my wife, 'Watch, he'll find a way to get fouled.' He did, and he made the free throws to win the game."

Bruce Hale had a similar memory from Mikan's first pro year, when he and Hale were teammates on the Chicago Gears.

"We were playing the Royals in Rochester, and it was tough winning in Rochester, in that tiny gym with those fans. We always felt a win in Rochester was like two at home.

"The score was tied with a few seconds remaining. We had a timeout and he told us, 'Just get me the ball and I'll score.' He was so determined, I'll never forget it. When he got the ball, two guys grabbed his arms, but he just took them up with him and stuffed the ball, and that was at a time when stuffs weren't common."

One other note: In two separate playoff series, Mikan averaged more than 30 points a game, at a time when 20 points in a game was a considerable feat.

Because he was such an outstanding player, and because he made the teams he played for winners, Mikan was the top gate attraction in the league. More than anybody else, he made pro basketball respectable.

And with it all he remained level-headed, seemingly untouched by the fame and adulation. "He's a good person," said Hale. Amazingly, those around the league who were getting crushed regularly by Mikan and the Lakers agreed.

Unlike the stars of today, who are usually high school All-Americans and recruited heavily by colleges across the nation, Mikan got no attention as a high school player at Joliet (Illinois) High School. He was tall but not well co-ordinated, he wore glasses, and he had missed most of one season with a broken leg. Nobody recruited him. On his own, he enrolled at DePaul University.

During his freshman year at DePaul, he was invited down to Notre Dame to work out during the Christmas holidays. "I had hurt my ankle just before that, and it seemed every pass that was thrown at me in that practice was thrown at my ankles," remembers Mikan today. "I kicked more three-point field goals that day than any of their kickers on the football team.

"After the practice, the coach, George Keogan, came up to me and said, 'I think you'd better go back to DePaul. You'll make a better scholar than athlete.' Well, he was wrong on two counts. A couple of years later, after I'd scored 50 points in a game against Notre Dame, I reminded him of that, but all he said was, 'You win some, you lose some.'"

One man saw the potential in Mikan: Ray Meyer. Ironically, Meyer had been an assistant at Notre Dame at the time Mikan had worked out there, and he also told Mikan he'd be better off at a small school. Then, Meyer got the chance to coach DePaul. When he arrived and saw Mikan, he said to himself, "There's my future."

"He was an awkward kid at first," remembers Meyer, "but he just kept improving. I guided him, but he had talent, and he just kept getting better and better. The superstars are like that. They have something inside.

"George always had great instincts for the game, and he was such an intelligent player. If you told him to overplay a guy, he would. If you told him to ignore fakes, he could do that. You only had to tell him once, and he picked it right up."

It was a good combination, Meyer and Mikan, because George was willing to work very hard to improve, and Meyer was a young coach willing to work equally hard to gain a reputation. Between them they tried all the normal training methods and some highly unusual ones.

"I hired a girl to teach him to dance," says Meyer now, "to improve his co-ordination. I would shoot—I was a pretty good shooter in those days—and have him trying to block shots. I had watched boxers get ready for fights and I noticed they skipped rope a lot to improve their co-ordination, so I had George do that."

Meyer tried something else: He put Billy Donato, a 5′5″ guard who was very quick and a good ballhandler, at mid-court with the ball; Mikan was supposed to try to stop him. "At first, Donato got by easily," says Meyer, "but as time went on, Mikan got better and better, and he learned, when he was beat, how to get the ball from behind."

By his sophomore year, Mikan was a much improved player, but he still had one glaring flaw: He could only go one way. "I could only shoot a right-handed hook," he says, "and everybody was overguarding me. We, Ray and I, decided I'd have to go the other way, so I worked hard on a left-handed hook, and in the long run, that turned out to be more accurate."

Long after he coached Mikan, Meyer remembered him with great fondness. "George was an unusual boy," he said. "Basketball was very important to him, but he also was determined to get his law degree. He always had his priorities right."

And, in fact, he did get his law degree in 1948, showing the same determination off the court that he did on. "I had to go back to school in the summer," he says. "Boy, that was hard, but it was very important to me."

By the time he was a senior, Mikan was awesome. When DePaul won the NIT, for instance, he set ten individual records, including 53 points against Rhode Island and a three-game total of 120. The pros could hardly wait to get him.

By that time, Mikan was ready for the pros, though it had only been in the last couple of years of his college career that he had thought of playing professionally.

"I didn't really think of a professional career at the time I started college ball," he says, "because the pros at that time were playing in small towns and I just didn't think of it as possible employment. But by the time I finished, well, it had become something in which you could make quick money.

"We used to go down from DePaul to watch the World Tournament in Chicago, and that was interesting, and there were some DePaul graduates playing pro ball, so gradually, it became something I was interested in."

Mikan actually turned pro while he was still in college although, of course, after he had completed his college playing career. The Chicago Gears signed him in time to play in the World Tournament (he also played in a few exhibitions before the tournament). He couldn't quite make the Gears a champion, as they lost to Oshkosh 72-66 in the semifinals, but he scored 100 points in five games and was named the tournament's Most Valuable Player.

The next year he played only 25 games because of the dispute over his contract, but he averaged 16.5 points a game in that stretch, the highest average in the league although nothing compared to what he would do later.

In the playoffs he started to show what a dominating force he would be as he scored 217 points in 11 games as the Gears roared to the title, taking Rochester three games out of four in the finals.

It was the next season, though, when he was assigned to the Minneapolis Lakers that Mikan's reign of glory really began. For six straight seasons, he averaged more than 20 points a game: 21.3, 28.3, 27.4, 28.4, 23.8, and 20.6. In his seventh season, he slipped to 18.1, still good enough for fourth place in the league.

Because modern-day scoring figures are so much higher, it's necessary to put Mikan's totals into perspective. In the 1948-49 season, for instance, when he averaged 28.3 points a game, only Joe Fulks (26) and Max Zaslofsky (20.6) also topped 20 points. In 1949-50, when Mikan averaged 27.4, only Alex Groza at 23.4 also topped 20 points a game. The next season, when George set what was then a pro scoring record by averaging 28.4 points, only Groza at 21.7 and Ed Macauley at 20.4 were also in the 20-point class. Or, to put it another way, at a time when almost nobody else was scoring 20 points a game, Mikan was coming close to 30.

Nine times he scored more than 44 points in a game, and he went as high as 61. And there was more to his game than scoring. "He was one of the best all-round players I've seen," said Hale.

Joe Lapchick, the old Original Celtic and an excellent center himself, once said Mikan was the best passing center ever in basketball.

It was a skill Mikan had acquired because of his ability to judge the game and his own performance. "When my opponents ganged up on me," he said, "that meant some of my teammates were free. So, I started concentrating on handing off or passing to players breaking around me."

Everything revolved around Mikan, as it had with his other teams, too. He would come down court in the Lakers' deliberate offense, set himself up near the basket and then maneuver to get open for a pass.

Once he got the ball, he would either work for his own shot or pass to a cutting teammate, who was usually open for a good shot because of the defensive concentration on Mikan.

"We played in a more controlled style than they do today," says Mikan, "with a lot of picking and blocking out. I always thought it was better that way because the guys knew where they were going to go and you knew what to expect."

Teams tried everything against George, double- and even triple-teaming him. That didn't work because he would pass to the open man. They tried rough stuff. In those days, every rookie got worked over good in his first few games to see if he could be intimidated. Mikan, because he was so good, got even rougher treatment. It didn't bother George, although it did concern him that he was getting cut around the eyes because of his glasses.

George was very nearsighted and needed his glasses. "I tried contact lenses but couldn't get used to them," he says. "I finally had glasses made similar to those used in railroads or in plants, hardened glass with steel rims and rubber over the rims. I used a rubber band to keep them on my head."

Unable to stop him on the court, other teams tried to legislate a reduction in

Mikan's effectiveness. "I was responsible for the goal-tending rule, and they widened the six-foot lane to 12 feet to try to stop me.

"Strangely enough, that was better for me because I could maneuver better. Before, they'd throw a low zone at me and I couldn't move. I'd just have to use brute strength to go to the basket. But this way, I could drive and pivot and go either way. I think it helped me develop into a better player."

Mikan was also partially responsible for the eventual adoption of the 24-second rule, a rule he likes because it's speeded up the game. "There were some guys in the league then, like Bob Cousy and Slater Martin, who could dribble for half an hour and nobody could take the ball away from them. But who wants to watch the ball being pumped up and down all night?"

"We played one game at home against Fort Wayne when they deliberately came in and stalled. They won the game, 19-18. It was a Father-Son night for us, and that really hurt us. Fort Wayne had a coach, Murray Mendenhall, who thought winning was everything, but of course, in the pros, it's entertainment, too."

As a result of games like that, the 24-second rule was eventually adopted.

In Mikan's seven full seasons with the Lakers the team won five titles and finished second twice. In the playoffs they were even better, winning six times out of seven (the one time they lost was when Mikan broke his leg). And, of course, George's first team, the Chicago Gears, had also won the playoffs, giving him a run of seven out of eight. That's dominance!

Mikan didn't do it alone, of course. The Lakers had other outstanding players, and their front line of Mikan, Jim Pollard, and Vern Mikkelsen was as good as the game has ever known.

Pollard, in particular, was outstanding. An All-American at Stanford, he had been in the service for three years and then had played two years of AAU ball in San Diego and Oakland before joining the Lakers the same year that Mikan did.

Pollard at 6'5" was an outstanding jumper, and a smooth all-round player, strong defensively and an excellent rebounder. He didn't score nearly as much as Mikan, averaging a shade over 13 points for his career, but he was a good shooter and a varied one, sometimes shooting a one-handed set, sometimes a jumper, and sometimes driving to the hoop.

It's possible that Pollard would have been recognized as a better player if he hadn't been in Mikan's shadow. Opponents spoke quite highly of him. Bones McKinney, for instance, called him the "greatest cornerman ever," and added, "On another club, no one would touch him. He can do everything on a basketball floor and do it with finesse." Fred Scolari, another opponent, talked of Pollard's all-round skills and said, "He is better than most big men and decidedly better than the little men."

But Pollard put the matter of playing with Mikan in better perspective. "Sure," he

Jim Pollard modified his game to fit in with George Mikan but was still spectacular enough to make the Hall of Fame for his play with the Minneapolis Lakers.
(Hall of Fame)

said, "I might have been able to do more things with another team, but it was not exactly a big, bad mistake to get with Mikan. That guaranteed a winner."

Mikan and Pollard worked well together, once they got to know each other's games. It took awhile, though.

"When I first came to the club," says Pollard, "I had trouble when I drove to the basket because Mikan would always turn to the basket to be in position for a rebound when anybody else started there. That meant his man automatically went with him.

"We talked about that and I finally convinced him to wait just one count. That way his man would stay in the middle. If that man left Mikan to cover me, then I could flip the ball to George for an easy basket."

Mikkelsen was another fine player, big (6'7½", which is probably the equivalent of about 6'10" in today's game) and strong. "For years, he was called 'Old Workhorse,'" remembers Pollard.

Mikkelsen wasn't a good outside shooter, but he worked well inside with a two-handed overhead shot and a hook shot. He was an outstanding rebounder and a good defensive player against big forwards. In today's game he would be classified as a strong forward.

"We complemented each other," notes Pollard, "because I had the quickness and agility Mikan and Mikkelsen lacked, so I could take any forward who had some quickness and they could take the bigger, stronger guys."

That Laker team also did something virtually no other team of the era did: With Mikan, Mikkelsen, and Pollard up front, they made offensive rebounding a key part of their game.

"We'd try to get guys to take a soft shot so there would be a short rebound if it missed," remembers Pollard. "That was tailor-made for us, especially with Mikan and Mikkelsen. In addition to being big and strong, George was absolutely the most competitive guy I ever saw. He'd go through a brick wall to get the ball.

"And then when we got the rebound we'd just go right back up with it, instead of passing it out and trying to set up another play."

As good as Pollard and Mikkelsen were, there was never any question that Mikan was the key to the team, a point that was underscored when he retired; the Lakers never won another championship until they were moved to Los Angeles.

Mikan's retirement came after the 1953-54 season, the last one played before the advent of the 24-second clock. He knew he was starting to lose his effectiveness, and he was not an athlete who had to hang on because he had nothing else he could do.

After one year in retirement he came back for one more try; that was a mistake. He was only a shadow of his old self, averaging only 10.5 points a game in 37 games before making his retirement permanent.

But that last disappointing season can't erase the great memories of when big George Mikan dominated pro basketball. He was truly the greatest.

7. Scandal!

Although the pro game was making great strides at mid-century, college basketball was still the more popular attraction. One thing changed that, virtually overnight: the college basketball scandals of 1951.

The scandals erupted at a time when interest in college basketball was at its peak. There seemed to be great teams everywhere: Oklahoma A&M had won two straight NCAA championships in the mid-'40s; Kentucky had won back-to-back NCAA titles, and an earlier NIT championship, over a period of four years; Bradley, though it hadn't won a championship, had been runnerup in both the NCAA and the NIT tournaments in 1950.

But the greatest story of all was the City College of New York (CCNY) team of 1950, coached by that old Celtic, Nat Holman, which had won both the NCAA and NIT titles in the same year. No other team had ever done that, and now no team can, because teams can no longer play in both tournaments.

CCNY was a clever, intelligent, hard-working team, in the mold of Holman, who had exhibited exactly those qualities when he was a player. (In 1976, an official proclamation from the Boys' Athletic League named Holman as the outstanding basketball product ever to come out of New York, a city which has produced Kareem Abdul-Jabbar [then Lew Alcindor] and Julius [Dr. J] Erving, among others.)

Holman drove his team relentlessly. He had no patience with mediocrity. He regarded himself as a teacher and, just as a student would be expected to learn something in a class, Holman felt that a player who had had a year of his coaching should show dramatic improvement.

Players often resented Holman's tactics, and he had teams which came close to rebellion in the years immediately after World War II, when war veterans were playing. But nobody denied that he was an excellent coach.

In the 1949-50 season the Beavers lacked great height, with Ed Roman the tallest player at 6'6", but Roman was more effective than his height would indicate because he knew how to block out for rebounds and he used his bulk (240 pounds) to great advantage.

And the fact that there were four players of relatively equal height (Roman, Irwin Dambrot, and Floyd Lane at 6'4", and Ed Warner at 6'3½"), gave Holman great flexibility. Defensively, players could switch without creating great mismatches.

Offensively, Holman could move Roman out of the pivot to hit a soft one-handed set from outside, while moving one of the other three inside to overpower a defender.

When the Beavers won both the NCAA and NIT tournaments they were dubbed the "Cinderella team." As always with any New York-based team in any sport, they received a remarkable amount of publicity.

Then, the next season, the story broke: The CCNY players had taken money to "shave" points, winning by less than the point spread established by the betting line. Other players on other teams had, too, but because the Beavers were the champions, their downfall had the greatest impact.

In retrospect it is easy to be cynical about the chain of events. A few players went to jail, but nothing really changed in the college game. Ten years later, another scandal broke, and it would surprise nobody familiar with the pressures and temptations of the college game if still another broke tomorrow.

But at the time there had to be a scapegoat, even beyond the players themselves. Because the first news of the scandal broke in New York, the city, Madison Square Garden, and the "big-time atmosphere" were seen as the villains by those outside metropolitan New York, many of whom had reasons to hate New York that had nothing to do with basketball.

College basketball should not be played in Madison Square Garden, went the litany, because there were too many gamblers to tempt the players. College basketball should be returned to college fieldhouses where, theoretically, gamblers could not approach the players: a wholesome atmosphere for a wholesome game.

So, Madison Square Garden—which had been the backbone of the college sports with its doubleheaders and tournaments—was deemphasized. The NCAA tournament, which had been played for seven of the previous eight years in the Garden, was played in Minneapolis in 1951 and has been moved around the country since, played everywhere but New York. The NIT, which remained a New York series, became a tournament which gets only those teams that do not qualify for the NCAA; before the scandal it had been at least as important as the NCAA tournament.

The pros moved into the vacuum. Somebody, after all, was going to play in the Garden; if the colleges left, the pros would play there. And because of the media concentration in New York, those who played there would get the most publicity.

The reason for the change wasn't just New York. Though the NBA still had some "minor league" cities, it was also moving into the big cities at the time when the colleges were pulling back to smaller towns to avoid the "big-time" taint. The ascendancy of the pro game started at that very point.

And then the scandal spread. It wasn't limited to sinful New York after all. In Peoria, Ill., some Bradley players had accepted bribes. In Lexington, Ky., too. At the first news of the scandal, Kentucky coach Adolph Rupp had bragged, "They couldn't touch my boys with a ten-foot pole." As it turned out, gamblers didn't have to worry about poles; they could reach the Kentucky players with outstretched hands with money in them.

And that last revelation, finally, reached into the pro game, to the heart of the Indianapolis Olympians.

The 1945-49 Kentucky Wildcats was the best team college basketball had known to that point, winning one NIT title and just missing another and winning back-to-back NCAA titles in 1948 and '49. Even today, that team would probably rank in the top five of all time.

Though it was a well-balanced team with excellent depth, there were two unquestioned stars: guard Ralph Beard and center Alex Groza.

Beard came from an athletic family. His grandfather had been a track star and baseball player at Vanderbilt. His father, Ralph Sr., had been a minor league baseball player. A stepbrother, Frank, later became a top golfer.

Ralph was a versatile athlete who lettered in four sports—football, basketball, baseball, and track—in high school, but his No. 1 sport was always basketball, from the time he tossed small balls into a miniature basket over his bed as a small child.

At Male High in Louisville he led his team to the school's first state championship. He was heavily recruited—though Kentucky always had the inside track—and it was no surprise when he became a college star.

Groza was a different matter. Though he was 6'5" (but only 165 pounds) when he graduated from high school, he didn't receive a single offer of an athletic scholarship.

The spurned Groza had no choice but to enlist in the Army. As it happened that was the best thing that could have happened to him, because in his 21-month tour of duty he matured physically. When he was released in 1945 he was 6'7" and 210 pounds. Rupp was tipped off about Groza and he offered him a scholarship, which Alex gratefully accepted.

As a freshman, Groza was still developing his skills. Because he lacked the overwhelming size of George Mikan and Bob Kurland, he depended more on movement. He could score from inside with a hook shot or move outside and shoot from there. Rupp brought him along slowly that first year.

Beard, in contrast, was a starter from the beginning, and the star of the team, too. He was a prototype guard, with his great speed and versatility. He could shoot effectively from outside or drive past a defender who played him too closely, and he was also an excellent passer.

Beard led the Wildcats to a 28-2 record in his freshman season, but because LSU won the Southeastern Conference, the 'Cats couldn't go to the NCAA. They settled for the NIT and beat Arizona and West Virginia to reach the finals. Tied, 45-45, with Rhode Island in that final game, Beard was fouled with just seconds remaining. He sank the free throw to give the Wildcats a 46-45 win and the NIT title.

The next year, Groza and another talented sophomore, Wallace (Wah Wah) Jones, joined Beard in the starting lineup. Beard was named to All-America teams and the Wildcats went 34-2, but their season ended in disappointment when they were beaten, 49-45, by Utah in the NIT.

There was still plenty of glory ahead, however. As juniors, Beard, Groza, and Jones were joined in the starting lineup by Kenny Rollins and Cliff Barker. On the bench were Jim Line and Walter Hirsch, good enough to be starting for most teams. The Wildcats won the SEC during a 36-3 season, which put them in the NCAA. They won the first of their NCAA titles with a lopsided 58-42 victory over Baylor in the finals.

Because 1948 was an Olympic year, the Wildcats had another chance for glory. In the Olympic trials, they advanced easily to the finals against the Phillips 66 Oilers. The Oilers were amateurs only in the sense that athletes in Communist countries are today; they were on the Phillips' payroll, but their primary job was to play basketball. With Kurland as the team's star, the Oilers were probably only a small cut below the top pro teams of the time.

Kurland dominated Groza in the game, and Barker broke his nose in the first half. So, the Oilers won the game, but only by 53-49. Beard scored 23 points and Oilers coach Bud Browning said, "Ralph Beard is absolutely the best basketball player I ever saw."

The Phillips and Kentucky starting units made up the U.S. Olympic team that year and, except for a 59-57 squeaker over Argentina, the United States team swept easily through the Olympics. Their average winning margin was 37 points, and in the finals, the Americans swamped France, 65-21.

The next season, when Beard, Groza, and Jones were all seniors, was the best yet; all three made the All-American teams, and the Wildcats, with a 29-1 season record, were voted the No. 1 team in the country in the Associated Press poll.

The Wildcats were favored to become the first team to win both the NIT and the NCAA. That dream ended when Loyola upset Kentucky in the NIT finals, 67-56, but the Wildcats redeemed themselves at least partially by winning another NCAA title. In the final game, Groza scored 25 points and Kentucky beat Oklahoma A&M, 46-36.

Naturally enough, the great Kentucky players turned pro when their collegiate careers ended, but they did it with a big difference—as a unit.

Beard, Groza, Jones, Barker, and Joe Holland became the nucleus of the Indianapolis Olympians, a name that was a natural derivation from the Wildcats' Olympics success.

The five players, with Lexington sports editor J. R. (Babe) Kimbrough, owned 70 percent of the club's stock. Kimbrough was the club's president; Groza, Beard, and Barker were listed as vice-presidents, Jones was the secretary and Holland was the treasurer. Barker was the playing coach.

Each player received a $5000 bonus and a $5000 salary, good money in those days, in addition to what he got from his stock.

Barker was the only Kentucky player who didn't start; Bruce Hale joined Beard, Groza, Jones, and Holland as starters.

It was a unique combination, and as such, a great gate attraction. Even though the name on the front of the uniform shirt was Indianapolis, with minor league connotations, Ned Irish was eager to book the Olympians into Madison Square Garden, where they ranked only behind George Mikan and the Minneapolis Lakers as an attraction.

They played well, too, winning 39 games and losing 25 in their first season, good enough to win in the NBA's Western Division. As in college, Beard and Groza were the team's stars, though the emphasis was reversed. In college, Beard had been the bigger star, but the slower-developing Groza was reaching his peak as a pro. In his rookie season, Groza was second only to Mikan in scoring with a 23.4 average, and he led the NBA in field goal percentage with 48 percent.

"Groza was the first of the new breed of centers," said teammate Hale, "because he was a good ballhandler and could put the ball on the floor. The way he played Mikan, he'd come out to the top of the key and if George didn't come out—and he usually didn't—he'd pop the jumper. If George did come out, he'd drive around him. He certainly would have been one of the all-time greats."

Beard was less spectacular in his rookie season, but he averaged a solid 14.8 points a game and gained an excellent reputation around the league.

"I played against every good little man," says Fred Scolari, a nine-year pro veteran who was with the Washington Caps when Beard broke in, "and Ralph Beard gave me more trouble than anybody I ever had to guard. Bob Davies and Bob Cousy were slower than me, so even when they made great moves, I could sometimes catch up, but Beard was the fastest player I ever had to guard. He and Groza would have been two of the very best ever to play the game."

The next season was another good one for Groza and Beard. Groza again finished second to Mikan in scoring, this time averaging 21.7 points a game, and again led the league in field goal percentage, with 47 percent. Beard, ninth in NBA scoring as a rookie, moved up to seventh with a 16.8 average.

As a team, the Olympians had not done so well. With the NBA condensing from an unwieldy 17 teams to 12 for the 1950-51 season, the Olympians had been placed in the Western Division with Minneapolis and Rochester, the two best teams in the NBA, along with the Fort Wayne and Tri-Cities franchise. With a 31-37 record, the Olympians finished fourth in their division.

Nonetheless, the future seemed bright for the Olympians. After paying the bills, the franchise had $27,000 left in the bank. The players had gotten another $10,000 in salary and bonus, just as in the first year, and stock in the club was $10,000 a share.

Beard and Groza had both been named to the NBA All-Star team that year (with

Mikan, Ed Macauley, and Bob Davies) and could be expected to keep improving for at least a couple of years. Beard had also played minor league baseball his first two years out of Kentucky, but he was so enthusiastic about his basketball career that he gave up on baseball. "I had never played better basketball in my life," he said. "I planned to play pro ball until my legs fell off."

He never got a chance. On October 19, the Olympians were en route to Moline, Ill., for an exhibition game. They decided to take a detour to watch the Rochester Royals play the College All-Stars at Chicago Stadium, because the All-Stars were coached by Adolph Rupp.

Hale was there when it all blew up. "I had been walking out of the stadium with Beard and Groza, but I fell behind while I was talking to Lester Harrison, owner of the Royals. After a bit, I looked ahead and saw that Groza and Beard each had a guy beside them. I thought at first they were 'Kentucky Colonels' come to congratulate them, but when I caught up, the guys flashed badges and told me to go on."

Beard and Groza were taken to the Cook County jailhouse and confronted with testimony from gamblers that they had shaved points while playing for Kentucky. (They had been so efficient that they had lost the Loyola game in the 1949 NIT, a game they almost certainly would have won if they hadn't been concerned about the point spread.)

From this distance in time, Beard's and Groza's actions are understandable. They were playing in a morally ambiguous atmosphere. Their coach, Rupp, had visited the home of Ed Curd, Lexington's best-known bookmaker, and had telephoned Curd at least once to inquire about the point spread on a game, though Rupp denied ever betting. Kentucky players who had played well in games often received money, from $10 to $50, from Rupp or one of the "Boosters," and they had had money stuffed in their pockets after their Olympic win. Given all that, it is easy enough to see how they could have succumbed to the lure of the gamblers, who were, after all, only asking them to win by less than the point spread, not actually lose.

But none of those extenuating circumstances mattered at the time. Only the fact that Beard and Groza had shaved points counted. To placate the public, NBA commissioner Maurice Podoloff banned the two players from the NBA for life. He had no other choice.

Podoloff also gave the players 30 days to dispose of their stock in the club, which went from $10,000 a share to $1000 with the revelations.

The NBA, of course, was tremendously affected by the loss of Beard and Groza. The other franchises threw 13 players into a pool from which the Indianapolis franchise could select to replace the two players, and the Olympians actually had a better record (34-32) that year without Beard and Groza than they had had with the two players the year before.

But the glamour was gone. The Olympians were just another team, with mostly journeyman players. No longer were they welcomed into Madison Square Garden.

The story was the same at home. Though the team was intact for two more years, it did not prosper. After the 1952-53 season the team folded, and Indianapolis would be without a professional basketball team until the American Basketball Association started nearly two decades later.

Another damaging revelation was to come, this one involving a referee, Sol Levy, who was charged with conspiring with Salvatore Sollazzo to fix six NBA games in the 1950-51 season. Levy was charged with fouling out star players early when the fix was on.

Interestingly, Levy was charged with a misdemeanor, not a felony, because there was no statute in the bribery sections concerning referees. That technicality eventually got him off without any penalty. Though a three-judge panel ruled him guilty (by a 2-1 vote), an appeals court overturned that verdict, ruling that Levy was not subject to the bribery laws, which applied only to gamblers and athletes.

There were rumors, never verified, that a few NBA players were involved in fixing games, but in retrospect, the NBA came out remarkably clean at the time, especially in comparison with the college game.

By the time the collegiate investigations were finished it was determined that games had been fixed in 22 cities in 17 states. Gamblers and players had discussed some 90 games, and at least 49 were actually fixed. Thirty-three players were involved.

In contrast, no pro player was even charged with fixing a pro game. (Beard and Groza, of course, were arrested because of their collegiate activities.)

The only incident of any kind involving a player came later, in the 1953-54 season, when Jack Molinas, a rookie with Fort Wayne, was found to be betting on his team. Molinas said he bet only on his own team to win, and small amounts, but commissioner Podoloff quickly banned him from the league because player contracts expressly forbade players betting. (Molinas did not learn from the experience. Years later, in still another college scandal, he was convicted of fixing games and went to prison.)

There were several logical reasons why the pro game was relatively untouched by scandal. For one thing, it was more difficult to fix a pro game. In a college game there were usually one or two players who did most of the scoring; on a pro team, almost all the players were good shooters, and if one player was off, another could take up the slack.

The temptation to accept a bribe was less for a pro, who was getting paid, than a collegian, who was not. The pros were older and thus less susceptible to the pitch of a smooth-talking gambler.

But the most telling reason was probably that fewer people cared about the pro game. A gambler could get a lot more money going on a college game, so it was in his best interest to concentrate on the collegians.

On balance, then, the NBA benefited from the scandals. Breaking the collegiate lock on Madison Square Garden was critical, and the pros no doubt gained some fans who had been shocked by the college scandals.

But despite that, the pro game still lacked something. It had the best players, but the rough, foul-ridden style of play that had emerged often kept those players from playing at their best. Something had to be done. That something was what is still probably the most radical rules change ever made in a major team sport: the 24-second clock.

8. 24 Seconds to Shoot

Two problems had always plagued basketball, and in the NBA in the early '50s, they were interrelated.

The first was fouling. In its purest form basketball is a joy to watch because its players are probably the best athletes among those playing team sports, as measured by speed, agility, and reactions.

But too often, in the early years of the NBA, that pure athletic ability would be negated by tactics that more properly belonged in the wrestling ring. Defenders would tug and shove and push offensive players before a shot was taken, knowing that even if a foul were called, the player would get only one shot and would not have a chance to make two points on a field goal.

The other problem was making certain that each team had an equal opportunity to score. In theory, this had been accomplished by the elimination of the center jump years before. The center jump had enabled a team with a tall center to control the ball, because the ball was jumped after every basket. When that was eliminated the team which had just given up a score took the ball out of bounds, giving that team a chance to score itself.

In practice, though, this just encouraged the team that was leading in the late minutes of a game to stall: Why take a chance on shooting and missing, which would give the other team a chance to score and cut into or obliterate a lead?

This, in turn, encouraged the trailing team to foul, because this might be the only way it could get the ball back. It was especially important to foul a player early, perhaps even as he was bringing the ball upcourt, because this saved time and gave up only one free throw.

Thus, the closing minutes of an NBA game, which should have been the most exciting, were often brawling, foul-filled times, which turned off all but the most partisan of fans. The NBA unquestionably had the best players in the world, but they were not being allowed to show their superiority.

There was a third element, too: television. The medium was still in its infancy, of course, and the rights fees for games were still a relatively small item, only supplementing gate receipts. But in the 1953-54 season, the league had gotten a national contract with NBC-TV, and commissioner Maurice Podoloff and the league owners certainly realized the importance and impact of that.

So it was only natural that a televised game became the prime catalyst for change. That game was a March 20, 1954, game between the New York Knicks and Boston Celtics, won by Boston, 79-78.

The game took an extraordinary three hours to play, mainly because of the frequent fouling and equally frequent complaints to the referees over calls. It demonstrated all the roughhouse tactics that players had embraced. There was nothing new, but the fact that it was on national TV was new. Not only the fans in the arena itself but a far broader audience of stay-at-homes was watching, and it was hardly conceivable that any of those watching would want to come out to a game after that.

That game, and the many others similar to it, was still fresh in the minds of the NBA owners when they met little more than a month later, on April 22. They were ready for change.

Syracuse owner Dan Biasone came up with an idea: a time limit on possession of the ball. He proposed that the limit be 24 seconds because, if each team took its full time in shooting, that would still permit 120 shots to be taken, 60 for each team.

The time limit may have seemed restrictive, but it really wasn't. Actually, teams had been shooting an average of each 18 seconds in the previous season. Teams had ten seconds to bring the ball to half court and seldom used that much time, so they would have anywhere from 14 to 20 seconds to run off a normal play. For the pros, most of whom did not run complicated plays, that was enough.

But the new rule would prevent stalling to protect a lead in the closing minutes. It would prevent a team from virtually freezing the ball for the whole game, as Fort Wayne once had done in a 19-18 win over Minneapolis. The rule was adopted by the owners.

The 24-second rule was so important that the other changes the owners made at that meeting generally have been overlooked, but they were important, too.

For the first time, owners established a limit on *team* fouls, not just individual fouls. After six team fouls in a quarter the fouled player would get an extra shot. That meant a fouled player had a chance to make two points, so it removed the incentive to foul a player before he got a chance to shoot a field goal.

The owners also decided to make a distinction between an offensive and defensive foul. Since offensive fouls were merely overaggressive plays made to score points, they would be treated differently from defensive fouls, which were attempts to get the ball. Henceforth, offensive fouls would be counted on the individual totals but not as a team foul. Equally important, the fouled player would not get a free throw; instead, his team would get the ball out of bounds. Thus, those long walks to the other end of the floor for a free throw could be eliminated.

Finally, the owners decided that a backcourt foul would bring two shots, so there was no reward for fouling a player as soon as he started bringing the ball upcourt to save a few seconds.

In that one meeting, the NBA owners changed their game tremendously and probably saved the league. It is hard to believe that the old-style game being played in the NBA to that point ever would have attracted the numbers of fans the league needed to survive. The new rules allowed players to demonstrate their great skills. Though there has been tinkering with rules since, the essential framework of the modern game was laid in that meeting.

Even today, the idea of a time limit is a controversial one. It is used in the Olympics (in the form of a 30-second limit) and it has been tried by some college conferences, but not yet permanently adopted. The women pros, in the Women's Basketball League, use a 30-second limit.

In the NBA, though, the only controversy since the rule was adopted has been over the actual time. There are some who would like to couple making the zone defense legal with a relaxing of the rule to 30 seconds. But nobody within the pro ranks ever talks seriously about eliminating the time limit. They all know what a difference it has made to their game.

Though it would be a couple of years before teams fully adjusted to the 24-second clock, the difference it made in the game was evident in its first year of use.

It effectively eliminated the style of play the Minneapolis Lakers had used to dominate the league. The Lakers would come downfloor deliberately and wait for George Mikan to get in position before they would try to run anything. No team would ever again be able to play that deliberately. (Coincidentally, Mikan retired that season, but his retirement had nothing to do with the new rule; he had obviously been declining as a player and felt it was time to retire.)

It made the fast break more important than ever. A team had to get the ball downcourt as quickly as possible; if the fast break didn't result in a shot, a team would still have plenty of time left to work a play.

Scoring jumped dramatically, almost 14 points a team, to an average of about 93 points. The Boston Celtics scored more than 100 points 45 times in the season, and they averaged 101.4 points a game. Some of the gloss was taken off that by the fact that the Celtics gave up 101.5 points a game.

Individual scoring also increased. Neil Johnston, Paul Arizin, Bob Cousy, and Bob Pettit all averaged more than 20 points a game, and Frank Selvy was close at 19. Ironically, the Philadelphia Warriors, with high scorers Johnston and Arizin, finished last in the Eastern Division. There was still more to the game than just scoring.

The new rule also was a factor in the shift of power, from the West to the East and from the older, dominant teams to the younger ones.

The Lakers, with Clyde Lovellette replacing Mikan at center, finished second in the West and wouldn't be a winner again until they moved to Los Angeles.

The Rochester Royals, who had been just a half-step behind the Lakers for nearly a decade, were caught in transition, winning only 29 games and losing 43. There was irony there, too, because the Royals would have benefited greatly if the 24-second clock had been used earlier, when the speed their players had had in their youth could have been exploited. It is not unreasonable to think that the Royals, not the Lakers, would have been the dominant team of their era if the 24-second rule had been in effect then.

The teams which made the best use of the new rule were Fort Wayne and Syracuse. In Fort Wayne, the Pistons had little choice. Owner Fred Zollner had hired Charley Eckman, a colorful, voluble referee, to coach his team. Eckman had almost no plays, so the Pistons simply ran and free-lanced.

The choice of the 32-year-old Eckman might have seemed bizarre to others, but it was a perfectly reasonable selection as seen by Eckman himself.

"Having officiated for seven years in the BAA and NBA," he said at the time of his appointment, "plus several college conferences, I believe I have formed a good working knowledge of professional basketball. The opportunity to coach was a personal challenge. I have looked forward to the day when I could accept that challenge."

The way Eckman told it then, he had decided a couple of years before, while officiating at a playoff game between the Minneapolis Lakers and Rochester Royals at Rochester, that he could be a coach in the NBA.

The game was tied with eight seconds left, and the Royals had the ball. When they called a time out, Eckman edged toward the huddle just to hear what they planned to do. Here's the way he told the story to Cliff Keane at the time:

> Coach Les Harrison was the first to speak. He's frantic with excitement. He says, "So, what do we do, gang? Speak up."
>
> Bob Davies is first. And Bob says, "I can drive on my guy and make the hoop. Give me the ball."
>
> "Sounds good to me," answered Harrison. "So, we'll give the ball to Davies, huh?"
>
> "No, hit me," said Bobby Wanzer. "I can set on my guy. He's giving me a lot of room. I'll throw it in."
>
> "That sounds good to me," said Harrison. "So, we'll give the ball to Wanzer, huh?"
>
> "No, I got the shot," said Jack Coleman. "My guy is playing me loose. I'll whip it in from the corner."
>
> "That's a good idea, too," said Harrison, tugging madly at his belt. "Unless someone has some other suggestion . . ."
>
> "I got George [Mikan] and I'll throw a right-hand hook on him," said center Arnie Risen. "George won't dare foul me with only eight seconds left."
>
> And then the time-out period ended, and as the players started to take their positions, I'm thinking about what went on in that huddle. Four guys want to make a play. The only guy who hasn't said a word is Bull Johnson. There's one ball to shoot and four players want to do it. I can't wait to see what develops.

The whistle blows and Rochester throws the ball in bounds. Who is going to shoot—Risen, Davies, Wanzer, or Coleman?

The first thing I know, I look under the basket and there's Johnson all alone. He's the only guy in the huddle who hasn't said a thing.

The ball goes to him. He throws it in the basket. Rochester wins. The place is going wild. People are rushing players off the floor, and I walk toward the exit, behind Harrison.

He's getting pats on the back from all sides. People are calling him a wonder for his strategy. They ask him how he thought out the play. And darned if he doesn't tell them exactly how he planned to get Johnson loose under the basket.

So, right then and there, I decided even I could coach in the NBA.

Eckman was a master storyteller and, though he swore that story was true, there may have been a little, uh, exaggeration in it. But he did prove that year that a lengthy coaching background wasn't essential for success in the NBA.

Charley kept his players relaxed all season with his excellent sense of humor, so they played their best. With players like Max Zaslofsky, Andy Phillip, and Frank Brian in the backcourt, and Larry Foust, George Yardley, Mel Hutchins, and Bob Houbregs up front, their best was formidable. They won the Western Division title with a 43-29 record.

The Syracuse Nationals, who had finished second in the East the year before, this time won handily by five games over the New York Knicks, with a 43-29 record that matched the Pistons.

The Nats were a well-balanced team with one definite star, Dolph Schayes, who averaged 18.5 points a game. In the backcourt, Paul Seymour and George King were quick guards who could move the Nats' offense. Seymour averaged 14.8 points a game while ranking fourth in the league in assists; King was sixth in assists.

At center, Red Rocha had come out of retirement to have a good year, and he was complemented by rookie Johnny Kerr. They combined to score almost 22 points a game (11.3 for Rocha, 10.5 for Kerr), and Kerr also demonstrated excellent passing ability from the pivot.

The playoffs eventually matched Fort Wayne and Syracuse for the championship, and the final series was as exciting as any that had been played to that point.

The Nats won the first two games at home. The Pistons, forced to use an Indianapolis gym because their own was unavailable, came back to win three straight.

Back in Syracuse, Dolph Schayes scored 28 points to lead the Nats to a series-tying 109-104 win. The final game came down to the final 12 seconds, tied at 91-91. George King was fouled and sank a free throw to give the Nats the lead, and then the Nats stole the ball to protect the lead and win the game.

Dolph Schayes could have been the great Jewish player the New York Knicks were looking for but instead starred for the Syracuse Nationals. *(NBA)*

It was the first time in seven years that the East had won in the playoffs and confirmed the swing of power from the West; the East had also won the All-Star Game that season.

More than that, though, it was fitting that the man who had come up with the rule that saved the game, Syracuse owner Dan Biasone, turned out to be the man who benefited most from it in its first year.

There was an amusing footnote to the first season of the 24-second clock. At the annual meeting of the Metropolitan Basketball Writers Association, the writers mounted a 24-second clock above the head of Maurice Podoloff—unknown, of course, to Podoloff—as the NBA president began to speak.

At the end of 24 seconds, the clock went off with a loud buzz, startling Podoloff and bringing a roar of laughter from his audience. After his initial shock, Podoloff joined in the laughter. It was easy to accept the joke because the experiment had been such a success.

9. From Arizin to Zaslofsky: Some Early Stars

Very quickly, the 24-second rule would also literally change the color of the game. With the premium on speed, black players would increasingly take over pro basketball. Indeed, the game would become a polished version of the game that was played on so many city playgrounds, most of them in the black neighborhoods. Hence, its nickname: The City Game.

But in the early '50s, though the color line had been officially broken, all the stars of the game were still white players. Those years would be the last when that was true.

One of the stars of those years started his career in the '40s, but was still a top player in the early '50s. You don't hear much of Max Zaslofsky now, but there was a time when Red Auerbach was crushed because he couldn't get Zaslofsky in a dispersal draft and had to settle for Bob Cousy; more will be said on that later.

Zaslofsky was an excellent shooter, nicknamed "The Touch" for obvious reasons. In his first four pro seasons, first in the BAA and then the NBA, he made the All-League team each time. Playing for the Chicago Stags of the BAA in the 1947-48 season, he led the league in scoring with a 20.7 average, and for three seasons he averaged more than 20 points a game.

Because his best years came before the 24-second rule, Zaslofsky's career scoring record doesn't seem impressive compared to current marks, which has probably hurt his reputation. But over a ten-year career, he averaged nearly 15 points a game, quite respectable totals for the era in which he played.

Zaslofsky also became a symbol of the way the game was changing, even while he was playing. At 6'2" and a willowy 174 pounds, he was big enough to play forward when he began his career, but by the time he ended it, he had been moved back to guard. In today's game, of course, he would be small even for a guard.

Some players had more influence on the game than others. One of the most influential of the era was Paul Arizin, the great jump shooter for the Philadelphia Warriors.

"He was the first true jump shooter," says Fred Scolari, who saw them all in that era. "He was the first I saw who used the kind of shot they all use now. He was something to behold, a marvel the way he could shoot."

The jump shot was discovered by accident, Arizin said. Playing in a Catholic league in Philadelphia, where games were often played on dance floors, he found that he would often slip or slide if he tried a hook shot or a drive. But when he jumped he could maintain his balance, and the ball went into the basket.

He kept the same shot for the rest of his career, and he was so successful that writers sought different ways to describe his shot. Try this one from a Philadelphia newspaper: ". . . flicking the ball on the crest of his leap like a man riding an invisible surf, this is Arizin's moment of expression."

Funny, and all that time Paul just thought he was shooting a basketball.

Arizin's career was highly unusual. He didn't even play high school ball in Philadelphia, and he nearly became a pro without playing collegiate ball, either.

While he was in high school he preferred to play recreational league basketball. He enrolled at Villanova and, as a freshman, continued to play in recreational leagues.

But a talent like his could not be ignored forever. Arizin averaged better than 30 points a game, and Eddie Gottlieb, owner of the Philadelphia Warriors, heard about him. But before Gottlieb had a chance to talk to Arizin, Villanova coach Al Severance talked Paul into joining the Wildcats.

As a sophomore, Arizin was on the bench for seven games, but once he became a starter, he led the team in scoring. As a junior he averaged 25 points a game and led Villanova to the NCAA championships, where they lost to eventual winner Kentucky.

As a senior, Auizin was even better, averaging 26 points a game. He scored as high as 85 points in a game against the Philadelphia Navy Air Materials Center, but that total didn't count on his record because it wasn't achieved against a four-year school. Even without that game, though, he led all major college scorers.

And Gottlieb, who had narrowly missed signing Arizin earlier, made sure this time, making Arizin the first-round choice of the Warriors before the 1950-51 season.

As a physical specimen, Arizin seemed an unlikely star. He was small for a forward, at 6'4" and 210 pounds, but he made up for that with his timing and great jumping ability. He had both asthma and a sinus condition, and opponents could hear him panting as he came down the floor. But that didn't prevent him from playing 40 minutes a night, game in and game out.

As a scorer, there have seldom been any his equal. He not only had a fine shot, but he also had the ability to sense when a defender was leaning too much one way or the other; at that point, he would immediately go up with his shot.

As a rookie, Arizin averaged a strong 17.2 points a game, but he was even better in his second year as a pro, scoring 25.4 points a game and breaking George Mikan's hold on the NBA scoring leadership.

Arizin had his career interrupted at that point for a two-year hitch in the Marines, but it didn't seem to affect his play. In the three seasons following his return from the Service, he averaged 21, 24.2, and, finally, 25.6 points a game. The last mark gave him his second NBA scoring title, and on three other occasions, he led the Warriors in scoring.

Paul reached the 10,000-point club faster than any man before him, and, when he retired, he had a career total of 16,266 and an average of 22.8 points a game.

Even with that, his career had its disappointments. He obviously lost a chance to further enhance his scoring totals when he lost two years to the military, and he retired while he could still play, when the Warriors moved to San Francisco.

In his last year with the Warriors, Arizin still averaged better than 21 points a game (a mark that was obscured by Wilt Chamberlain's incredible 50.4 average that same season), so it seems Paul could have played at least another couple of seasons.

Staying in Philadelphia he played in the Eastern Basketball League, where he was the Most Valuable Player.

The Warriors in those years had exceptional luck in developing top scorers. Joe Fulks had been the first, Arizin was the second, and then Neil Johnston came along to match George Mikan's string of three straight scoring championships. In fact, between Arizin and Johnston, the Warriors had the top scorer five times in one six-year stretch.

Johnston, who had played collegiate ball at Ohio State, had started his professional career as a baseball pitcher, but had had to quit because of a sore arm. Turning to pro basketball, he became a starter—and the league scoring champion—in his second year.

He was a solid, unspectacular player who relied chiefly on a hook shot, though he would occasionally go to the outside and hit a set shot. He was also an excellent rebounder, in the top ten for most of his career; once, he led the league, and for a time he had the NBA record of 39 rebounds in one game.

Johnston was an incredibly consistent player. In his best five-year stretch, his scoring average hardly varied, from a low of 22.1 to a high of 24.2.

That consistency probably lowered his fan appeal because Johnston definitely lacked charisma. Ultimately he became the Warriors' coach as his eight-year career was ended by a knee injury and by the presence of a rookie who definitely did not lack charisma: Wilt Chamberlain. And the Warriors tradition of producing scoring champions continued.

Another player who is seldom heard of today is George Yardley, but it was Yardley who had the distinction of becoming the first NBA player to score more than 2000 points in a season.

(above) Easy Ed Macauley starred for the Boston Celtics and then, traded for the draft rights to Bill Russell, returned home to help the St. Louis Hawks win a championship. *(Hall of Fame)*

(left) Paul Arizin was the first to shoot a jump shot as modern players do, and he became a great scorer for the Philadelphia Warriors. *(Hall of Fame)*

Yardley, like Arizin, didn't look like a basketball player: He had a meager 190 pounds spread over his 6'5" frame, and he was prematurely bald. But he had an incredible jumping ability and seemed almost to hang in the air at a time when he should have been returning to the floor.

He naturally made most of his points on a jump shot, and he had studied how defensive players tried to stop a jump shot. Seeing that defenders tended to go straight up and go for the ball, Yardley developed a number of moves he could make in mid-air to keep a defender from blocking his shot.

It was no surprise that Yardley used his intelligence to make himself a better player; he had been a good student, majoring in civil engineering at Stanford.

Because he wanted to play on the 1952 Olympic team, Yardley passed up an offer from the Fort Wayne Pistons when he graduated from college in 1950, playing instead for the Stewart Chevrolet team in an AAU league in San Francisco. Then, in the '52 Olympic Trials, he broke his hand and lost his chance to play in the Olympics.

The disappointed Yardley then joined the Pistons and had a mediocre rookie season, averaging only nine points a game. He nearly quit but was persuaded to continue his career by Charley Eckman, who started his coaching career with the Pistons as Yardley was entering his second season.

Nicknamed "The Bird" because of his jumping ability and personal appearance, Yardley steadily improved his scoring averages, to 17.3, 17.4, and 21.5, in his next three seasons.

The next season, he moved just past the 2000-point barrier, scoring 2001 points on a 27.8 average.

Oddly, he was traded after that great season to the Syracuse Nationals. He played one more season, averaging 20.1 points a game, and then retired, with a career point total of 7590 and an average of 19.0.

His record? It didn't even last a season. Chamberlain broke it in Yardley's last season—Wilt's rookie year—and more than doubled Yardley's totals two seasons after that. Which is no doubt why George Yardley's name doesn't ring many bells with basketball fans.

Ed Macauley didn't set any scoring records, but he was so talented that the New York Knickerbockers were once willing to buy an entire team just to get Macauley.

Macauley had been an All-American center at St. Louis University, where he had been such a smooth player that he had acquired the nickname of "Easy Ed."

He signed with the hometown St. Louis Bombers, reportedly for $30,000 for two years, and had a fine rookie season, averaging 16.1 points a game. But Macauley wasn't enough to either make the Bombers a winner or a good gate attraction, and the team folded before the next season.

Hearing that the Bombers were about to fold, Knicks' owner Ned Irish offered to buy the franchise, just to get the rights to Macauley. The Knicks needed a center, a problem that has plagued the team for most of its existence (though not now, with Bill Cartwright).

But Irish had never made many friends among NBA owners, and they weren't ready to do him the favor of allowing him to have Macauley. Instead, the league set up a dispersal draft for the Bombers players. Macauley, easily the best player on the team, went to the Boston Celtics, then the weakest team in the NBA.

At 6'8" and 190 pounds, Macauley lacked the brute strength to compete with some of the NBA giants, but he compensated for his lack of strength with his grace and agility. He could do it all and he made it look easy, whether he was shooting a hook or driving for the basket. At his best, he was unstoppable, as he proved by bombing George Mikan and the Minneapolis Lakers for 46 points on March 6, 1953, the best scoring night of his career.

Macauley's value, though, was more in his consistency than in big scoring splurges. In his six seasons with the Celtics, he never averaged under 17.5 points a game, and he was always among the scoring leaders. Never one to shoot indiscriminately, he was also among the leaders in field goal percentage.

Before the 1956-57 season, Macauley was traded back home to the St. Louis Hawks (with Cliff Hagan) for the draft rights to Bill Russell. Everybody remembers that Russell made the Celtics the best team in NBA history, but the deal was a good one for the Hawks, too. In Macauley's two full seasons in St. Louis, the Hawks won two Western Division titles and took the NBA crown the second year by defeating the Celtics.

Macauley was still only 30 when the next season started, but he knew he was no longer the player he had been. After 14 games he retired as a player and took over as coach and general manager of the team.

In his two seasons as coach the Hawks were divisional champions twice, but in 1962 Macauley retired to go into private business. Perhaps he felt he had nothing left to prove; if so, he was right.

As good a shooter as Ed Macauley was, he wasn't as good as one of his teammates on the Celtics—Bill Sharman. For pure shooting ability, there may never have been anybody better than Sharman.

Probably more than any other player, Sharman reduced shooting to a science. He never took shots from outside his range, which was 20 feet. He never shot off-balance or in a hurry—unless it was necessary because there was hardly any time left on the timer or in the game, of course. He shot with the same fluid motion whether he was attempting a field goal or a free throw.

Bill was especially deadly from the foul line, where he converted at a .883 percentage for his career, winning the NBA foul shooting title seven times. He and Rick Barry are unquestionably the finest foul shooters in NBA history.

Sharman was an all-round athlete, good enough to have a shot at making the

Bill Sharman set foul-shooting records and teamed with Bob Cousy in one of the top backcourts of all time, before going on to be an outstanding coach and executive. *(Hall of Fame)*

Brooklyn Dodger team as a third baseman. In fact, he enjoyed playing both baseball and basketball for a time, as much because of the way his image changed as for any other reason. "When I play basketball, I'm 'Little Bill,' " he once noted. "But when I play baseball, suddenly I'm 'Big Bill.' " He was right. At 6'2", he was usually smaller than almost everybody else on the basketball court, but his size made him a big third baseman.

But Sharman was always at least a shade better as a basketball player than a baseball player—he had broken Hank Luisetti's conference scoring record while a forward at USC—and he eventually chose basketball, when he decided he had to make a choice between sports.

It was a wise decision. He and Bob Cousy made a superb pair in the Celtic backcourt. Cousy was the better all-round player, of course, but when it came time to get those important points, nobody was better than Sharman.

Bill always knew exactly what he was doing. "I aim for the back rim," he said. "I've found that most shots are missed short because players get tired. Their shots start bouncing off that front rim. But if you shoot for the back rim, you get three factors working for you. First, most players shoot with backspin. If a backspinning ball hits the front rim, it skids away. But if it hits the back rim, the 'English' practically forces it into the basket.

"Second, if you overshoot and miss the back rim, you still have a chance for a cheap basket. The ball can bank in off the backboard.

"Third, the rim of the basket has an eighteen-inch diameter, the basketball about nine inches. So, if you shoot for the rear rim, you have a nine-inch margin for error."

It was analysis like that, and his great natural ability, that made Sharman such a good player, four times a first team All-Star during his career.

Sharman went on to become an excellent coach after his playing career, with his analytical mind helping him produce winners in two NBA cities—San Francisco and Los Angeles—and for an American Basketball Association franchise in Utah, as well.

With the Los Angeles Lakers, Sharman finally went to the front office, but years after his playing career had ended he still had his great shooting skills. During the Lakers' training camp in 1980 Magic Johnson challenged Sharman to a free-throw shooting contest. Johnson made 23 of 30. Sharman sank 28 of 30. You don't mess with the master.

As good as these players were, there were two others who stood apart in the '50s—Bob Pettit and Bob Cousy.

Pettit was the classic example of the player who made good because of his fierce competitiveness. He probably ranked, in fact, with George Mikan as the player who made the most of what he had. When he turned pro, Pettit was supposed to be too thin and not a good-enough jumper, but he probably became as good a forward as has ever played in the NBA.

Critical evaluations were nothing new to Pettit. He had been cut from his high school team as a sophomore because he was too awkward. His answer to that was to go out to the backyard—and shoot and shoot and shoot. As a 6'4" junior he made the team; as a senior he played well enough to attract some collegiate scholarship offers, though there was never any doubt in his own mind that he would play for Louisiana State University in his home town of Baton Rouge.

Pettit grew to 6'7" early in his college career, and he developed a full repertoire of shots. By the time he was a senior he was 6'9"—but only 200 pounds—and an All-American, averaging 30 points a game.

But he had played center in college; coming to the Milwaukee Hawks, who had 6'11" Charlie Share in the pivot, he would have to play forward. Many lesser players would not have been able to make the adjustment, but it was just another challenge to Pettit.

Years later, Pettit explained his philosophy. "As you go along in life and work hard, you reach new plateaus of accomplishment. With each plateau you reach, the demands upon you become greater, and your pride increases to meet the demands.

"You drive yourself harder than before. You can't afford negative thinking, so you always believe you'll win. You build an image of yourself that has nothing to do with ego—but it has to be satisfied.

"When I fall below what I know I can do, my belly growls and growls. Anytime I'm not playing up to my very best I can count on a jolt of indigestion." There can't have been too many of those cases of indigestion. Pettit was a good player when he came into the league and he kept improving until he was the best.

Shooting was never a problem even though he had to switch positions; he averaged 20.4 points a game as a rookie. What defeats most big men who have to switch from center to forward is ballhandling. A center seldom has to take more than a dribble or two; often he just goes up with the ball when he gets it. A forward must put the ball on the floor. If he can't drive his defender will play him so tight that he'll never get a shot off.

Pettit learned that lesson very quickly. He worked very hard on his ballhandling and dribbling, and the results showed immediately. He became an excellent driver, and he handled the ball extremely well on the break. His versatility made him almost impossible to guard.

Because he worked so hard his game seemed easy. He was a smooth shooter and an excellent rebounder, using finesse and positioning to overcome the strength of heavier men and the jumping ability of more gifted players.

Ed Macauley, who was much the same type of player (though not as good), became Pettit's coach for two years, and he appreciated what Pettit was doing, probably more than anyone else.

An inner drive made Bob Pettit the best forward of his era and, some still think, the best of all time. *(Hall of Fame)*

"He doesn't make a lot of noise," said Macauley, talking about Pettit's professionalism. "He always knows exactly what he wants to do and how to go about doing it. This is a guy who knows his business. You don't have to tell him anything."

His statistics were overwhelming. Twice he led the league in scoring, and for his first ten years he placed in the top five in the league as both a scorer and rebounder. In the 1955-56 season he led in both scoring and rebounding.

He was the league's Most Valuable Player twice, and in six other seasons he was at least fourth in the voting. He was chosen to the all-league first team for ten consecutive years. Even in his final season, when injuries kept him out of 30 games, he was named to the second unit, as he finished seventh in the league in scoring.

He was the first to score 20,000 career points, finishing with 20,880, and he grabbed 12,849 rebounds. His career averages were 26.4 points and 16.1 rebounds a game.

As good as he was in the regular season, Pettit was even better in the special games. In the All-Star Game, for instance, he was MVP three times and shared the honor a fourth time.

The highlight of his career undoubtedly was 1958, when he brought the Hawks—by then moved to St. Louis—their first NBA championship in a six-game final against Boston. In that sixth game he scored 50 points—including 19 of the last 21 for the Hawks. That's taking charge.

Bob Cousy has long been considered the finest ballhandler of his generation, and perhaps of all time, but as in the case of Pettit, there were questions about his ability when he turned pro. The coach who later praised him, Red Auerbach, originally didn't even want him.

Cousy had been an All-American at Holy Cross, a gifted ballhandler and a fine scorer, and there was considerable pressure for the Boston Celtics to grab the (virtually) home town boy. Auerbach resisted that pressure.

Auerbach could have taken Cousy as a territorial pick, but he chose instead to go for the 6'11" Charlie Share in the summer of 1950. His reasoning was that the Celtics needed a good big man more than they needed a good little man. There was nothing wrong with that reasoning—except that Share turned out to be only a mediocre big man and Cousy became a great little man, which changed the equation considerably.

Auerbach, of course, was lambasted by the Boston press for passing up Cousy, who was immensely admired throughout New England. And in this case, the fans and writers knew more than the professional did.

But what is never remembered is that a lot of other clubs passed up Cousy, too. Sometimes, it was understandable; Philadelphia, for instance, picked Paul Arizin.

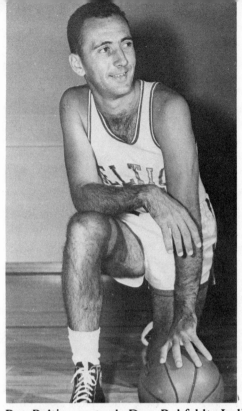

Bob Cousy, shown in a rare moment of repose, was a magician on the court. *(Boston Celtics)*

But Baltimore took Don Rehfeldt, Indianapolis took Bob Lavoy, and Syracuse chose Don Lofgran; none of them was ever in danger of making the Hall of Fame.

And the owner who finally selected Cousy, Ben Kerner of the Tri-Cities franchise, immediately traded him to Chicago for Frankie Brian, an established star.

In the volatile world that was pro basketball then, changes came frequently, and a series of changes eventually forced Cousy on the unwilling Auerbach, to his later gratitude.

The first change was the folding of the St. Louis Bombers franchise in June. As noted earlier, in the dispersal draft, the Celtics got Ed Macauley. That eliminated their need for a center, and the Celtics didn't even sign Share, their No. 1 pick.

Then, just before the league season was to start in October, the Chicago franchise folded. Everybody thought there were two quality players—Max Zaslofsky and Andy Phillip—and New York, Philadelphia, and Boston all wanted one of the two, preferably Zaslofsky.

NBA President Maurice Podoloff decided the only fair way to operate was to draw names out of a hat. Ned Irish drew first for the Knicks and got the prize— Zaslofsky, who was everything a New York player should be, a great scorer, four time All-Star and Jewish, to boot.

Philadelphia's turn came next, and Eddie Gottlieb drew Phillip's name. Though he would have preferred Zaslofsky, he was happy with Phillip, a great playmaker who was coming to a team which had one great scorer (Joe Fulks) and had drafted another (Arizin).

That left Boston with Cousy, and Auerbach was steaming. As part of the deal, it had been agreed before the draw that the team that got Zaslofsky would pay $15,000 to the league, the team that got Phillip would pay $10,000 and the team that got Cousy would pay $8500.

Irish and Gottlieb were quite willing to pay for the players they had drawn, but Auerbach was in a position of having to pay for a player he could have gotten free (through the draft) and didn't want. "He'll have to make the team," said the angry Auerbach of Cousy.

Well, he did. There may never have been a player like Cousy (though Fred Scolari thought he spotted some of Bob Davies' influence on Cousy's style). He was a marvelous, exciting player, who probably did more than any other player at the time to create a positive image for the NBA; and eventually, he was the catalyst for the NBA's greatest team.

Cousy could amass impressive statistics (50 points in a playoff game against Syracuse in 1953, for instance) but what made him special was the fact that he could make plays that nobody else could—or even attempted.

He passed the ball in a dazzling variety of ways, even behind his back, the pass for which he became most famous. "I don't use the behind-the-back pass as often as people think I do," he once said. "When I use it, I have a good reason for it. When a situation develops where I can help the club with a certain maneuver, I go ahead with it."

And that was the key to his game. Auerbach had trouble with Cousy's style at first because Red believed the simplest pass, the most direct, was the best; Cousy's passes were seldom simple. His teammates had trouble catching his passes at first, because they were unprepared for the ball to come their direction. But eventually, they learned not to worry how the ball was coming, just to realize that it would come if they were open. Cousy always found a way, and Auerbach came to appreciate that.

He had superb reflexes and great peripheral vision, physical assets that (along with a very large pair of hands) enabled him to do remarkable things.

Despite his 50-point game, Cousy's admirers often pointed to two other examples of his wizardry as being even more impressive. One was a game against the New York Knicks in 1954, when the Knicks were leading, 93-89, with 30 seconds left. Cousy stole the ball twice and converted each time in those 30 seconds to tie the game and force an overtime. The Celtics finally won in double overtime—and Cousy scored 12 of their 20 points.

There was another game in New York, this in 1960, when the Celtics had the lead with 23 seconds left. Cousy dribbled away the time, and no Knicks player could get close enough even to foul him. Wrote Jimmy Cannon in the *New York Journal American* the next day, "If Cousy never put the ball in the basket, he'd still be the most respected man in the league."

For eight consecutive years he led the league in assists. For ten straight years he was named to the all-league team, and he played in 13 All-Star Games.

And in the end he even convinced his coach. At banquet after banquet, Auerbach would say, "Every kid who can dribble a basketball gets called another Cousy. Well I've got news for you. There ain't nobody as good as Cooz. There never was."

10. Bill Russell—Defense

Because basketball is played with only five on a team, one player can make a big difference, so the NBA has always been star-oriented. Sometimes, an individual player can dominate the whole league. The late '40s and early '50s had clearly been the George Mikan Era. In 1956, the Bill Russell Era was about to begin.

There were marked differences between the two. Mikan's forte had clearly been offense, though he was a solid defensive player. Russell's strength was just as obviously his defensive play, though his rebounding was also the key to his team's offense.

Mikan had been coveted by all the professional teams; there was never any doubt that he would be an outstanding pro and a great gate attraction. Not everybody was as convinced about Russell. Some questioned whether he could be an offensive force in the NBA, since he was such a poor shooter. Others wondered whether, playing against the bigger and stronger pros, he could dominate the game defensively as he did in college.

One who didn't doubt Russell's ability at all was Red Auerbach, coach/general manager of the Boston Celtics. Auerbach had coveted Russell for two years.

Auerbach had put together probably the league's most exciting team at Boston. Bob Cousy and Bill Sharman were unquestionably the best backcourt in the league; Cousy, Sharman, and Ed Macauley were among the top ten scorers in the league. Jim Loscutoff had joined the team as a rookie the previous year and had played well, giving the team defensive muscle and good rebounding.

But the Celtics had one obvious weakness—defensive rebounding. Because they couldn't get the ball off the boards with enough consistency, they couldn't make maximum use of their fast break—and Auerbach was the most fervent proponent of the fast break in the league. Nor could they keep opponents from getting second and third shots at the basket.

The problem was that they were, in effect, playing with three forwards. Macauley was an excellent shooter and a great athlete, but at 6'8" and 190, he couldn't muscle inside on the boards. At his best he had been a weak rebounder for a center, never averaging in double figures during an MBA season. In the 1955-56 season he had slipped badly. On his own team he was only fourth in rebounding; Cousy, a 6'1" guard, had 70 more rebounds during the year.

Without a dominant defensive-rebounding center the Celtics were much the weakest defensive team in the league. Though they averaged 106 points a game, by nearly three points the highest in the league, they gave away nearly all of that advantage by yielding 105.3 points a game. New York (100.6) and Minneapolis (100.3) were the only other teams that gave up more than 100 points a game, and the defensive leader, Fort Wayne, yielded only 93.7.

"I had to have somebody who could get me the ball," says Auerbach now. "I'd been tipped off about Russell by my college coach, Bill Reinhart of George Washington, when Russell was only a sophomore. Bill said Russell was the greatest defensive player and the greatest rebounder he'd ever seen."

Some teams that might have wanted Russell were discouraged by two factors: 1) The Harlem Globetrotters were also seeking Russell, which meant at best that his asking price would be higher than normal and at worst that he might not even play in the NBA; and 2) Russell had made it clear that he would play for the U.S. Olympics team; because the Olympics were being held in Melbourne, Australia, the basketball competition would be held in November and early December, which meant Russell would miss about two months of the NBA season.

Auerbach wasn't deterred. He was thinking in terms of a full career, so he was willing to give up the first two months if he had Russell for the years to come. And even a cursory examination of Russell's history would have made it clear that the proud Russell would never have played for the Globetrotters, whose basketball was secondary to their clowning. Russell wanted to be taken seriously.

But first, Auerbach had to get into position to draft Russell. The Celtics were drafting sixth. It was generally believed that two other teams were seriously interested in Russell—Rochester, drafting first, and Minneapolis, drafting third.

Rochester passed on Russell, drafting Sihugo Green of Duquesne, because the Royals decided they couldn't afford Bill's asking price. (In light of the astronomical salaries of recent years it is astounding to realize that Russell was asking only about $25,000 a year and actually settled for less. Benchwarmers get quadruple that now.)

St. Louis was second in line. Probably, Hawks' owner Ben Kerner would not have drafted Russell, for several reasons: 1) Russell's price; 2) the fact that Kerner already had an outstanding big man in Bob Pettit who, though a forward, carried the rebounding load a center normally would; and 3) the fact that St. Louis was a border town and not the best place for a black to play or live at the time. (In fact, years later, when the Hawks moved to Atlanta, one of the primary reasons was because St. Louis would not support a team which had become primarily black by that time.)

Auerbach knew, though, that Minneapolis would take Russell if St. Louis didn't, so he got on the phone to Kerner and offered to trade him Macauley for the rights to Russell.

Bill Russell transformed the Celtics from an also-ran into a team which won a record 11 championships in 13 years. *(Boston Celtics)*

Macauley, of course, was a native of St. Louis and a big hero there; he would be a big promotional plus for the Hawks and, on a team where he wouldn't have to do a lot of rebounding, a definite playing asset.

He wanted to return to St. Louis, too. He was near the end of his career. He had already asked Auerbach if it would be possible to work a trade so he could go to the Hawks.

"His son had been sick," says Auerbach, "but it isn't true that he would have quit if we hadn't traded him. He told me that if nothing could be worked out, he would be perfectly happy to come back and play in Boston."

Auerbach didn't have to put Macauley to the test on that. Kerner demanded another player in the deal—Cliff Hagan, a 6'4" forward who had been an All-American at Kentucky before going into the Army. (Auerbach had drafted both Hagan and Frank Ramsey before they went into military service; Ramsey, of course, later became a star with the Celtics, the first to play the "sixth man" role for the team, able to come off the bench and score points as either a guard or a forward.)

The deal was struck and Auerbach drafted Russell, but he had a long time to wait before he could get Russell's signature on a contract. The U.S. Olympic Committee, in one of those misguided attempts at protecting athletes from the professionals, insisted that year that each Olympic team member sign a pledge that he intended to stay an amateur. Thus, Russell signed the pledge, which meant he couldn't even talk to the Celtics.

Meanwhile, the Globetrotters had also made a public offer to Russell of $50,000. Bill greeted that with his laconic humor. "That's $50,000 a year more than I've been making," he said.

In actual fact, the Globetrotters' offer was $32,000, a sizeable one for the times even if less than two-thirds of what they were "offering" through the newspapers. It's unlikely, though, that Russell ever seriously consider that offer.

As soon as the Olympics were over—Russell had led the United States team to the championship—Bill signed with the Celtics for what was said to be $20,000 a year for two years.

It turned out to be easily the most important signing since Mikan had joined the Chicago Gears a decade earlier. Russell led the Celtics to an unprecedented string of championships (a streak which will probably never be equaled and possibly not even approached). He made the NBA a much more attractive venture.

There was one more ramification: The fact that Minneapolis was unable to draft him probably doomed the Lakers in that town. Attendance eventually declined so dramatically that the Lakers had to be moved, to Los Angeles. But had Russell played for the Lakers they would have been the NBA's top team again, and their attendance certainly would have reflected it. As it turned out, Russell was the only one of the NBA's four dominant centers—Mikan, Wilt Chamberlain, and Kareem

Abdul-Jabbar being the other three—who did not play for the Lakers, either in Minneapolis or Los Angeles.

Who was Bill Russell that he should have this kind of effect on the game? Well, for openers, he was a young man who hadn't even been able to start every game as a high school senior, at McClymonds in Oakland, California.

Strictly on potential, University of San Francisco assistant basketball coach Hal DeJulio suggested Russell be given an athletic scholarship, which Russell eagerly accepted. At the time, USF head coach Phil Woolpert had not even seen Russell play.

When Woolpert finally did see Russell, as a freshman at USF, he was not impressed. Russell was 6'7" and still growing, an awkward, gangling youngster who couldn't shoot and who didn't seem to have a very clear idea of what he was supposed to do on the basketball court. Woolpert admitted years later that his first thought was that USF had wasted a scholarship.

But Russell had some assets, even then. He was a tremendous leaper (he later high-jumped 6'10") and fast, with 49-second speed for the quarter-mile. He had quickness and excellent timing, and Woolpert could quickly see that he had a diamond in the rough—though very rough.

He was also impressed with Russell's determination and pride. Woolpert recalls a meeting with Russell in the office of the public relations director for the college, a young man named Pete Rozelle, when Russell said flatly that he would become an All-American.

The claim seemed absurd at the time, but by the time Russell was a sophomore he had grown to 6'9" and his awkwardness was disappearing. By that time Woolpert could see how much potential there was. He deliberately didn't coach Russell much on offense nor did Woolpert put in many plays involving him, because he could see that otherwise there would be a tendency to make everything revolve around Bill. Woolpert believed strongly in the team aspect of the game, and he wanted every player to feel he was an important part of it.

What Woolpert got was a great team. In Russell's junior and senior years, the Dons won 55 straight games (the streak went to 60 in the year after Russell had gone, before it was broken) and two straight NCAA titles. Some thought it was the best college team of all time, better even than the 1948-49 Kentucky team.

It was a most unusual team because of Russell. By Woolpert's design the offense had few plays which gave him a chance to shoot the ball, but he got his points anyway. Other USF players would shoot from the outside or the corners and Russell would wait, poised, near the backboard. If the shot was off target he would leap into the air and guide it in.

Defensively, Russell enabled the USF guards—K. C. Jones and Hal Perry when

Bill was a junior; and Jones, Perry, and Gene Brown in his senior year—to gamble defensively. Often they were able to steal the ball; if they could not and their man went by, Russell was there to block the lane.

At times he seemed to be playing the whole floor. He could be on one side guarding his man when a player drove from the other side—but by the time that player got to the basket, Russell had swooped in to block his shot.

He demoralized some very good centers. There is probably no better example than the Holiday Tournament in Madison Square Garden in December of Russell's senior year. In consecutive games he faced Tommy Heinsohn and Willie Naulls and made them look like boys playing against a man.

Heinsohn of Holy Cross had scored 36 points the night before he faced Russell. Bill held him to 12 points while getting 24 points and 22 rebounds himself, and USF won. The next night Russell closed off the middle so thoroughly to Naulls (whose nickname, "The Whale," gives an indication of his size), that Naulls conceded the middle to Russell and went outside for his shots. USF won easily, 70-53.

Russell was so awesome a presence that he forced coaches into bizarre strategies. The best-remembered one was the stall-freeze tactic employed by Cal's Pete Newell. At one point, Cal center Joe Hagler held the ball for 8½ minutes. USF finally won the low-scoring game, 33-24.

Everybody assumed that Newell was trying to keep the game from getting out of hand, but he explained years later that he was concerned about the effect Russell would have on his team.

"The year before," he said, "Russell had blocked so many shots against us that our players were looking over their shoulders for a month. I didn't want that to happen again. I wanted to spread out their defense and keep him on one side. I didn't care about that game, but I didn't want a demoralized team for the conference games we had coming up."

And that's why Auerbach wanted him for the Celtics.

While Russell was off in Australia proving—if there were any doubt—that American basketball was the best, the Celtics had to make do. Fortunately for Auerbach, even without Russell, he had a stronger team than the year before.

With his territorial draft pick, Auerbach had selected Heinsohn. Though Heinsohn's natural pro position was forward, he was a good enough rebounder to play center until Russell arrived, and he was an excellent shooter who was always willing to put the ball up . . . hence, his nickname: Ack-Ack.

As a backup at center, Auerbach had the veteran Arnie Risen, who was still capable of good play if he didn't have to play for long stretches. Forward Jack Nichols was an excellent rebounder (he had led the Celtics in that department the year before), and the Celtics had signed veteran Andy Phillip as a capable backup for Cousy and Sharman.

So, even without Russell, the Celtics were a good team; they sprinted out to a 13-3 record, mainly on the strength of a ten-game winning streak, to take an early five-game lead.

But it quickly became obvious that the Celtics still did not have the rebounding strength they needed to make the maximum use of their scoring talents. They had slipped back to a 16-8 mark by the time Russell finally reported for action on December 22. He played 21 minutes and scored only six points—but he also got 16 rebounds and the Celtics beat St. Louis, 95-93, with Sharman and Heinsohn scoring baskets in the last ten seconds. And the Bill Russell Era had begun.

Those who had doubted that he could be as effective as a pro as he had been as a collegian soon had their doubts erased. Because he played only four months, Russell didn't get the Rookie-of-the-Year award (that went to teammate Heinsohn), but there was no doubt he was a great player.

As a rookie, Russell averaged only 14.7 points a game, far down the scoring list, but Russell's game was never one of statistics. Only his rebounding totals were truly impressive, and even there he was surpassed by Wilt Chamberlain. Russell's greatness came primarily because of factors that could not be judged statistically.

First and foremost, of course, was his defense. "Nobody had ever blocked shots on the pros before Russell came along," says Auerbach. "He upset everybody. The only defense they could think of was to dish out a physical beating and hope he couldn't take it." Which turned out to be a lost hope, because Russell, though slender, was a tough physical specimen.

Russell not only blocked shots; he kept them in play. Since he came along, many centers have developed techniques to block shots, but most times when shots are blocked, the ball goes out of bounds and the team gets another chance to score. When Russell blocked a shot, he usually directed it to a teammate. Occasionally, he would make such a thorough block that he would be able to control the ball himself.

He was able to do this because of marvelous timing and extraordinarily long arms. (The story is told of a time in his college days when USF played Oregon State in the NCAA Western Regionals. Hoping to "psych" Russell, Oregon state coach Slats Gill proposed that a photographer take a shot of Russell and 7′3″ Oregon State center Swede Halbrook reaching for a ball. Halbrook held the ball up—and Russell reached up and curled his palm around the top of the ball! So much for psyching!)

Russell almost never got faked out of position. He would wait, poised, and leap at precisely the right instant, as the ball was released. Unlike many centers who make grandstanding swats at descending shots and get called for goal-tending, Russell hit the ball on the way up and rarely got a goal-tending call.

He picked his spots carefully. He was aware that he couldn't block every shot, and he didn't try; if he could get 10 percent of the shots his man took in a game it was a big evening. But he concentrated on getting the shot blocks at the critical moments, when the other team really needed a basket or, conversely, when his team needed a spark to get going.

Even when he thought he could block every shot, he didn't try to. Philadelphia center Neil Johnston, for instance, was an obvious target. Because Johnston shot his hook at such a low trajectory, Russell thought he probably could block nine out of ten. But if he did that, Johnston would simply stop shooting the hook and go to a tougher shot—or pass the ball to a teammate. So, Russell blocked just enough of Johnston's hooks to make the Philadelphia center think and worry about it; as a result, Johnston seldom shot effectively against the Celtics.

As he had with USF, Russell made the Celtic guards much more effective. Cousy and Sharman (and later K. C. Jones and Sam Jones) could gamble on defense, going for the steal and what would then turn into a fast break bucket, because Russell was protecting the middle. There were no more easy baskets against the Celtics.

His rebounding became an offensive weapon for the Celtics because he whipped out an outlet pass as soon as he grabbed the ball, and Cousy or Sharman got moving before their opponents could get back defensively. That probably pleased Auerbach more than anything else, because he had long believed an effective fast break was the key to winning.

Offensively, he fit perfectly into the Celtic game because his skills were complementary to the others. He didn't shoot a lot, but there was no need to on a team that had Sharman, Heinsohn, and Cousy. He set screens, he passed off, he rebounded—and he shot often enough to keep the opposition honest. His field-goal percentage was fairly high despite his lack of pure shooting ability because he was smart enough to take only the shots he had a reasonable chance of making. A lot of better shooters could have done well with that strategy.

It was indeed amusing that, in the first few weeks Russell played, many of his San Francisco fans, unable to see the Celtics games and not realizing the makeup of the team, complained that Russell wasn't being passed the ball by the Celtic guards. In fact, he was getting it as often as he did in college, but he was smartly passing it off to better-shooting teammates.

There is much to be said for the Russell style. It's easy for a center to be a high scorer because he is the biggest man on his team and he is usually near the basket. Even Russell could have scored more had he chosen to.

But because Russell usually set up teammates with screens or passes he made them more effective. Russell made the Celtics more than the sum of their parts. Wilt Chamberlain, because the team had to be sublimated to his individual skills, usually made his teams less than the sum of their parts. And that's why, despite his overwhelming personal statistics, Chamberlain was never as highly regarded by basketball people as Russell.

Russell's greatness, though, went beyond his physical abilities. His great pride was as big a factor in his success.

He was never content to do less than his best, and the more important the game the better he wanted to play. That can be measured statistically by the fact that he scored and rebounded better in playoff games than in regular season. It can also be measured by the stories people tell of his nervousness before games.

Woolpert first noticed that at USF. Russell would go through bizarre actions before a game. Imaginary aches would overwhelm him. He would discover his socks were bunched or his shorts were chafing. One shoulder would seem to droop and he would feel a pain there. A leg would almost buckle when he stood up and his eyelids would start twitching.

Before the most important games Russell would imagine extreme ailments—such as appendicitis. He would barely be able to limp out onto the court, but once out there he would tear the opponent apart. Woolpert came to look forward to those ailments, because the worse Russell felt before a game, the better he played.

That pride often made Russell a difficult man to deal with, especially for people who didn't understand that he was a complex man and wanted to be treated as a whole person, not just as Bill Russell, Basketball Superstar.

Coming from a poor black neighborhood in Oakland, he had been conscious of racial bias all his life. Probably he thought that things would be better when he reached the top. What he discovered, of course, was that, although being a basketball star opened some doors for him, being black kept a lot of them closed.

More and more he spoke out against what he saw as examples of racial prejudice. Sometimes he was in error. He once charged Woolpert with racial bias, which was exactly the opposite of the truth; Woolpert had been under a lot of pressure at USF because he played three and sometimes four blacks in the lineup at a time when few top college teams had even one.

But often Russell was right when he spoke out against racial bias. The problem was that he was speaking to a white audience, which did not view injustices in the same way Russell did.

It didn't help that, when he came to the Celtics, he was the only black. Playing or practicing, the Celtics were together; Russell later recalled a time when Risen, a man he had never met before coming to the team, offered to stay late at practice to help him with his play. But off the court the white players went one way and Russell went another.

It didn't help that Boston was a racially tense city (as it is still); that, in the '60s, the losing Bruins hockey team usually outdrew the winning Celtics: because, many said, the Bruins were a white team.

Nor did it help that Russell was the first black superstar. He wasn't in quite the position that Jack Robinson had been in baseball in 1947, in that other black players had preceded him. But it was still a time when the league's stars were all white players. As with Robinson in '47, Russell was expected to ignore racial taunts and slurs and to speak only to basketball questions. Fans were shocked when Russell spoke his mind.

Russell has since modified his racial views. In his book, *Second Wind,* done with Taylor Branch, he comments that when he became coach of the Seattle SuperSonics, pro basketball had come full circle: The Sonics had 11 blacks and one white. Off the court, he noted, the blacks went their way and left the white player to his own amusements. That, concluded Russell, was no real improvement over the situation he had faced.

And, though Russell's accusatory remarks usually got the biggest press, his humorous side was an equally important part of the man's personality. His famous, high-pitched, infectious laugh could often be heard echoing through the Celtic dressing room, and in his recollections of those times the funny moments play a big role.

He loved the game in a way only the best players can. In *Second Wind,* he talks of a special kind of joy that came when everybody was playing well, not just his own team. It usually happened, he noted, when three or four stars really got into the flow of the game, playing at their very best.

"The feeling would spread to the other guys, and we'd all levitate. Then the game would just take off, and there'd be a natural ebb and flow that reminded you of how rhythmic and musical basketball is supposed to feel."

It didn't take long for Russell to make his presence felt in the NBA. Not two weeks after he joined the Celtics, some coaches and owners claimed that he was trying to play a one-man zone and that he was goal-tending.

Eddie Gottlieb, owner of the Philadelphia Warriors, was especially livid after a loss to the Celtics. He said he would make a protest on at least one call.

"Our Paul Arizin went underneath for a simple layup and as the ball headed down toward the basket, Russell batted it away. If this isn't goal-tending I want somebody to tell me what it is. He goal-tended at least three different times and was called for it only once."

Gottlieb added that "at times, Russell tries to play a one-man zone. He stands under the basket and waits to try and bat shots out."

Sour grapes, retorted Auerbach. "When we made the deal for Russell nobody thought he was going to be so good. He has far exceeded everybody's expectations. None of his blocks of shots have been on the downward flight. He has marvelous timing. He catches the ball on the upward flight."

Jocko Collins, at that time supervisor of NBA officials, said that he didn't think Russell was goal-tending, or that he was playing a zone.

"I've seen him follow his man in a weave," said Collins. "I've seen him come out and pick up players like Neil Johnston and Bob Pettit. He doesn't stand in one spot. Therefore, how can you say he is playing a one-man zone?"

Gottlieb soon backed down, sheepishly admitting he had not protested Russell's play and did not intend to.

"He's not doing anything radically wrong," said Gottlieb. "I guess he played the zone defense in college and sometimes might unconsciously lapse into it. But there's nothing to protest."

It may have been that Gottlieb's change of mind came about when he looked at the box office receipts. Throughout the league, the Celtics, with Russell the star attraction, were drawing record crowds.

Though he was forcing other teams to change their style of play, Russell preferred at that time to emphasize the problems he was having in adjusting from the college game to the pros'—problems which were less evident to others.

"In college," he told Darrell Wilson of the *San Francisco Chronicle,* "you run into a strong guy now and then, but up here, they're all that strong. They all know how to screen you off the boards and they all do it.

"I'm starting my second trip around the league and picking up pointers all the time. I think I'll make it."

Russell noted that other teams were pulling their centers away from the basket to draw him out of rebounding range. "I got outside with these fellows," he said, "but I usually don't make a career out of it. Unless my man is breaking up the game, I keep one eye on the backboard."

With Russell keeping at least one eye on the backboard at all times, the Celtics swept to the Eastern Division title by six games over Syracuse. Cousy led the league in assists and Sharman in free-throw percentage, but the key statistic was probably Russell's league-leading 19.6 rebound average.

The Celtics swept the Nats in three games in the first round of the playoffs. Everybody assumed they would do the same to St. Louis which, though it had finished in a three-way tie in the West and then beaten the Pistons in the first round of the playoffs, had actually been below .500 during the season, 34-38.

But the Hawks were a much better team than any they had played during the season. That had always been the opinion of Ben Kerner, who had fired Red Holzman in mid-season for not doing better, and the Hawks proved it in a tremendously exciting playoff series.

The first game, in Boston, went into double overtime. Bob Pettit had 37 points for the Hawks, Sharman scored 36 for the Celts; but the game was decided when the

Hawks' Jack Coleman threw in a desperate shot with only 30 seconds left and the 24-second clock running out.

The second game, also in Boston, was an easy win for the Celtics, 119-99, but the Hawks took the lead again when they won, 100-98, in the third game, on their home court. Had they won the fourth game, the Hawks could have taken a commanding lead, but the Celtics rallied for a series-tying 123-118 win.

The Celts then seemed to take command when they blew out the Hawks, 124-109, in the fifth game at Boston. Two days later, in St. Louis, with the score tied at 94-94, Cousy missed a free throw and Cliff Hagan came back to score in the final second to tie the series once more.

Now, it was all down to one game, in Boston, and it could hardly have been more dramatic. The team which could have drafted Russell, St. Louis, was playing the team that had, Boston. Starting with Russell, Cousy, and Pettit, you could have formed an all-star team from those playing that would be the equal of virtually any that could be chosen from all those who have played in the NBA.

The new 24-second rule had upgraded the tempo and brought new fans to the game. Auerbach and Kerner, exchanging insults between complaints about the officiating, were creating copy themselves. Probably more than ever before, the NBA had the attention of the sports public.

There was one other important factor. April 13, when the final game was played, was the Saturday before the opening of the baseball season. Baseball at that time was unquestionably the country's No. 1 sport—the National Pastime, as baseball officials reverently called it. The top writers in the country followed baseball. They had all been south to the training camps. Now, they had returned north, and a good number of them came to cover the Celtics-Hawks final.

Sometimes a game that gets such tremendous advance attention turns out to be a stinker, as the players turn cautious or grow fearful of the consequences of the mistakes. Not this one—this one was a corker.

Everything seemed to be in the Celtics' favor. Certainly, the Celts were the better team, and they were playing at home. Six times during the game they seemed ready to take a commanding lead and blow the Hawks out.

But the Hawks were riding one of those streaks that teams sometimes hit, and six times, they rallied back. The last time, with a minute and a half to play, they actually took the lead.

That lead didn't last, and, with 13 seconds to play, Cousy hit a free throw to give Boston a 103-101 lead. Was that it? Hardly. Pettit was fouled, sank both free throws—and the game went into overtime.

With just a few seconds left in overtime, the Celtics had a 113-111 lead, but then Coleman hit a jump shot and the game went into a second overtime.

In the second overtime, the Celtics took a two-point lead, at 125-123, when Jim Loscutoff sank a foul shot.

St. Louis player-coach Alex Hannum had one last trick: a play the Royals had used when he had played in Rochester. Knowing that the clock doesn't start until a player touches the ball in bounds, Hannum heaved the ball at the opposite back-board. If the ball hit there and if Pettit could get the rebound, there was time for a score-tying basket.

Hannum's throw did hit the backboard and Pettit did get the rebound. He put the shot up and it rolled around the rim—and out. The Celtics were champions.

It was the first of 11 championships for the Celtics in Russell's 13 years with the team, the last two as player-coach. Certainly, it wasn't all Russell. As he noted himself, one of the big reasons for the team's success was balance and the fact that everybody knew his role. ". . . I wanted to lead the league in rebounding. Cousy wanted to lead the league in assists. Sharman wanted to lead the league in field goal attempts, and Red wanted to lead the league in technical fouls and fines."

But in the end, the main man was Russell. Players changed—Cousy and Sharman were replaced by K. C. Jones and Sam Jones, sixth man Frank Ramsey was replaced by John Havlicek. Even the coach changed, finally, as Auerbach yielded the reins to Russell. Russell was the one constant through the 13 years; when he retired, the Celtics plunged to sixth place.

That lesson was not lost on anybody. On the occasion of the NBA's thirty-fifth anniversary, the 1980-81 season, sportswriters and sportscasters voted on an all-star team covering all 35 years. The choice as best player in the NBA's history: Bill Russell, of course.

11. Wilt Casts a Long Shadow

Bill Russell the best player of all time? What about Wilt Chamberlain? Wilt always thought of himself as the greatest, and he certainly has the statistics to support his claim.

Chamberlain's statistics are awesome. Nobody else even comes close. In his 14 years he scored a record 31,419 points. One season he averaged 50.4 points a game and scored 100 points in one game; nobody has approached those figures, and almost certainly, nobody ever will.

Rebounding was supposed to be Russell's game, but Chamberlain was, statistically, a better rebounder, too. He finished his career with 23,924 rebounds, averaging 22 a game. In one game, he got 55 rebounds—against Russell.

Stung by criticism that his scoring kept his teammates from doing their best, Wilt concentrated on passing the ball and led the league in assists one year, the only center ever to do that.

Team play? Russell was supposed to be the ultimate team player, and yet Chamberlain played on two of the best teams in NBA history—the 1966-67 Philadelphia 76ers, voted the best NBA team by writers and broadcasters, and the 1972-73 Los Angeles Lakers, who won 69 games and a record 33 straight.

Though Chamberlain was labeled a loser because his college team failed to win an NCAA championship and his pro team so often finished second to Russell's Celtics, each team he played for (Philadelphia Warriors, 76ers, and Lakers) did better after he joined than before; and, in each case, set a club record for wins.

Chamberlain often appeared to be a man playing among boys. He was unquestionably the strongest man to play the game, and it did not pay to get him aroused; once, he knocked Clyde Lovelette out with one punch. Yet he seldom lost his temper, and players would push and shove him at will and he would not retaliate.

"I think he knew he was so much better than everybody else that this was the only way he could make it halfway even," says his former teammate, Al Attles, who has remained a friend of Wilt's. "I don't think he was bothered as much by players leaning on him in the pivot as everybody else thought at the time. And I'm sure he felt that if he ever lost his temper and started pushing back, with his strength, it would be chaos out there."

He had outstanding speed; in college he had run the quarter-mile in less than 49 seconds. He was a great leaper, high-jumping 6'7" as a track man. Though his great size left him open to taunts that he was good only because he was big, the truth was that he was an outstanding athlete, the first seven-footer who could not be called a "goon."

Off the court he was a pacesetter, too. He was the first to push salaries up to levels commensurate with other sports, and sometimes beyond.

He played for nine coaches and was often accused of being responsible when a coach was fired, and yet, he says there was only one coach he couldn't play for—Butch van Breda Kolff, coach of the Lakers when Wilt arrived.

Attles, who became a coach for the Warriors long after Wilt had left, feels that the talk about Chamberlain being hard to coach should be put into perspective.

"I think it's silly to say you're going to treat every player the same," says Attles. "You have to have some rules that they all accept, but basically you have to treat them as individuals, and obviously, the player's ability enters into that.

"Anybody who thinks Kareem [Abdul-Jabbar] gets the same treatment as everybody else on the Lakers is crazy. You never heard much about Russell causing trouble, but I remember that when Red Auerbach retired, the reasoning in making Russell the coach was that you'd eliminate any problems that way.

"Wilt had certain things he liked to do, and you just had to go with that because he had such great ability. Could I have coached him? I'd certainly have been willing to try."

To put Attles' remarks into context, it should be noted that he coached Rick Barry, who is certainly in everybody's top-ten prima donna list, and won an NBA championship.

It should also be noted that Chamberlain changed his game more than any other star ever did, depending on the coach and the makeup of the team.

He was an excellent businessman, investing his money so that he wouldn't have to do anything after retirement. He has varied interests, and in the basketball off-season he frequently traveled to other countries.

An aura has always surrounded Chamberlain. Next to Muhammad Ali, he is certainly the best-recognized American athlete throughout the world. Years after his retirement he does commercials identified only as a "famous tall person"; those watching know instantly who he is.

Controversy followed him throughout his career. He threatened to quit after his first season because of the hammering he took on the court. Early in his career, he signed his name to a magazine article entitled, "My Life in a Bush League." Predictably, it did not make him popular throughout the league.

Once, he and Ali talked of meeting in a heavyweight championship match. It was probably never more than hype on Ali's part, but Wilt was ready to go and was disappointed when Ali's entourage backed away from it.

It is axiomatic in sports that a superstar is never traded in his prime, and yet Chamberlain was traded twice, by the Warriors to the 76ers and by the 76ers to the Lakers. In each case the team that traded him got almost nothing in return; the chief motive was to get rid of Chamberlain.

Coaches like Alex Hannum and Bill Sharman, who explained to Wilt exactly what they expected from him, won championships. Coaches like van Breda Kolff and Neil Johnston, the Warriors' coach when Wilt was a rookie, seemed determined that Wilt would play their way *or else*; and they found out what the "or else" meant when the coach got fired.

Inevitably, Chamberlain was compared to Russell, though it was comparing apples and oranges. The two men were very different in physical makeup and ability, and in temperament; and they were playing in much different environments.

Russell had the advantage not only of playing with a great team but playing with the same one throughout his career, so the transition from year to year was a smooth one.

Chamberlain played for three teams, all very different from one another. The Warriors were largely average players, and he was expected to carry the load; the 76ers were a superbly balanced team, the only one comparable in that sense to Russell's teams; and the Lakers, when Wilt arrived, had two of the greatest ever to play the game, Jerry West and Elgin Baylor.

Hal Greer, a great guard for the Syracuse Nats (who became the Philadelphia 76ers), tries to get by Philadelphia Warriors' Tom Gola. That tall fellow off to the right is Wilt Chamberlain. *(Golden State Warriors)*

Naturally, Chamberlain's play differed on those teams. He was, for instance, criticized for shooting so much with the Warriors, but the team was designed that way. "The players had been selected to fill in around Wilt," points out Attles, who played on that team. "We were supposed to feed Wilt, and he was supposed to shoot. It would have been detrimental to the team if he hadn't shot a lot."

Russell was much smaller than Wilt (the lesser by four inches in height and as much as 60 pounds in weight) and could not match Chamberlain in strength. But he was much quicker and more agile, and that showed in the way they played defense.

Chamberlain was a massive presence in the middle. Opposing players seldom drove the lane because Wilt would be there to block the shot. But Russell had much more range. He was able to move well out to the corner to harass a shooter and still be able to get back to protect the middle. Chamberlain was not that mobile.

There was a difference in their shot-blocking styles, too. When Russell blocked a shot, his team usually got the ball. When Wilt blocked a shot, it usually went out of bounds, so the other team got another chance.

Thus, Russell had more effect on the other team. Because he picked his spots to block shots he often forced players to change their styles, since they were always conscious of Russell's presence.

Chamberlain sometimes intimidated opponents because of the sheer physical force of his shot blocks. But a player who could keep his cool could accept a certain number of shot blocks as part of the game against Chamberlain, knowing that his team would probably get the ball back and he'd get another shot.

Auerbach, admittedly prejudiced, summed it up this way: "Russell was a shot blocker; Chamberlain was a shot swatter."

Though Chamberlain had the statistical edge in rebounding, Russell also had a slight edge there because he was so quick with the outlet pass for the fast break, a skill Chamberlain did not really master until near the end of his career.

Offensively, there was a huge difference between the two. Russell was always a poor shooter, relying on tips and dunks for most of his points, and the Celtics always had other players to rely on for their scoring.

Until the end of his career, when he concentrated on defense, Chamberlain was the focal point of his team's offense. Ironically, though, many considered him a poor shooter.

When he first came up, Chamberlain shot a fall-away jumper (some thought because he wanted to prove that he could do something that didn't depend on his height). His coaches gradually convinced him that it was better for him to go to the basket, not away, so that he would be in position to rebound if he missed the shot.

Before long, Chamberlain was getting almost all of his points inside, on short jumpers, tips, and dunks. He was such an imposing physical force inside that it was virtually impossible to deny him the ball and, once he had it, to stop him from going to the basket. He always had a high shooting percentage because he didn't attempt shots outside the ten-foot range—and his detractors insisted he couldn't have made them.

Yet, in practice, Wilt practiced shots from all over and made a high percentage. In fact, he seldom practiced the kind of game he played. "He liked to take the best shooter on the team and challenge him to a game of 'horse'," says Alex Hannum. "I remember when we drafted Bud Koper with the Warriors and Koper hit about 20 shots in a row from outside in practice. Wilt challenged him. I didn't see it, but Wilt has always insisted he beat Koper."

It was the same way with his foul shooting. His detractors always pointed to Chamberlain's lack of success at the free-throw line as proof that he wasn't a shooter. When he retired, Chamberlain was barely over 50 percent at the free-throw line, and he had seasons when he averaged well under that.

Again, in practice, it was different. "When I first came to the Warriors," says Attles, "there were some good free-throw shooters, guys like Paul Arizin and Tom Gola. And yet, in practice, when they'd have little contests, Wilt would often beat them. I guess it just got to be a mental thing in games. I know he tried everything, standing back of the line, to one side, but nothing worked for him."

His poor foul shooting definitely hurt Chamberlain, and some insisted it cost his teams as many as ten wins in a season, though that seems farfetched. Because they feared him shooting from the field far more than the free-throw line, opposing players hammered him even more as his career progressed. At times, Chamberlain seemed to be backing away from fouls because he didn't want to go to the line.

Also, Chamberlain often seemed to be obsessed with his personal marks, to the detriment of his game—and not just in the scoring totals.

One of his most incredible records, for instance, is the fact that he never fouled out of a game. But there is no question that Chamberlain changed his game when he got to four fouls, because he wanted to preserve that record. (There is also no question but that he would have fouled out of at least one game except that no referee wanted to be the first to whistle that sixth foul.)

He also was very proud of his iron-man record. He almost never came out of a game, and one season averaged 48.5 minutes a game, a fact made possible because he played in some overtime games that season.

But he paced himself to do that. All big men pace themselves. Russell would occasionally lope back upcourt on offense, pausing at midcourt to see if his teammates could score without him so he could stay back on defense. Chamberlain, because he played virtually every minute, probably paced himself more than most. In early and mid-career it was usually his defense that suffered, because he wouldn't get back. In late career, he would work hard on defense and loaf downcourt on offense.

Chamberlain's theory was that he stiffened up when he came out of the game (he had trouble getting back into the flow after half-time) and was better off staying in the game.

"I know he used to say that if he stayed out five minutes it would take him ten to get back into the flow," says Attles, "so even if he played poorly for five minutes, it was better to have him in the game than on the bench. I could see his point when I was a player, but I think I'd have to talk to him about that if I were coaching him."

But in the context of Chamberlain's entire game these are almost nitpickings. He was a very great player, so awesome in his physical abilities that other players feared him, even Russell. There is, in fact, considerable evidence that Russell deliberately played on Chamberlain's good, trusting nature to keep him from unleashing his complete ability.

During their careers, Chamberlain and Russell seemed to be good friends. They would often meet each other at airports and have dinner together. Chamberlain would laugh at Russell's outlandish jokes and join in when Russell let loose that high-pitched cackle that masquerades as a laugh. In turn, Russell would constantly compliment Chamberlain, talking of his great ability; when Wilt was criticized because his teams didn't win championships and Russell's did, Russell would say that he was surrounded by a better team than Chamberlain was.

And in the games that Russell played against Chamberlain it was obvious that they were friendly rivals. "There was no animosity," says Attles. "We often wondered about that. We'd see Wilt do things against other players that were downright mean, but he always played like he was afraid of hurting Russell. One time, Russell got his wrist hurt when he tried to stop Wilt from dunking and when he was asked about that, he said it felt like trying to block a 16-pound shot. We wanted Wilt to do that kind of thing more often, be more aggressive against Russell, but he wouldn't do it."

Then, in Russell's final game, the Celtics played Wilt's Lakers in the seventh game of the championship playoff. Wilt came down hard on his knee after taking a rebound with five minutes left in the game. He later compared the feeling to the numbness that occurs when you hit your "funny bone," and he asked to be taken out of the game.

The Lakers, who had been behind by as much as 21 points early in the fourth quarter, were closing the gap fast on the aging Celtics by that time. When his knee recovered, Chamberlain told van Breda Kolff that he was ready to go back into the game. Van Breda Kolff told him that Mel Counts, who had replaced Wilt, was playing well and helping the team. Though Wilt twice more asked to go back into the game, van Breda Kolff stubbornly kept him on the bench until the end of the game, which the Celtics won.

Some time later, speaking to a group of college students, Russell criticized Chamberlain for taking himself out of the game, saying that nothing short of a broken leg was reason to come out in the closing minutes of a championship contest. There happened to be a reporter in the room at the time, and the story quickly went out over the wire service.

That caused a rift between Chamberlain and Russell, and the two haven't spoken since. "I've always thought that was sad," observes Attles. "The two of them had been so close, and they meant so much to the game, I thought they'd remain friends."

The interesting thing, though, is that the rift seemed after awhile to be one-sided. Chamberlain, though angered by Russell's comments, got over his anger, but Russell never seemed to want to make up. Chamberlain was still playing and Russell was doing television work on pro basketball, but Russell resolutely refused to try to interview Chamberlain.

There are those who think, therefore, that Russell feigned a friendship with Chamberlain only to keep Wilt from playing all out against the Celtics. Certainly, it seems more than coincidental that Russell's only public criticism of Chamberlain came after Bill had retired. He picked his spot carefully.

"If he did that intentionally, he's a smart man," says Attles.

Well, nobody ever accused Bill Russell of being dumb.

That psychological gamesmanship seems all too typical of the relationship between Russell and Chamberlain. Wilt always seemed to be coming out second-best in any battle of images.

For instance, when his salary soared to $150,000, the Warriors announced it as $100,000 because they didn't want other players demanding salaries in line with Wilt's real one. The Celtics promptly announced that Russell would get one dollar more than $100,000, so in the public's eyes, Russell was the higher paid and theoretically more valuable of the two.

During his career, Wilt was named the starting center in the All-Star Game seven times, Russell only three. Yet, Russell was named Most Valuable Player five times and Wilt four, and when it came to voting at the thirty-fifth anniversary, writers and broadcasters voted for Russell as the best, not Chamberlain.

"I believe in the 'hate the big guy' theory," says Attles. "Wilt could do so much, people just disliked him. It isn't just journalists, either. I really enjoyed playing with Wilt and I always thought players should really like him because he had so much to do with making salaries higher, but I know when I started coaching, I heard players say they wouldn't vote for Wilt for MVP because they didn't like him."

As Chamberlain has commented so often, nobody roots for Goliath.

Chamberlain didn't exactly sneak up on people. He scored 32 points in his first varsity game as a sophomore in high school. Later in the year he tied the Pennsylvania state record with 71 points against Roxborough, the team that was to be his special pigeon. As a junior he scored 74 against Roxborough; as a senior he scored 90 against the team! This, remember, was in a 32-minute game. Minute for minute, that was the equivalent of 135 points in a pro game.

Overbrook High lost only three games in the three years Wilt played there, while winning 58. Though he was often taken out of lopsided games, he averaged nearly 37 points a game.

Playing in the Catskills Mountain league in the summer, Chamberlain was coached by Red Auerbach, who tried to persuade Wilt to attend a Boston-area college so the Celtics could take him as a territorial draft pick.

But Auerbach, smart as he was, was no match for Philadelphia owner Eddie Gottlieb, who convinced the other owners that he should be allowed to make Wilt a territorial pick out of high school, which had never been done before.

"We were fighting for survival in those days," Gottlieb said later. "Hometown boys were big at the box office. I wasn't the only one to want it. Cincinnati got Jerry Lucas that way."

But, as Gottlieb knew, there was no real comparison between Chamberlain and Lucas as players.

Gottlieb drafted Chamberlain in 1955 as a "future." Probably Wilt could have played professionally right then. As it turned out, he would have been better off.

He was pursued by every major college, some two hundred offers in all. He chose Kansas. Why? There were rumors of money deals, which Wilt denied. But he did admit later that he got lots of bills from Kansas alumni after winning games. There seemed to be no other compelling reasons for him to go there.

His college career was largely a disappointment. Since freshmen were not eligible for varsity play at the time, he was a sophomore before he could play on that team. By that time the legendary Phog Allen had been forcibly retired at age 70, a disappointment to both Chamberlain and Allen. Wilt had hoped to play for Allen, and Allen had hoped that recruiting Chamberlain would enable him to stave off retirement for three years.

Allen's assistant, Dick Harp, took over, and Harp was no more than an average coach. Nor was Kansas an outstanding team. Wilt was so good that the Jayhawks made it to the finals of the NCAA tournament the first year, losing in triple overtime to undefeated North Carolina. In Chamberlain's junior year, with the team depleted by graduation, they didn't even make it to the NCAA tournament.

A disillusioned Chamberlain dropped out of school and joined the Globetrotters for a year. He made good money for the time—apparently about $65,000—but it was basically another wasted year for Wilt. To prove his point that he was an athlete and not a freak, he played guard for the 'Trotters.

So, Chamberlain spent four years treading water, in a sense, but he had no choice:

At the time, players could not be drafted out of high school; they were only eligible for the pros when their college class had graduated.

"Wilt was one of the few who could have played in the pros right out of high school," said Gottlieb. "Gola was another. Wilt was ready. He made mincemeat out of All-Pro centers like Neil Johnston in the Catskills. We had Johnston, but Wilt would have started for me."

But though his fellow owners had changed one rule for Gottlieb they wouldn't change the other for fear of alienating the colleges, which were the pros' farm system.

Wilt was every bit as good as expected when he finally became a rookie, becoming the first player to be voted Rookie of the Year and Most Valuable Player simultaneously, averaging 37.6 points a game. It was, like most of Chamberlain's accomplishments, a record, but it was only the beginning.

The second year, his scoring average went to 38.4 a game, and his third season was like nothing anybody had ever seen or likely will ever see again.

Frank McGuire was the new coach of the Warriors that year, and he wanted Wilt to shoot more than he ever had. His theory was simple: With Wilt scoring 38 the year before, the team had finished second—to the Celtics, of course; with Wilt scoring 50, he believed the Warriors could win.

McGuire was also the first to change Wilt's style, weaning him from the fall-away so he would be in position to rebound his missed shots.

The coach also talked to the other players on the team so they would know what was expected of them. He especially had to convince Guy Rodgers, who feared (like most players) that his salary would suffer if his scoring did. McGuire assured Rodgers that he would speak up for him at negotiating time. Rodgers' scoring average fell from 12.8 to 8.2, but his assists went up from 6.7 to 8.0.

Before the first practice, McGuire showed the team a basketball on which he had drawn lines sectioning it off. The biggest section, he explained, belonged to Wilt; the smaller part to the rest of the team.

Thus encouraged, Wilt put the ball up at a record pace that year, 47 times a game, and averaged 50.4 points a game. That was an absolutely stupefying statistic. For a player to score 50 points in a game was, and is, a remarkable feat. It was unimaginable that one player could average that.

Game after game, Wilt was putting up those big numbers, but there was one that stood out above all the rest: On March 2, 1962, he scored 100 points against the New York Knickerbockers.

Ironically, the feat was accomplished in the small town of Hershey, Pennsylvania, one of the barnstorming stops that the pros made in those days, instead of on either the Warriors' or the Knicks' home court. Only 4112 watched the game.

Athletes often talk of those days or nights when they're "in the zone," when they reach a level of performance that they can seldom duplicate. This was one of those nights for Wilt.

The tipoff came earlier. Gottlieb and Ike Richman, a part owner of the Warriors, were playing a target-shooting game. They were scoring 400 to 500 points a game and learned that 1800 was the record. They bet Wilt he couldn't hit 1000. He took the bet and won.

They kept raising the score and the bet, and Wilt kept winning. Finally, he hit 2000 points on the game. His next target was the Knicks, and they were no more of a problem.

Darrall Imhoff started at center for the Knicks that night. Imhoff had been known as a great defensive center at Cal, but he got into foul trouble early that night trying to stop Wilt.

Cleveland Buckner replaced Imhoff at center, but it really made no difference who was playing there that night. Wilt just kept scoring and scoring. Even his free-throw shooting was superb that night; he wound up hitting 28 of 32.

The point totals kept rising. At halftime, Wilt had 41; at the end of the third quarter, he had 69.

"We really weren't thinking about 100," said Attles, "and Wilt never said anything to us about it. There wasn't much we could do different. We'd been feeding him all year, so it wasn't like McGuire could suddenly tell us to start feeding Wilt.

"The Knicks tried everything they could to stop him, especially fouling. I remember one time he was even fouled in the backcourt. But of course, he was hitting his foul shots that night, so that didn't work.

"We weren't really conscious of how many points he had until the fourth quarter. We were used to seeing him score unbelievable amounts, anyway. Then Dave Zinkoff, the public address announcer, started announcing after each basket how many points Wilt had."

With just under eight minutes left, Wilt hit a fadeaway to reach 79, a regulation game record. With five minutes left, he reached 89. The Knicks slowed the game down as much as possible under the 24-second clock, and he didn't score for the next two minutes and 15 seconds.

Then, he heated up again, sinking three free throws and two fadeaways. A looped pass from York Larese was dunked, and Wilt was at 98 with 1:19 left.

Then, trying for the magic 100, Wilt got anxious. He intercepted a pass but missed a jumper. On the next offensive sequence, he missed a shot, grabbed the rebound but missed the next shot, too.

Finally, Ted Luckenbill grabbed the rebound off Wilt's missed shot and passed it back out to Joe Rucklick, who lobbed the ball high toward the basket. Wilt soared up to smash it through, and he had his 100 points.

For the game, Wilt had shot 63 times from the floor, hitting 36, and had hit 28 of 32 free-throw attempts. All were single-game records.

McGuire's strategy for the season almost worked. With Wilt pouring in 50-plus points in 46 of the 80 games, the Warriors again finished second to the Celtics in the regular season. But McGuire had planned all along that the regular season would be basically a warmup for the playoffs, and he almost pulled it off.

In the final playoff series the Warriors took the Celtics right down to the seventh game. The game was a furious one, tight all the way.

The Warriors led at half-time, 56-52, and 81-80, after three periods. The Celtics then spurted and led by as much as ten points with five minutes to play, but the Warriors came back strongly.

Wilt played magnificently down the stretch, even hitting two free throws to cut the Celts' lead to 107-104 with a minute to play. The Celtics, using all the time on the 24-second clock, shot and missed.

With 20 seconds left to play, Wilt grabbed a missed Philadelphia shot and went to the hoop, slamming the shot through. Fouled by Russell, he made the free throw—his fourth in a row—and the score was tied, with 16 seconds left.

But the Celtics came back and stalled the clock down until Sam Jones hit a jumper with two seconds to go. The Warriors had a chance only for a desperation play. Tom Gola tossed the ball in from mid-court, aiming it at Chamberlain near the basket, but Russell deflected it as the buzzer ended the game.

It was a bitter end to what had been a great season for Wilt and the Warriors, and it was all too typical of the disappointments that marred his professional career. There were a lot of excuses. Referee Mendy Rudolph had made two controversial calls against Chamberlain, one on goal-tending and the other on an out-of-bounds play. Gola was hurt, and Rodgers fouled out of the game, as he had in two others during the series. But whatever the story, the Celtics had won and Wilt's team had lost, and he would be saddled with the reputation of a "loser," despite his great individual play, through most of his career.

In retirement, Wilt remains—in Alex Hannum's classic phrase—"just like any seven-foot millionaire who lives next door."

He lives in a huge house in Bel Air, California, which he had built, and which he named Ursa Major; for those who don't understand the Latin, it loosely translates as the Big Dipper, the nickname Chamberlain always preferred for himself.

Everything in the house is built to his proportions, including a 45-foot-high stone fireplace and a 72-square-foot master bed with a mirrored roof, which rolls away to reveal the sky at a touch of a button. The house, 8300 square feet in area, sits on two acres of property. It is a monument to Wilt, who feels he has never received enough recognition. It is also a good investment; Chamberlain says he bought it for $2 million and estimates it is now worth $10 million. If he could find another seven-foot millionaire to buy it, that is.

Wilt has dabbled in sports since his retirement, with a volleyball team for awhile and as coach of a women's track team at another time. There have been reports that he was ready to come out of retirement to play for an NBA team, but nothing happened. The suspicion is that teams are just mentioning Wilt's name for the publicity value. In retirement as in his playing days, Wilt Chamberlain casts a long shadow.

12. Westward Ho!

The Minneapolis Lakers were in serious trouble, and the NBA was about to live up to its name as the *National* Basketball Association for the first time.

In the early years of the NBA, of course, the Lakers had been the glamor team, the dynasty. George Mikan was virtually unstoppable in the middle, and when the smoke cleared after the playoffs, the Lakers were usually the winning team.

But Mikan had retired after the 1953-54 season and it was all downhill for the Lakers after that. (Mikan did return for the 1955-56 season, but he was only a shell of the great player he had been and he wisely retired for good after that season.)

Clyde Lovellette, an All-American center from Kansas, had replaced Mikan in the middle for the Lakers, and at first glance, seemed much the same kind of player. He was roughly the same size as Mikan, and an excellent shooter and rebounder.

But Lovellette did not have the competitive fire of Mikan (probably nobody else did, either), nor was he the force in the middle on defense that Mikan was. His scoring and rebounding statistics were comparable to Mikan's, but nobody thought he was the same kind of dominating player that Mikan had been.

At times the Lakers even tried Lovellette at forward, first when Mikan came back in the 1955-56 season and later when the seven-foot Walter Dukes was acquired.

But the lumbering Lovellette was a defensive liability at forward, and he was more effective playing inside on offense, too. Soon, the Lakers disposed of both Lovellette and Dukes and brought in Larry Foust to play center, but that was shuffling bodies, no more. Foust was the same type of center as Lovellette, and neither was ever confused with Mikan.

Even with Mikan, though, the Lakers would have had great problems, because the game was changing. The 24-second clock, combined with the widening of the foul lanes, had made the Lakers' deliberate, muscle style of play obsolete. Now, the emphasis was on speed, on the fast break; and the Lakers were a plodding, ineffectual team.

The other stars who had combined with Mikan to make the Lakers great were also going. Forward Jim Pollard retired the same season Mikan did, and though Pollard was never the force that Mikan was, his all-round game (defense, rebounding, scoring) was badly missed by the Lakers. Vern Mikkelsen, the very model for what would become known in later years as a "power forward," was slowing down, though he didn't retire until after the 1958-59 season.

The first post-Mikan year wasn't too much of a slippage: The Lakers' 40-32 mark wasn't far from the 40-26 record of the season before. But the Mikan Lakers had won both their divisional championship and the playoffs; the next year, the Lakers finished second in the division and lost in the second round of the playoffs.

It quickly got worse, going to 33-39 and 34-38 in the next two seasons and then plunging to an embarrassing 19-53 record in the 1957-58 season.

There was one consolation to that record: Because it was the worst in the league, it qualified the Lakers for the first pick in the college draft, which meant the chance to draft Elgin Baylor.

Baylor had been an All-American in college his final year, but because he had played at an obscure college against indifferent and mediocre opposition for the most part, it was only in that last year that most of the sporting public had heard much about him. But to those involved in the sport, he had been well known long before that.

He had played his high school ball in Washington, D.C., historically one of the most productive areas in terms of prep basketball talent. Because he had not applied himself in the classroom as he had on the basketball court, his grades were not good enough to get him into a major college, and so he wound up at the College of Idaho, where he was to play both football and basketball.

After he got there, the College of Idaho cut back on athletic scholarships and cut down on the sports program in general, so Baylor transferred to Seattle University.

Because of his transfer, Baylor had to sit out one year before he would be eligible for intercollegiate competition again, but he was worth waiting for. In his senior academic year (junior as far as intercollegiate competition went), Baylor led an otherwise ordinary team to the finals of the NCAA tournament.

Kentucky, a much superior team, won the NCAA championship, 84-72. But Baylor, playing with cracked ribs and plagued by fouls, scored 25 points and made believers of those who had thought his impressive statistics were the result only of inferior competition. That tournament confirmed what those in the Seattle area already knew: that Baylor was the best college basketball player in the country.

Baylor wasn't big, as basketball players go; at 6'5", he was small for a forward and smaller even than some of the men who have played guard in the NBA. But he was a tremendous jumper, and Seattle even used him in the pivot at times. In the pros he would lead his team in rebounding for the first seven years of his career.

But even more important than his jumping ability was his body control. Baylor was the first player who would change directions while he was in the air, to maneuver for a shot or make a pass.

The best example of his body control was the way he handled a fast break. Baylor would come downcourt with the ball in the middle, with teammates on his right and left. When he got to the free-throw line, he would leap into the air. Depending on

Elgin Baylor became the prototype for the modern forward, a high-jumping player who was both a great scorer and rebounder. *(Los Angeles Lakers)*

how the defense reacted, he could pass to a cutting teammate on either side—or take the ball in himself.

Defenders didn't know until they committed themselves which way Elgin would go—and they weren't alone. "When he went up," says Alex Hannum, who coached teams against Baylor many times, "Baylor didn't know what he would do, either."

In conventional play, Baylor was just as good. There has probably never been a forward who could drive for the basket better than Baylor, and maybe only Rick Barry and Dolph Schayes have ever been as good. He was indefensible. If a defender laid back to stop Baylor from driving, he'd pop a medium-range jump shot over him. If the defender moved up to stop the jump shot, Baylor would simply drive past him for the basket.

He was tremendously strong. In the pros he filled out to 225 pounds; his Laker teammates were convinced he could be the heavyweight champion if he trained for it. He could not be moved out of rebounding position, and though he was giving away several inches to his opponents he often outjumped them for the rebound.

His one weakness was defense, but his coaches were more than willing to overlook that because of all the other things Baylor brought to the party.

Baylor could have returned to college for one more season because he had not completed his eligibility, but there was no reason to. He had never pretended to be a scholar, and he had nothing left to prove athletically in college. He was ready to turn pro and take his money.

At that news Bob Short breathed a deep sigh of relief. Short, a man of many hats (he was a trucking executive and a power in Democratic state politics), had bought the club from the original Laker owners, Max Winter and Ben Berger, in 1957. With the team declining so rapidly on the court, attendance had dwindled to practically nothing. Short has since said that he might have had to fold the franchise if he couldn't have gotten Baylor in the draft.

Baylor was everything that he was expected to be in that rookie season. He led the Lakers in virtually every measurable department that year. He was the team's leading scorer (fourth in the league) at 24.9; the team's leading rebounder (third in the league) with 15; and even the leading playmaker, with 4.1 assists a game. He topped the team in shooting percentage (41 percent), in minutes played (and second only to Bob Pettit in the league), and in personal fouls. Only in free-throw shooting, where his 78 percent was second to Mikkelsen's 81, did Baylor trail a teammate.

And Elgin was only warming up. In his second season, he broke Joe Fulk's NBA scoring record with 64 points in a game against Boston. The next season he raised that to 71 in a game against the Knicks.

Wilt Chamberlain later obliterated Baylor's scoring record with a 100-point effort against the Knicks, whose contributions to league history were entirely negative in those days, but Elgin's 71 points remains a league record for forwards.

But those who saw him play remember the number of points he scored less than the fashion in which they were scored, and the times he scored them. He was at his best in the clutch. "Elgin always found a way to get the job done," says Hannum.

Everything would seem to freeze when he got the ball and the Lakers needed points. He had an involuntary neck twitch which never seemed to bother him but drove defenders crazy because, while they were watching the twitch, Elgin would go past them to the hoop.

If he missed, Baylor always seemed to be there to get his own rebound and put the ball up again. No statistics have ever been kept on this, but those who watched Baylor in his prime are convinced that he got more points off rebounds of his missed shots than any other player in history.

His versatility was underscored in the 1962-63 season, when he was second in the NBA in scoring with a 34.0 average, third in free-throw percentage at .837, fifth in rebounding at 14.3, and sixth in assists, with a 4.8 average. And only Chamberlain played more minutes that year.

Through the second half of his NBA career, Baylor was plagued by knee problems; after the 1963-64 season, he was never again as good a player as he had been earlier.

But Elgin Baylor operating at 70 percent was still much better than almost any other player operating at 100 percent. When he retired, Baylor was the third leading scorer in NBA history with 23,149 points and the No. 2 rebounding forward (behind Bob Pettit) with 11,463. And in the thirty-fifth anniversary voting, he was selected as one of the all-time forwards.

With Baylor, the Lakers improved to a 33-39 record in the 1958-59 season, but though Elgin boosted his scoring to 29.6 points a game in his second season, the Lakers fell back to a disastrous 25-50 season. Baylor's college coach, John Castellani, had started the season as the new Lakers' coach, replacing Johnny Kundla, who had coached the great Laker teams; but Castellani didn't last the season, being replaced by old Laker star Jim Pollard.

That did it for the Lakers in Minneapolis. Attendance was down once again and Short was ready to move the club, though he remained in Minneapolis himself.

Until then the NBA had been strictly an Eastern and Midwestern league, but the new site for the Lakers would be Los Angeles, which meant the league would now stretch from East to West.

Ned Irish, whose New York Knicks would be one of the teams which had to travel across the continent, complained of the added travel costs, but there were compelling reasons to move the franchise from Minneapolis to Los Angeles.

In Los Angeles, there was a new 14,000-seat Sports Arena; in Minneapolis, the Lakers had an old 10,000-seat arena, which they seldom filled, of course.

There were far more people living in Los Angeles, but the gap between Los Angeles and Minneapolis would widen even further because the California city was growing so rapidly.

Having a franchise in Los Angeles, the nation's entertainment capital, would do a lot for the league's image. Although Minneapolis has since gotten major league teams in both football and baseball, many still associated it with cities like Rochester and Syracuse and a bush league past.

So, the deed was done. Ironically, the franchise kept its nickname, though it was no longer appropriate. The nickname of Lakers was a natural for a team in Minnesota, a state which claims to have 10,000 lakes; but the only fresh water in the arid Los Angeles area has to be pumped in from elsewhere.

It was an ideal time for Short to move his team to a new city because he was about to get another star to go with Baylor.

The big prize in the draft that year was Oscar Robertson, the great University of Cincinnati player who many think is the best, in terms of all-round skills, ever to play basketball. The Cincinnati Royals had a lock on Robertson because their record was the worst in the NBA, giving them the first-draft pick, and Robertson could be a territorial pick.

But 1960 was an exceptional year for college basketball talent. The U.S. Olympic team that year had had Robertson, Jerry West, Jerry Lucas, Terry Dischinger, Walt

Bellamy, Bob Boozer, and Adrian Smith, all of whom would become outstanding NBA players. Not surprisingly, the United States won easily.

Drafting second that year, the Lakers got West, who was almost as good a choice as Robertson. Not as big (at 6'3") or as strong as Robertson, West was nevertheless an exceptional shooter, a superb passer, an outstanding floor leader, and such a great leaper that he sometimes moved into the pivot in his college years. He had incredibly long arms, measuring 81 inches from tip to tip—the arms of a man 6'9" or 6'10".

West was an exceptional college player, a two-time All-American who led his team to the NCAA finals as a junior (the favored Mountaineers lost, 71-70, to Cal).

But as good as he was as a college player, he was even better as a pro. In part, this was because the pro game allows more avenues of expression for the greatly talented. But it was also because of the kind of individual West was. Like all great players, he was driven to excel, and he was never satisfied to remain at one level of performance, however good it might be.

In college, despite his great statistics, opponents knew he would drive only to his right. Defenders would overplay him a full step to the right—although, even then, Jerry often got his basket. When he came to the pros, West worked long hours on his own to learn to drive to the left, and he became a complete player.

West's chief offensive weapon was his jumper, which he shot with a feathery touch. He was impossible to stop because he needed no breathing space to launch his shot. He would go up so quickly that his defender would be left on the floor to watch as West flicked his shot toward the basket.

As a scorer, West was proficient enough to finish his career with the third-highest total in NBA history at the time, but he was far more than a scorer. Nobody, in fact, has ever worked harder on both ends of the court.

As long as he played, Jerry was his team's floor leader, bringing the ball upcourt and running the offense. In the mid-'60s, for instance, he had a four-year stretch in which he led his team in scoring and assists each year.

And he played superbly on defense. On almost any team responsibilities are split. If a guard is a high scorer he is usually assigned to the weaker offensive guard on the other team, because a coach wants his high scorer to be fresh for offense—and he doesn't want to take a chance the scorer will foul out of the game. But West always took the other team's scoring guard, and he usually shut that guard down. Nobody played better defense.

Most important, he did it when it counted. In the big games, when a basket meant the difference between winning and losing, Jerry West wanted the ball. He made so many of those big shots that he became known as "Mr. Clutch," which became the title of his autobiography.

Oddly, there were some who thought West wouldn't make it as a pro. Nobody doubted his ability, but there were questions whether his wiry, 175-pound body could hold up to the pounding, night after night. In college, West had played with incredible intensity, diving for loose balls and playing at the top of his ability game after game. But a college season involves only 30 games, more or less; a pro season, with exhibitions and playoffs, can exceed 100. It didn't seem likely West could maintain his pace over a pro season as he had done in college.

By now, of course, we know that West answered all the questions. His style of play did get him injured frequently; his nose was broken 14 times in his career, for instance. But he played through his injuries, game after game, season after season, and any talk of great NBA guards always revolves around Oscar Robertson, Bob Cousy, and Jerry West.

It took West part of his rookie season to get acclimated to the pro style. He averaged 17.6 points a game in that rookie season, a sensational performance by most standards but the only season in his career in which West scored fewer than 20 points a game.

Battle of the best: Jerry West tries to drive by Oscar Robertson.
(Los Angeles Lakers)

By his second season, West was the player we all remember, averaging 30.8 points a game, and he was well on his way to a superb career. In his third season, he scored 63 points in a game (against the Knicks, naturally) to set a scoring record for guards. The record has since been broken by Pete Maravich's 68. Again, Maravich's spree came against the Knicks.

West was joined on the Lakers by his college coach, Fred Schaus from West Virginia, as Baylor had been joined by his college coach. There, the similarity ended. Schaus was an excellent mentor who understood the pro game. He became an outstanding coach, and later executive, in the NBA.

The Lakers' improvement coincided with West's. During his rookie year, when Jerry took awhile to hit top gear, the Lakers improved only to 36-43, good for second place in the west.

But when he hit his stride in his second year the Lakers jumped up to a 54-26 mark, and for most of the rest of his career, the Lakers were the best in the West.

Once an NBA team was settled in Los Angeles it was inevitable that there would eventually be one in San Francisco, too. That had been the pattern in other sports. The Dodgers had moved to L.A. and the Giants to San Francisco in the same year. The Los Angeles Rams and San Francisco 49ers had been rivals for well over a decade.

It was a natural rivalry to have teams in the two cities, and it made sense from a travel standpoint; Eastern teams could play in both cities instead of making the trip out to play just one team. But it took two years for the other shoe to drop, and for a team to locate in San Francisco.

Preliminary talks started shortly after the Lakers moved west, as Franklin Mieuli talked with NBA commissioner Maurice Podoloff about the possibility of an expansion team for San Francisco.

Mieuli was a radio-TV production man who had minority interests in both the 49ers (10 percent) and Giants (about 5 percent). He remembers his conversation with Podoloff, coming while the 49ers were in New York to play the Giants. "He told me there was no chance San Francisco could get an expansion team," says Mieuli, "and I wasn't even thinking of an established team moving out here."

As a footnote, San Francisco did have a professional basketball team at the time—the San Francisco Saints of the American Basketball League, a rival league which had been formed by Abe Saperstein.

The Saints had Phil Woolpert, formerly of USF, as their head coach, and their best-known player was Kenny Sears, who had played his college basketball at Santa Clara, 45 miles south of San Francisco. But neither Woolpert nor Sears was enough to pull in fans. The Saints folded after one season and the league lasted only halfway through the next.

Then, in 1962, negotiations began to move the Warriors from Philadelphia. Diners Club executives Matty Simmons and Len Mogle approached Eddie Gottlieb with a magnificent offer of $850,000 for the team. "At the time, remember, clubs were selling for like $250,000," says Mieuli.

The Warriors had been struggling for years, though Philadelphia was and is a great basketball town. Gottlieb's problem was that the interest was mainly in college basketball.

Gottlieb had tried to capitalize on the collegiate interest by signing former Philadelphia college stars such as Paul Arizin and Tom Gola. As already explained, he had persuaded his fellow owners to amend the territorial pick rule so he could get Wilt Chamberlain, who played his high school ball in Philadelphia.

The Warriors were still playing second banana in Philadelphia, but Gottlieb, one of the pioneers of pro basketball, had never seriously thought of selling the club. But the offer of $850,000 was too good to resist. He accepted it, and also agreed to serve as a "consultant" for one year.

So, the deal was struck. But Simmons and Mogle wanted to get San Francisco interests involved in the team, knowing that absentee ownership can often be fatal to a sports franchise. They decided to try to sell two-thirds of the club to San Francisco interests, and Mieuli got back into the picture.

"My main client with radio productions at that time was KSFO, which belongs to the Golden West network," explains Mieuli. "Gene Autry owned Golden West, so I got to know him pretty well.

"The Diners Club guys had gone to Autry to ask him if he'd be interested and he said no, that if he were ever interested in pro basketball he'd be trying to get the Lakers from Short. But he mentioned my name to them and told them I'd be a good man to talk to because of my radio-TV background. They'd certainly need help in that area, even if they didn't have me involved in the club.

"Simmons sent his accountant, Bernard Solomon, to talk to me. Solomon told me there would be a franchise moving out. I had no idea which team he was talking about, and I didn't show very much interest.

"'So,' he said, 'maybe I should tell you what the franchise is.' He told me it was the Warriors, and the wheels really started spinning in my head then.

"If you remember, at that time the big rivalry was between the Warriors with Wilt Chamberlain and the Celtics with Bill Russell. The Warriors and Celtics would meet in the Eastern playoffs, and that was the big matchup. Whoever won, and it was usually the Celtics, would then beat the Lakers in the finals, but that was really kind of anti-climactic.

"I figured that if the Warriors moved to San Francisco the big rivalry would come in the finals. The big series would be the matchup between the Warriors in the West and the Celtics in the East."

So, Mieuli agreed to work with the Warriors in radio and TV productions and also to buy 10 percent for a "rooting interest." Then, Solomon asked him if he had anybody else who would be interested. Did he!

Mieuli had gotten his 49er stock because principal owner Tony Morabito was a friend and had allowed him to buy in. He'd gotten his Giants' stock because owner Horace Stoneham had tipped him off when Joan Payson sold her Giants' stock so she could buy the New York Mets.

"Ever since, I'd had friends telling me, 'Jeez, Franklin, are you ever lucky. Nobody ever tells me about deals like that. If you hear of anything else, let me know.'

"So, when I heard this, I went around to all my jock-loving friends and told them about it. I even got my banker in on the deal."

But that first year in San Francisco was an absolute disaster for the Warriors. Arizin didn't come west with the team, taking an early retirement so he could stay in Philadelphia. Coach Frank McGuire also quit rather than come west, and Bob Feerick (a former pro player who had gone to school at Santa Clara) was named coach. The Warriors, 49-31 the year before, exactly reversed their record and finished a badly beaten fourth.

"The Diners Club guys were going crazy," remembers Mieuli. "They were in New York, and they were phoning Gottlieb every two minutes. They got Eddie to make a trade, Tom Gola for Willie Naulls, for cosmetic purposes. Well, Naulls got here and went into shock. He had never played with a player like Wilt before. He was a guy who needed the ball, and now he was being asked to be a feeder. He never did play well for us."

The Warriors were also bombing at the gate, losing $250,000. The Diners Club people wanted out. So did some of Mieuli's friends who he had brought in. "I never oversold it," he says, "but when guys get involved in sports, their business sense just goes out the window."

Though the club had been officially sold, Gottlieb actually still owned most of it, because only 25 percent of the sale price had been put down. Mieuli talked to Gottlieb, asking for more time so he could take over the Diners Club share. "I mortgaged everything I owned," he says.

Some of the other minority owners defaulted on their payments on the operating loss. Under the terms of the agreement, that meant their stock percentage went down, which made Mieuli's go up. Eventually, he got control of the team. By the mid-'70s, when he bought out the last of the minority owners, he had complete ownership of the team.

Mieuli's first act when he took over control of the team was to bring in a new coach, Alex Hannum, who had both played and coached in the league. Hannum's first move was to change the Warriors' whole attitude.

"When we went to training camp, I really emphasized physical conditioning," says

Hannum. "It was a brutal camp. Some guys couldn't make it through. Wilt went right along with everything, of course, but that was the last training camp I was able to get him to. Every other year I coached him (with the Warriors and Philadelphia 76ers) he had a reason not to be there."

The Warriors had drafted Nate Thurmond out of Bowling Green that year. Thurmond had been an outstanding defensive center in college, but many wondered if he would be a good enough shooter as a pro.

Because the Warriors already had Chamberlain a lot of eyebrows were raised when they drafted Thurmond. But the Warriors were only following a basic rule of pro basketball: You can never have too many good big men. Surplus big men can be traded for more than smaller players of comparable quality.

Hannum moved Thurmond to forward. It was obvious that forward was not Nate's best position because he lacked the quickness to handle the more agile forwards in the league; he was used as a reserve in his rookie season. But he gave the Warriors some flexibility, especially against big forwards, and he was a factor in the Warriors' much-improved play.

The big man, though, was still Chamberlain. Hannum was one of the coaches who got the most out of Wilt in his career. "The big thing was, you couldn't ever try to con Wilt," says Hannum. "He was too smart to fool. You had to be very honest with him."

Even Hannum had his problems at times with Chamberlain—those close to the team at the time claim that Hannum once challenged Wilt to a fight over a disagreement on strategy, a challenge which Wilt refused, fortunately for Hannum—but Wilt played very well that year, averaging a league-leading 36.9 points a game. The Warriors did another flip-flop, this time winning 48 games and losing only 32, to finish first in the West.

Despite losing to the Celtics in the playoffs, the Warriors' season was good enough to make fans think they'd be consistent contenders for a time. But the next season, they took another nosedive.

As usual, Chamberlain was right in the middle. Wilt had suffered from stomach pains before training camp, which caused him to miss both the camp and exhibition games. Eventually, his ailment was diagnosed as pancreatitis.

When he returned to action, he scored at an even higher rate than the season before—38.9 points a game—but the team played poorly, perhaps because of the emotional upheaval created when it seemed that Chamberlain might not play at all.

The Warriors lost 16 of their first 21 games. Despite his scoring, Chamberlain had never been big box office in San Francisco. Now that the Warriors were losing before small crowds, Chamberlain's salary was a big liability. And as long as Wilt remained with the team, Thurmond would have to play out of position.

Hannum and Mieuli have contradictory versions of what happened next—which shouldn't be surprising. The two were never close (Mieuli eventually fired Hannum, and neither has anything good to say about the other now), and communication was always a problem.

Mieuli says, "Hannum kept coming in and holding his head in his hands and saying, 'That guy (Wilt) is driving me up the wall. We're going to wind up going outside and he'll kill me.'

"Meanwhile, he was also telling me how great Nate was going to be. I'm listening to this and I'm thinking I have to make a change."

Hannum says the two talked over the possibility of a trade on the way to St. Louis for the All-Star Game. "We went over the pluses and minuses," says Hannum, "and my conclusion was that there were more pluses. I didn't want to trade Wilt."

Mieuli snorts at that. "The only guy who was against trading Wilt was Gottlieb. He said, 'You can't trade the franchise.' But I told him we weren't drawing with Wilt."

One thing Hannum and Mieuli agree on: Franklin was determined to trade Chamberlain before leaving St. Louis. And he did, trading Chamberlain to the Philadelphia 76ers (the former Syracuse team which had just that season been moved to Philadelphia) for Lee Shaffer, Connie Dierking, and Paul Neumann.

It was a shocker at the time, but it should have been a good deal for the Warriors. By trading Chamberlain, they were able to move Thurmond to the middle, and Nate became an outstanding center. Neumann was a good guard, which the Warriors needed; Dierking was a good backup center.

The key to the trade, though, was Shaffer. A 6'7", 230-pound forward, he had played three seasons in the NBA averaging 16.8 points a game, but had not reported that year because of a contract dispute. If he could be persuaded to play, he would be a valuable player for the Warriors, a solid player in the Bailey Howell/Tom Heinsohn mold who could score and rebound.

"Alex had gone down (to Shaffer's North Carolina home) to talk to Shaffer," says Mieuli, "and Shaffer told him he would come out and play for us. So, we made the deal."

After the trade was announced, of course, Mieuli was besieged by phone calls from writers and broadcasters. One phone call was different, though.

"I picked up the phone and heard this sobbing voice," he says. "It was Shaffer's wife. She said, 'I just heard the news. I hope you didn't make a decision based on what Lee told Alex last week, because he isn't going to play.'

"At the time I thought it was just another case of a hysterical wife who maybe didn't want to make another move. But, she was right. Shaffer never played again in the NBA."

When Shaffer didn't report, it made the deal a bad one for the Warriors. It didn't help, either, when the 76ers, with Chamberlain, went on to the NBA finals, while the Warriors limped through a disastrous 17-63 campaign.

But in the NBA, dramatic changes come quickly. Because the Warriors and Knicks were so bad that year each got two picks in the draft before anybody else. With the Warriors' second pick, they took Rick Barry, a gate attraction, who was to make the team a winner.

And so, the Warriors became a solid franchise, as the Lakers had been from the moment they moved. The NBA's western expansion was a success.

13. The Greatest Team of All Time?

Rick Barry came along at the perfect time for the San Francisco Warriors. He was almost too good to be true, the All-American boy come to life. On the court, he was a spectacular, dynamic player, the kind who brought fans out of their seats with incredible plays. Off the court, he was tall and handsome, married to his college sweetheart, the daughter of his college coach, Bruce Hale. Their story was a natural for the special sections in the Sunday newspaper, and thus, Barry brought the Warriors publicity they would never have gotten otherwise.

It is not too strong a statement to say that Barry saved the Warrior franchise. San Franciscans are a provincial, skeptical bunch. They do not readily accept stars from other areas, which is one reason Wilt Chamberlain hadn't been a big draw in San Francisco. They much prefer either players who grew up in the area or at least started their professional careers in San Francisco.

In Barry they had the kind of player they could accept. Though he had been an All-American in college, other players were better known; his greatest fame, by far, came after he arrived in San Francisco. It didn't hurt, either, that he was the son-in-law of Bruce Hale, who had played in the area, at Santa Clara.

Nor did it hurt that he was white. That was the issue nobody wanted to talk about publicly but was probably the major topic of conversation for NBA executives in private.

The league was turning black, and owners and general managers were concerned that white fans—then as now, far more whites attended games than blacks—would not pay to see black players.

The year before Barry came into the league, four of the first five scorers and seven of the first ten were black. Nine of the top ten rebounders were black. The first five assist producers were black.

The biggest stars in the league were Chamberlain, Bill Russell, Elgin Baylor, Oscar Robertson, and Jerry West. Only West was white.

So, though nobody would be quoted on it, all around the league, teams were glad to see Barry become a star. Because there is no gate-sharing in the NBA, the home teams got all the benefit of the increased gate when the Warriors were on the road. But the Warriors were home half of the time—and they got all the benefit then.

The ironic aspect of all this was that the Warriors almost didn't get Barry. If the league hadn't put in a special drafting procedure that year, Barry would have played somewhere else. And the history of the NBA would have been quite different.

Since 1961, the two last-place teams in each division had flipped a coin to see who would get first pick. In 1965, for one year only, the two last-place teams—the Warriors and New York Knicks—each got two picks before anybody else drafted.

The Knicks won the coin flip, so they drafted first and fourth. The Warriors drafted second and third. On their first pick, the Knicks took Bill Bradley, the Princeton All-American, though Bradley would spend the next two years as a Rhodes Scholar at Oxford University.

Since the Warriors had the next two picks, it didn't make any difference in which order they selected the players. But it is a fact that coach Alex Hannum's first choice was Fred Hetzel, a 6'9" All-American forward from Davidson. Hannum was not nearly so high on Barry, though he was persuaded by others in the Warrior organization to take Rick.

At the time, Hannum's reasoning seemed sound. Hetzel was an excellent outside shooter and a strong rebounder. Barry was a skinny 6'7" with no outside shot. In college, the bulk of his points had come inside, from driving or picking up "garbage" shots. There were many who questioned his ability to be a good pro.

But, as coaches and general managers will tell you, the one thing that cannot be measured is an athlete's heart, or desire. Barry had that desire, and Hetzel didn't. Hetzel played six years, his first two with the Warriors, in the NBA, but was never more than a journeyman. Barry became a superstar.

In his rookie year Barry averaged 25.7 points a game, fourth in the league, though he had not yet developed an outside shot. He was a tremendous driver and, though he was not a great jumper, he had great body control. He would twist and squirm in mid-air to take an off-balance shot—and the shot would go in. His style was neither pretty nor classic, but it was effective.

Barry was also a superb free-throw shooter. His style was something out of an almost forgotten era; the two-handed underhand shot. Players had gotten away from that style, probably because it didn't look good, but Barry was deadly effective with it. That first year he was second in free-throw shooting average at .862 and scored an average of seven points a game on free throws. Only West and Robertson, established stars, scored better.

Like all great players, Barry improved in his second season. By now, constant practice had developed an outside shot to go with his drives, and he was virtually unstoppable. He led the league in scoring with a 35.6 average, five points better than Robertson in second place and nearly ten full points better than his rookie year effort.

"I think that was probably Rick's best year," says Bill Sharman, who coached the Warriors that season. "He was young and full of enthusiasm, and he was at his physical peak."

It was not Barry's happiest year, though. Sharman had replaced Hannum, fired by Franklin Mieuli when the Warriors finished 35-45 and missed the playoffs in the 1965-66 season, and Barry was among those who disliked the change.

Hannum was always very popular with his players. Though he drove them hard in practice, he was an extroverted man who would go out after a game and drink with his players. Sharman was a much more private person. His relationship with his players was in the mold of most coaches: It ended after the game.

Sharman also had a different coaching style. He believed in light practices on game day, where players would come out and shoot around to get into the flow of the game. Every coach holds such practices now, but it was a novel idea then. "Some of the players objected to that," Sharman recalls.

The chief objector was Barry, who preferred to sleep late on game days. Rick was not reluctant to tell Sharman about it. Though he has never gotten the publicity that Chamberlain did for being hard to coach, Barry was probably just as difficult. He was always determined to go his own way, and just as determined that others would go along with him. In his later career, he even decided that he should be the one who decided where players would sit on airplanes.

In the 1974-75 season, Al Attles would build a championship team around Barry, and let the others work their styles into Rick's form of play.

Sharman, coaching Barry in Rick's second season, wasn't quite so accommodating. Barry resented that, and his smoldering resentment was one reason he jumped to the American Basketball League after the second season with the Warriors.

But, though he resented Sharman, Barry played extremely well for him. That may indeed, as Sharman says, have been Barry's best year. He was magnificent throughout, and not just during the regular season. The All-Star Game that year was played in San Francisco, and Barry was the game's Most Valuable Player.

Barry was by no means the entire Warrior team, of course. Nate Thurmond had come on strong since the Chamberlain deal had made room for him in the middle; though he missed the first 16 games because of a broken hand, he averaged 18.7 points a game for the rest of the year and an excellent 21.3 rebounds, second in the league only to Chamberlain.

Thurmond, because he played in an era of super centers—starting when Russell and Chamberlain were playing and finishing when Lew Alcindor Kareem Abdul-Jabbar was the best—seldom got the recognition he deserved. He was a superb center, adept in all phases of the game. He was a strong scorer, and excellent rebounder and unyielding on defense. Not as spectacular a player as either Russell or Chamberlain on defense, he was nonetheless very effective. He was a master of positioning, learning early that every center had a favorite spot from which he liked to shoot; Nate would simply occupy that spot and force the offensive man to change his game. That technique, unobserved by the casual fan, was the reason Abdul-Jabbar always said that Thurmond was the toughest center for him to play against.

Before he was fired, Hannum had had a long talk with Mieuli about the team's needs. "Owners always do that before they fire you," observes Hannum, sardonically. "They want to pick your brain, to find out whatever they can before they get rid of you." Hannum told Mieuli that he should trade Guy Rodgers, the team's playmaking guard, while Rodgers' value was still high.

Rodgers was an excellent playmaker, and he—and the Warriors—had thrived when Chamberlain was there, because nobody was better at getting the ball to Wilt than Rodgers.

But with Wilt gone, much of Rodgers' value was diminished. Thurmond was a steady scorer, but the offense didn't revolve around him; many of Nate's points came when he moved out to the top of the key and hit a jumper. The Warriors obviously no longer needed a guard whose chief asset was his ability to feed the center.

Thus, Rodgers' liabilities became more obvious. He had no outside shot to keep the defense from sagging off him. He was a weak defensive player who often only waved at his man as he went by.

When Sharman came in he pressed Mieuli to make the trade Hannum had suggested. So the Warriors traded Rodgers to the expansion Chicago Bulls for guards Jimmy King and Jeff Mullins, an All-American from Duke who had played a little for the St. Louis Hawks before being taken by Chicago in the expansion draft.

"It was a good deal for both teams," insists Sharman. "The Bulls were a young team and needed a playmaker."

Sharman is being charitable. Actually, the deal was a steal for the Warriors. Mullins moved right into the Warriors' starting lineup and became their most dependable scorer in the years after Barry had jumped from the team. King was a reliable reserve, scoring 11 points a game in the 1966-67 season, who would have had a longer career but for back trouble.

With all the parts together, the Warriors came on strong in the second half of the season to win the Western Division title by five games over the St. Louis Hawks. Then they beat Los Angeles and the Hawks in the first two rounds of the playoffs.

But nobody gave them much of a chance in the finals because they were meeting the team that was later selected as the best in NBA history—the Philadelphia 76ers.

As happened so often in that period in the NBA, the power seemed to be concentrated in the Eastern cities of Boston and Philadelphia.

The Celtics were coached for the first time by Bill Russell; Red Auerbach had retired from coaching after the previous season to concentrate on being general manager. Although Russell was fading as a player he still had enough left to lead the Celtics to a 60-21 record, the third best in their history.

This time, though, that glossy record was good enough only for second place. The 76ers had a 68-13 record, and it could have been even better; they were 45-4 when starting guard Larry Costello injured his knee. Costello missed the final 32 games of the season and played in only two playoff games.

"The key stat in evaluating that team," says Hannum, who had ironically bounced from the Warriors to the 76ers, "is the fact that it was before general expansion and before the ABA. The league was not diluted. Every night we were playing against quality players. There were no weak sisters to fatten up on."

The key to the team was the massive front line of Chamberlain, Lucius Jackson, and Chet Walker. "We had overwhelming physical strength," says Hannum. "As long as we could stay close to a team, we figured we could wear them down in the end."

The 76ers were even more physically overpowering than the old Minneapolis Lakers teams. Chamberlain was bigger, stronger and much more agile than George Mikan. Jackson was at least as strong as Vern Mikkelsen, two inches taller and a much better shooter. Walker was much the same type of player as Jim Pollard, quick and agile.

And in team balance and depth the 76ers ranked right with the great Celtic teams. Six players averaged in double figures, for instance. Chamberlain led the team with a 24.1 average, but Hal Greer was right behind with a 22.1 average, and Walker had 19.3 points per game at forward. Obviously, other teams couldn't double up on any one player, even Chamberlain, because there was firepower everywhere.

The team's depth was impressive. Before Costello was injured, they had Wally Jones coming off the bench, and Jones wound up averaging more than 13 points a game. Two excellent rookie guards, Matt Guokas and Bill Melchionni, backed up Greer, Costello, and Jones.

At forward, the 76ers had the luxury of having Bill Cunningham coming off the bench—and Cunningham averaged 18.5 points a game as a reserve!

For the first time, Chamberlain had the luxury of the kind of team Russell had always had, and he changed his style of play to accommodate his teammates, passing more and concentrating on the defensive end of the court. "Wilt didn't have to score," says Hannum, "and he had one of his best years."

Chamberlain's scoring average was the lowest of his pro career, and he lost the scoring crown for the first time. But he ranked first in shooting percentage and rebounding, and he was third in assists. His blocked-shots total rivaled that of Russell.

But the hardest part of the season was coming up—the playoffs. The year before, the 76ers had finished ahead of the Celtics in the regular season but, given a bye in the opening round of the playoffs, they had cooled off. The Celtics had blown them out, winning four of five games, and that had cost Dolph Schayes his job as coach, leaving an opening for Hannum.

Billy Cunningham goes to the basket as Chicago's Tom Boerwinkle tries to stop him and Norm Van Lier watches. Cunningham later became the coach of the Philadelphia 76ers. *(Philadelphia 76ers; William H. Gordon)*

There were some who thought the Celtics might beat the 76ers again in this playoff series. Despite the 76ers' great record, they had lost five of nine games to Boston during the regular season.

Both teams advanced through the first round of the playoffs by winning three of four games, the 76ers turning back Cincinnati and the Celtics beating the Knicks.

So, once again, it was the Celtics and the Warriors for the Eastern title—and, most likely, the NBA championship. It seemed a matchup, the Celtics' knowledge and skill against the 76ers' power. As it turned out, knowledge and skill were no match for power.

The series went only five games, with Boston winning only the fourth, a Sunday afternoon, nationally-televised game at home; the Celtics' sense of drama was obviously still intact. The other games were almost monotonous in their regularity: The Celtics would start strong, but the 76ers would wear them down by the fourth quarter.

Chamberlain was magnificent. In the first game, he got 32 rebounds and 13 assists. In the third game, he had 25 rebounds at halftime and finished with 41, a playoff record. But it was the fifth, final game which really proved the dominance of Wilt and his team.

The Celtics got off to an 8-0 lead and were ahead by 37-26 at the end of the first quarter. Midway through the second period, they had moved the lead to 59-43.

But then Wilt took charge, doing everything—rebounding, blocking shots, feeding teammates, and scoring himself. The 76ers spurted for a 22-9 streak and closed the deficit to 70-65 at halftime. It was still anybody's game.

The 76ers kept applying the pressure in the third quarter, and the older Celtics tried desperately to hold them off. By the start of the fourth quarter, Philadelphia had a lead of 100-94.

The Celtics had nothing left. The 76ers poured it on in the final quarter, leading by as many as 27 points at one stage before finishing with a 140-116 win. The Celtics' reign had finally come to an end.

The playoff between Philadelphia and San Francisco seemed almost anticlimactic, but there were some factors which made it intriguing.

One, of course, was that the Warriors had originally been a Philadelphia team. Chamberlain had been a Warrior and had been traded; Hannum had coached the team and had been fired, moving then to the 76ers.

It was no secret that many of the Warrior players still preferred Hannum to their new coach, Sharman, with his rigid discipline and long practices. Nate Thurmond guessed that a vote on Sharman among the players would have been about 7-5 against, though Nate said he would have voted for Sharman because the Warriors were winning under him.

Even the Warriors' broadcaster, Bill King (this writer's nominee as the best in the business, incidentally) and his color man, Hank Greenwald, had mixed emotions about the series. Both had been close to Hannum, and neither liked Sharman.

For the Warriors, too, the finals were almost anticlimactic after a riotous series with the St. Louis Hawks. Rick Barry had made an offhand remark about St. Louis being a town "for the birds" because they had the Cardinals in football and baseball and the Hawks in basketball. The remark was picked up by the Associated Press and printed in St. Louis newspapers, and the fans were determined to make Barry see the error of his ways.

The St. Louis fans booed Barry vociferously every time his name was mentioned on the public address system, and they threw eggs, tomatoes, and even Snickers bars (because Barry was doing commercials for the candy bar company at the time) onto the court. Warrior owner Mieuli had hired two special guards to stand behind the Warrior bench to protect Barry from the fans.

None of this bothered Barry, who reasoned that boos on the road are the equivalent of cheers at home. What did bother him was an ankle that he had sprained during the series. He had to take pain-killing injections so he could play.

"His ankle was an awful sight," says King. "It was several different colors—purple, gold, red. As I remember, he had to take something like seven injections before the game and another six at halftime. Fred Hetzel, who was always a little squeamish, had to walk out of the locker room. He couldn't stand to watch it."

The series went six games with the expected result—the 76ers winning—but the Warriors had a chance to pull off what would have been one of the two great upsets of all time.

King remembers two pivotal moments. "The first came in the first game," he says. "The score was tied and the Warriors had run the clock down to leave time for just one play. It was supposed to be a pick-and-roll with Barry and Thurmond.

"Rick got the ball and Wilt jumped out at him, as Nate rolled to the hoop. But Wilt got back and blocked Nate's shot, so the game went into overtime, and the 76ers won it, 141-135.

"As they were lining up for the tip to start the OT, Wilt said to Nate, 'Hey, man, I fouled the shit out of you on that play.'"

(Barry and Thurmond felt the same way. "Earl Strom was standing right there but never made the call," said Barry. "I couldn't believe it. Thurmond couldn't believe it.")

The dispirited Warriors lost the next one by 31 points, as Wilt got 38 rebounds, but they came home to San Francisco to win the third game as Barry scored 55 points and Thurmond gathered 25 rebounds.

But the 76ers came back to win the fourth game and take a 3-1 series lead back to Philadelphia, where they seemed poised to wrap it up. There were stories in the

Philadelphia newspapers that 76er owner Irv Kosloff had already bought plane tickets to Puerto Rico for the players, in anticipation of victory.

Perhaps that made the Warriors angry. Barry got 36 points, 26 of them in the first half, and Thurmond played great defense against Chamberlain in the closing minutes as the Warriors won, 117-109. The series would go to a sixth game, in San Francisco. If the Warriors could win that game, the series would go to its limit, and there were many who thought Chamberlain would be psyched out in a seventh game.

That brought up the second pivotal moment. "The 76ers were ahead by a point," says King, "and the Warriors had worked the clock down again to set up the same play, a pick-and-roll with Barry and Thurmond, that they had used in the first game in that situation.

"This time, Alex anticipated the play and Wilt stayed with Nate. Jackson had cheated a little and he jumped out at Barry. Wilt came back to him, too, and Rick had to take a double-clutch prayer shot. The ball hit the iron and bounced a couple of times, and then it fell out."

And that was it. Barry had scored 44 in the game, but it wasn't enough. Two meaningless 76er free throws made the final score 125-122, and the 76ers were champions.

Sharman thought it was fitting that the game ended with two 76er free throws because he saw that as the difference in the game. "They had 35 more free throws in that game than we did," he says. "We were ahead most of the way in that game, by 8 to 10 points, and I think referees sometimes lean a little the other way in that situation."

In the dressing room, Chamberlain was subdued, though he did drink some champagne and hug Hannum. He still felt the criticism for the failures of his previous teams, and one championship wasn't enough to erase that.

Hannum enjoyed the win much more, celebrating with his friends later that night. Some were 76ers, some were Warriors—or connected with them. Greer and Jackson were there. So were King and Greenwald, and the party was at Thurmond's apartment on Twin Peaks in San Francisco.

"It went all night," remembers King. "We got drunk and maudlin, talking about how Alex should still be with the Warriors. Alex was walking around with a half-gallon container of vodka and orange juice. I broke a glass and cut my hand. It was that kind of party."

Not until dawn did the party break up. Hannum and players returned to Philadelphia, where they were met by thousands of cheering fans at the airport. Alex couldn't say a word to them; he had lost his voice during the marathon party.

The 76ers' accomplishments spoke for themselves. They had won more games than anybody in NBA history. They had seemingly ended the long run of the Celtic dynasty. They had swept through the playoffs, winning 11 games and losing only four en route to their championship. They were a relatively young team, and it seemed they would win more championships before the team broke up.

Yet, even then, in the wake of victory, there were signs of the problems to come. Wilt was upset because the victory was called a "team victory." When his teams had lost, he noted, the losses had always been blamed on him; now he felt he wasn't getting sufficient credit for the win. It bothered him, too, that Barry was getting only praise for his high scoring, not blame because his team had lost—as had always happened to Chamberlain when he scored a lot of points in defeat.

It was almost as if Wilt felt that victory caused more problems than defeat. In *Sport* magazine he was quoted as saying, "In a way, I like it better when we lose. It's over and I can look forward to the next game. If we win, it builds up the tension and I start worrying about the next game."

Before the next season, there were additional problems. Chamberlain claimed that the 76ers' previous owner, Ike Richman, had promised him 25 percent of the franchise; Kosloff did not feel bound by that promise. Kosloff also claimed that some race horses Wilt and Richman had bought had been bought with 76er money, and therefore, the franchise owned half the stable.

Wilt renegotiated his contract and, in a provision kept secret at the time, it would end when the season did. This would be his last year in Philadelphia.

He missed almost the entire exhibition season and admitted later that he went into the season with no real enthusiasm. He was still miffed that his teammates, and Hannum, were getting so much credit for the championship.

It was a bad season for Hannum, too. He had wanted to be named general manager as well as coach. Instead, Kosloff brought in Jack Ramsey as general manager. Hannum started looking for another coaching job, though he stayed with the 76ers for the rest of the season.

Even with all the problems, the 76ers had too much talent to lose very often. Though they didn't match their sensational previous season, they again finished first in the East with a 60-20 mark.

But the competitive fire that championship teams must have was lacking in the 76ers. There was too much bickering. The 76ers felt that Wilt was too concerned about individual goals, and they were probably right. Chamberlain's goal for the season was to lead the league in assists—which he did—and teammates felt he was passing up shots so he could get assists instead. It was an ironic twist in the career of a man who had once taken far more shots and scored far more points than anybody in history.

In the Eastern finals that year it again came down to the Celtics and 76ers. This time the Celtics pushed the series into a seventh game, and the psychological pressure on Philadelphia was overwhelming; the 76ers had never won a seventh game and the Celtics had never lost one.

The seventh game was close to the finish, but the Celtics won it, 100-95. Wilt had only two shots, both tips, in the final quarter—because his teammates had passed the ball to him only four times in the quarter. Nothing could have shown more vividly how they had lost faith in him.

After the season Wilt was traded to the Los Angeles Lakers. Hannum got the coaching job he was seeking, with the Oakland Oaks of the newly formed American Basketball Association. The 76ers were through as a great team.

The greatest team ever? For one season, probably, but this was no dynasty.

Escaping the tight defense of Chicago's Jerry Sloan, Jeff Mullins lays one in for the Golden State Warriors. *(Golden State Warriors)*

14. The ABA Challenge

Imitation may be the sincerest form of flattery, but the NBA owners didn't feel flattered when the American Basketball Association (ABA) was formed before the 1967-68 season; they felt threatened.

Ownership of a sports franchise is economically attractive because sports are a monopoly business. An owner has an area to himself, or at the least, a sizeable portion of an area. With the college drafts that are used in basketball and football, owners have exclusive rights to the players drafted; there is no competition between clubs for players.

That cozy situation ended for the NBA owners as soon as the ABA went into business. There was direct competition at the gate only in three areas—New York/New Jersey, Los Angeles/Anaheim, and San Francisco/Oakland—but the ABA was bidding for the same players the NBA was. Veteran NBA players often got pay boosts by threatening to jump to the new league, and rookies' asking prices went up dramatically.

The ABA was formed by Los Angeles area lawyers and businessmen Gary Davidson, Dennis Murphy, and Jack Crist, among others; it was chiefly Davidson's ideas.

Davidson's model was not the NBA but the American Football League. The AFL had been laughed at when it started play in 1960, a funny little league where people threw the ball all the time and nobody played defense. But by the mid-'60s, the AFL had a national television contract and a star quarterback in New York, and it was a solid concern. Eventually, it merged with the NFL, and those owners who had bought franchises for $25,000 had properties worth millions.

That was the type of thing Davidson and his friends were looking for—a small initial investment parlayed into a large capital gain. The key was television. If the league could do well enough to get a national TV contract it could force a merger, as the AFL had done with the NFL.

So the league was formed for the 1967-68 season with teams in Pittsburgh, Minneapolis (called Minnesota), Indianapolis (called Indiana), Louisville (called Kentucky), New Jersey, New Orleans, Dallas, Denver, Houston, Anaheim, and Oakland.

Rick Mount, dribbling the striped "beach ball" that became the symbol of the ABA, was one of the early big names in the ABA, though he never quite lived up to his collegiate promise. *(Indiana Pacers)*

George Mikan was named commissioner; his reputation gave the league instant credibility with older fans, who remembered Mikan from his days with the Lakers.

Mikan, though, was never more than a figurehead; the league was run largely by men behind the scenes; perhaps the major one was an Indianapolis attorney, Richard Tinkham. George was there to say the right things in public, although he didn't, always: At the season opener in Oakland, he announced that he was "glad to be here in Oklahoma."

The new league differed from the NBA in three specific areas: Field goals from more than 25 feet counted for three points; a 30-second clock was used, giving teams six more seconds to work for a shot; and a red, white, and blue striped ball was used, instead of the regulation brown. The obvious idea was to attract attention with the ball, but the wrong kind of attention was attracted. The ABA was scorned as the "beach ball league."

There was no television contract for the first season, nor were there many name players. Of the college stars coming out that season, for instance, the ABA attracted only Mel Daniels and Randy Mahaffey among those picked on the first round by NBA clubs. Guards Louie Dampier, Bob Verga, and Bob Lloyd were also signed, and Dampier became one of three players (Byron Beck and Fred Lewis were the others) to play from start to finish in the ABA's nine-year career.

Almost all of the other players had shown that they couldn't make it in the NBA, for one reason or another. Cliff Hagan, an NBA veteran who was now over the hill, joined the new league. So did marginal NBA players like Ben Warley and Wayne Hightower.

Some players who had had a brief stint in the NBA before being dropped came into the league, a group that included Lewis, Larry Jones, and Les Hunter. Former college stars who had been cut by NBA teams got another shot, such as Donnie Freeman, Jim Hadnot, Willie Somerset, Ollie Darden, Levern Tart, and Walt Simon.

Connie Hawkins, Doug Moe, Roger Brown, and Tony Jackson—all of whom allegedly had marginal involvements with fixed games in colleges and had been barred from the NBA—joined the new league. Hawkins became a star and eventually made it into the NBA.

There were also some players who had been active in AAU ball, or in minor leagues. There were even some players who had been in the American Basketball League before it had folded.

With this motley group it was obvious that the first season of the ABA would be unspectacular, and it lived down to those expectations. But ABA owners had hopes of getting a bigger share of the college talent in the years to come, and they had one star waiting on the sidelines: Rick Barry.

Barry had jumped to the Oakland Oaks from the San Francisco Warriors for a variety of reasons. He didn't like Warrior coach Bill Sharman; he complained that basketball was work, not fun, under Sharman. His father-in-law, Bruce Hale, had been named coach of the Oaks. His feelings were hurt because he didn't think Warrior owner Franklin Mieuli truly appreciated him.

Mieuli's relationship with Barry was a strange one, an inevitable result because of the egos involved. Franklin sometimes talked of Barry as being almost like a son to him; the unspoken message was that Mieuli, as the father, knew what was best for Rick. Barry didn't always agree.

Certainly, Mieuli had been generous to Barry, not only paying him well but allowing him the use of a leased Porsche. But Franklin also felt that he should always pay Nate Thurmond more than Barry because Thurmond's defense and rebounding, which brought him far less public attention than Barry's scoring, were crucial to the team's success.

For the 1967-68 season, Mieuli bumped Thurmond's salary to $90,000, big numbers in those days and especially for a franchise that was only now beginning to get onto solid ground.

Then Mieuli offered Barry $40,000, plus a percentage of the gate, which could have brought Rick $75,000. In his desk, Mieuli also had a contract for a flat $75,000, which he would have offered Barry if Rick had said that that was what he wanted. Indeed, Mieuli said later he would have gone as high as $100,000, although he would have then also had to renegotiate Thurmond's contract to keep Nate slightly ahead. (In fact, after Barry jumped, Mieuli did escalate Thurmond's contract to $109,000, to demonstrate his gratitude for Nate's loyalty.)

Mieuli then went off on a European trip, confident that Barry would stay. He had totally misjudged his man. Barry was extremely sensitive to what he viewed as a slight by Mieuli. Meanwhile, the Oaks were pursuing Barry vigorously. From part-owner Pat Boone, Barry got the impression that he would be able to launch a show business career after his playing career was over. He was flattered and intrigued. He signed for $75,000, plus 15 percent of the Oaks, forgetting that 15 percent of nothing is still nothing.

When Mieuli returned, Barry met him in Franklin's office and told him that he had signed with the Oaks. Only then did Franklin show Rick the contract for a flat $75,000 that Rick could have had.

For both men it was an enormous blunder. Mieuli had had a young team which would certainly have won more championships in the years to come, and the game's brightest star. When Barry left, the team sagged and the excitement that had surrounded the team disappeared.

Barry had the world by the tail in San Francisco. Had he stayed with the Warriors he would certainly have made more money in salary and endorsements. He would have had far more recognition for his talents, which is very important to him.

Rick couldn't even play the first season after he jumped. A court ruled that he had to sit out the option year of his contract with the Warriors, though he was free to play with the Oaks after that.

The first year he played with the Oaks, Barry tore up his knee midway through the season. (That, of course, could also have happened if he had stayed in the NBA.) For three years, the bad knee limited his playing time, and it also changed his style of play. No longer would he drive up the middle so fearlessly as he had in his first two years with the Warriors.

His ABA experience was filled with disappointment for Barry. By the time he played for the Oaks, Hale had moved up to the front office (though the coach then was Alex Hannum, whom Barry liked).

He had been told, he says, that the club would stay in Oakland; if it did not, he would be released from his contract. But he never got that in writing and had to go to Washington when the franchise was moved after two seasons.

When the franchise was moved again, to Virginia, Barry rebelled. In a *Sports Illustrated* article, he ridiculed the area and said he did not want his sons to grow up with a Southern drawl. Earl Foreman, by then the owner of the franchise, traded Barry to the New York Nets—but not before Barry had signed a contract to return to the Warriors, after his ABA contract expired.

Barry was happy in New York. He reasoned that he could make a reputation that would enhance his chances of doing television work when he quit playing. He wanted to stay there, and Nets' owner Roy Boe offered Mieuli $750,000 for Barry's contract.

But Mieuli would not let go, and so the prodigal son finally returned, before the 1972-73 season. By then, though, Rick had paid a high price for his ABA experience. Had Barry stayed in the NBA, he likely would have become the highest scoring

Elvin Hayes of the Bullets is about to make a Wilsonburger of a shot by Dan Roundfield of the Atlanta Hawks. The ABA had tried to get Hayes in 1968. *(Washington Bullets; Gary N. Fine)*

forward of all time, but injuries and the fact that ABA totals do not count toward NBA records precluded that.

Because he played the bulk of his prime years in an inferior league it is difficult to measure his accomplishments against those of forwards like Bob Pettit and Elgin Baylor.

Having seen Barry play so many times, I believe he ranks with any forward who has played the game. He was a great scorer, a man who could get his shot when it was needed no matter what the defense did. He had incredible body control, able to get off a shot or a pass from the most contorted of positions. He was probably the best passing forward ever, and for the Warriors, it was like having a third guard when Barry was playing.

Yet, I can understand it when Barry is left off the all-time teams. He didn't play long enough in top-flight competition to deserve that kind of recognition, and it was his own fault.

Barry didn't really do the ABA much good, either, because his injuries kept him out so often. The ABA was desperate for stars in the first two years. Two well-known coaches, Alex Hannum and Bill Sharman, jumped to the new league in its second season, but coaches don't bring in fans. The top college stars, like Elvin Hayes in 1968, were still going to the NBA.

But the ABA owners thought they had a chance to get UCLA All-American Lew Alcindor, the biggest name in college basketball since Wilt Chamberlain. It was so important for the ABA to get Alcindor that owners banded together to make an offer of $1 million. A cashier's check in that amount was made out to Alcindor and handed to him. "Alcindor nearly fainted," says Fred Furth, then the ABA attorney. "He couldn't believe it."

But he didn't take it. Alcindor instead opted to sign with the Milwaukee Bucks, who had won a coin flip with Phoenix within the NBA for his rights; reportedly, he got $1.4 million in a multi-year package.

It's interesting to speculate on what might have been. Alcindor was such a big name then, and became such an outstanding pro, that he might have given the ABA the publc image it needed. That in turn might have gotten the league the national television contract it needed for survival.

When the ABA failed to sign Alcindor, many thought the league would collapse. Instead, the owners started fighting more fiercely for talent. The ABA's fight with the NBA was always a lopsided one and doomed to defeat, but the league would inflict a lot of scars on the NBA before it died.

Three NBA stars announced they had signed contracts with ABA teams, though they would not take effect for at least a year: Zelmo Beaty was going from the Atlanta Hawks to the Los Angeles Stars; Billy Cunningham from the Philadelphia 76ers to the Carolina Cougars; and Dave Bing from the Detroit Pistons to the Washington Caps.

An even more startling battle was being fought on the collegiate level. The NBA had always forbidden teams to sign players until their college class had graduated, less for moral reasons than practical ones: Nobody wanted to anger the colleges, which were acting as a farm system for the NBA.

But the ABA was desperate for college talent, and the Denver Rockets signed Spencer Haywood out of the University of Detroit after his sophomore year in a move that sent shock waves through the sports world and put the ABA back on the front page of sports sections throughout the country.

Haywood, a 6'8", 230-pounder, had been a star in the 1968 Olympics and an All-American in his one year of varsity play at Detroit (freshmen were not eligible for varsity competition at the time). He was a great talent, big, well coordinated, a good shooter, and a strong rebounder.

As a pro, Haywood never fully lived up to his potential, though he had some outstanding moments. He was the type of player who could be great when properly motivated but was indifferent much of the time. And he didn't last long in the ABA, jumping to the Seattle SuperSonics in the NBA after two seasons.

But Haywood was far less important for what he did than for what he represented. Freed from the restrictions of dealing only with players whose classes had graduated,

ABA owners could gather far more good talent—and the NBA was eventually forced to draft undergraduates, too.

There were some real nuggets to be had this way. The ABA even went after one high school graduate, Moses Malone, who signed with Utah after he had signed a letter-of-intent to go to the University of Maryland; he never played a minute at Maryland. Malone eventually became a star at Houston in the NBA, and many think he is the finest offensive rebounder in the game's history.

George McGinnis joined the Indiana Pacers after his sophomore year at Indiana University, and became a star almost immediately. A bull of a man at 6'8" and 230 pounds, McGinnis was awesome whether he had the ball or was going after it. He was a very strong rebounder and, though not an outstanding shooter, could move so well with the ball that he became a high scorer. His period of stardom was short because he never learned that it was necessary to at least occasionally play defense, and when he slowed down offensively he became a liability. But he was great copy for awhile.

George Gervin was another undergraduate who became a star, though the Virginia Squires, who drafted him, didn't know what to do with him at first.

Gervin played forward for the Squires, but when he was traded to the San Antonio Spurs he was shifted to guard. At 6'7", he simply cannot be handled by guards who are usually 3 to 6 inches shorter, and his deadly jump shot has made him a scoring champion.

But the best-known and easily the best of the players who turned pro early is Julius Erving, the fabulous "Dr. J." Erving is so good and so spectacular that he is often credited with keeping the ABA alive long enough to force a merger with the NBA. Without Erving, the league probably would have been forced to disband before 1976.

Erving was a late bloomer. He was not widely recruited as a New York prep and went to the University of Massachusetts, hardly a basketball power, because he liked the campus. In three years he averaged 20 points and 20 rebounds a game, but when he signed a four-year, $500,000 contract with the Virginia Squires it wasn't headline news outside the state.

But there are players who are better as pros than collegians because the pro game allows for more individual expression. Erving was one of those players. In the pro game he soared—literally.

Some have compared Erving's game to Connie Hawkins'. Others have seen traces of Elgin Baylor. But most agree that Erving is in a class by himself.

"Baylor always found a way to get things done," says Alex Hannum, "but Julius maybe has a little more physical ability. The way he plays, it's more like an art form."

Dr. J's game is one which seems to defy gravity. He can be on the wing, seemingly stymied by a defensive man, and suddenly leap over and beyond his defender to the

Connie Hawkins, at first barred from the NBA because of a collegiate scandal, got his chance in pro basketball in the ABA and then went on to the Phoenix Suns of the NBA. *(Phoenix Suns)*

basket. Coming down court on the fast break, he can take off at the free-throw line or even beyond and dunk. In mid-air he can twist and turn so that even a defender who can jump with him has no idea where the shot is coming from. He can dunk in every conceivable way. He is a wizard.

Mere statistics cannot show Erving's value nor describe his game, but it gives some idea of his talent to say that he averaged 27.3 points a game and was third in the ABA in rebounding with a 15.7 mark in his rookie year, and that he led the league in scoring with a 31.9 average his second year.

More important was the fact that he was traded to the New York Nets in '73. Erving led the Nets to two league titles and one runner-up position in his three years there.

With Erving as the most significant player, the ABA was finally beginning to attract top collegiate stars—even those who had graduated. Such players as David Thompson, Dan Issel, Bobby Jones, Artis Gilmore, Ralph Simpson, James Silas, and Marvin Barnes, in addition to those previously mentioned, came to the ABA.

Indeed, by the mid-'70s, many basketball people regarded the ABA as being roughly comparable to the NBA in overall quality. But the league had lost the image battle and too many of its cities were in minor television markets, so the league was never able to get that national TV contract it needed for survival.

Artis Gilmore, demonstrating the awesome power of his stuff shot, was a big star in the ABA before joining the Chicago Bulls. *(Chicago Bulls)*

Court battles held up the inevitable merger for a time, but on June 17, 1976, the NBA added four ABA clubs: Denver, Indiana, San Antonio, and New Jersey. Two other clubs, Kentucky and St. Louis, got a settlement. The war was over.

It had been a costly battle for all concerned. It's been estimated that ABA owners lost at least $50 million in the nine years the league operated. Those who hung on until they could be absorbed by the NBA probably came out all right in the long run, but even for them, it was no bonanza; for most owners, it was a disaster.

The league went through seven commissioners in nine years—Mikan, Jim Gardner, Jack Dolph, Robert Carlson, Mike Storen, Tedd Munchak, and Dave DeBusschere.

It left a lasting legacy. Salaries for players became astronomical during the ABA-NBA war, and they have not come down. The NBA had adopted the three-point rule which the ABA used. And players can be drafted before their college class graduates.

15. Knicks Notch Championship

In any sport a New York franchise occupies a unique position. Because of the concentration of media and advertising in Manhattan, a successful New York franchise is very important to the success of a league, particularly in the early years. The fact that Joe Namath was a bright young star in New York, for instance, was a big factor in the success of the AFL.

Yet, most people living outside New York have a generalized dislike and distrust of New Yorkers, a feeling often rooted in envy, and sports franchise owners are no exception. Many owners fear, too, that a New York franchise will dominate the league, because a New York team, able to charge higher ticket prices and make much more money from local TV and radio packages, has far more economic potential than other teams in the league. The example of the New York Yankees, past and present, is always there to remind owners how their worst fears can be realized.

All these factors were present in the NBA, and there was an added factor: Basketball is often called the "city game" because it is the game played most frequently in the inner city, and New York is the ultimate American city.

New York's Madison Square Garden had long been *the* place to play, first for the collegians and then, after the college basketball scandals had torn the sport apart, for the pros.

The Knicks had been one of the charter teams of the BAA, the forerunner of the NBA, and Knicks' owner Ned Irish, who also owned the Garden, had been a progressive thinker, insisting that the league comport itself as a big-time operation even at a time when it was not.

But Irish had never had much success with the Knicks, and there were few tears shed around the league because of that, even though it probably hindered the league's progress. Irish was an irascible man, seemingly unwilling to take the problems of other owners into account when he made his proposals. As a result, even when his ideas were sound they were often defeated by other owners.

Some of the Knicks' problems through the years had been a result of bad luck, some a result of bad decisions, and some a combination of both.

As mentioned in an earlier chapter, the Knicks had had a chance at Dolph Schayes when he came out of college, but because the BAA had a salary limit for rookies at the time, Irish could not offer the NYU star as much as Syracuse of the NBL could, and the Knicks lost a player who would have been both a great draw and a great player for years.

The 1960 college draft produced two super guards, Oscar Robertson and Jerry West, who went to Cincinnati and Los Angeles. The Knicks, drafting third, picked Cal center Darrall Imhoff.

Imhoff had been an excellent college player, leading Cal to a national championship and runner-up slot in consecutive years, but he lacked quickness and was a weak offensive player. As a pro, he was never more than a journeyman. Though he played several seasons, he is known chiefly for a negative reason: He started at center the night Wilt Chamberlain scored 100 points.

The next year, the Knicks had the worst record and were scheduled to draft first. Indiana's Walt Bellamy, who seemed to be the big man they so desperately needed, was available.

But that was the year the NBA put an expansion franchise into Chicago, the Bulls. Traditionally, owners of established franchises give expansion teams only leftovers, but this time, in a move obviously designed to punish Irish, the other owners decided to give the expansion Bulls first choice, with the Knicks relegated to second. Chicago, of course, took Ballamy.

Two years later the Knicks had a chance at Nate Thurmond, who could have been the big man they needed. They went instead for Duke's Art Heyman, a flashy player who seemed to be both a potentially outstanding player and the box office draw the Knicks wanted, the Jewish star that New York teams always seek. But Heyman was a bust.

Because of mistakes like these the Knicks won only two divisional titles in their first 23 years, losing in the playoffs each time. Ten times they had finished last, and another time fourth in a five-team division. They were so inept, they had become known as the team against which players set scoring records.

But, though it would take several years for the improvement to become obvious, the Knicks were starting to make their move in the '60s. Most of the credit goes to Eddie Donovan, who started the decade as coach and moved up to general manager, and Red Holzman, who was first Donovan's assistant and later the coach as the Knicks matured into world champions.

Donovan's first important move came in 1964, when he drafted Willis Reed—though Reed was not even the first player the Knicks took that year.

Reed was coming out of Grambling that year, and he was one of three good big men, the other two being Jim (Bad News) Barnes of Texas Western and Lucius Jackson of Pan American.

All three played in the Olympic Trials. Barnes and Jackson were very impressive and made the team. Reed, bothered by a cold, did not play well, and he was not selected. As a result, the status of Barnes and Jackson went up, while Reed's went down.

Donovan and Holzman had both scouted Reed in college, and they knew he was better than he had looked in the Trials. But, though they suspected he might have the most potential of the three big men, they wanted immediate help.

They also knew that Reed might last to the second round, but that Barnes and Jackson certainly would not. So, they went for Barnes as their first pick, the first of the draft, and then held their collective breath, hoping Reed would last.

He did, and the Knicks grabbed him. Later, when Reed became a star, there were constant references to him as a second-round pick, the implication being that he was a surprise. But at that time there were only nine teams drafting. Reed was the tenth player taken, which would put him before the halfway mark in the NBA draft of today. He was no surprise, except, perhaps, that he developed faster than Donovan and Holzman had anticipated.

His first year, in fact, Reed was Rookie of the Year, leading his team in scoring with a 19.5 average (Barnes had a 15.5 average at forward) and effectively plugging the middle on defense. The Knicks improved by nine games, though their 31-49 record still couldn't get them out of last.

The next year Donovan traded Barnes, with Johnny Egan and Johnny Green, to Baltimore for Bellamy, the center the Knicks had almost gotten five years before. That forced Reed to move outside, to forward. He did it uncomplainingly—it was not Reed's style to complain—and he played well there, though out of position.

That was the year, too, that the Knicks had two first-round picks in the draft. Donovan used them to pick Bill Bradley, the Princeton All-American, and Dave Stallworth, an All-American forward from Wichita.

For a time, it seemed the Knicks' bad luck would hit them again. Stallworth played reasonably well his first two seasons, averaging 12 and 13 points a game as a reserve, but then developed a heart problem and had to retire.

Meanwhile, Bradley had gone to England as a Rhodes Scholar, as the Knicks knew he would, and there was doubt that he would ever play professional basketball. Bradley himself thought he wouldn't; he was disgusted with the public and media attention he had gotten at Princeton and wanted out of the spotlight. It was not until his second year at Oxford that Bradley, who had not played basketball at all since his Princeton graduation, picked up a basketball again and started shooting. Only then did he realize he wanted to come back and test his skills against the best, so he joined the Knicks for the 1967-68 season.

The other pieces were starting to come together, too. In 1966, the Knicks picked up Cazzie Russell, the Michigan All-American. In 1967, they drafted guard Walt

The multi-faceted Bill Bradley, a Rhodes Scholar before playing in the NBA and a U.S. Senator after, made the most of his limited natural talents. *(New York Knicks; George Kalinsky)*

Frazier, who had led Southern Illinois to the NIT title that year and had thus become a popular player in New York.

Meanwhile, there seemed to be as many coaching changes as players changes. Donovan gave way to old-time Knick star Harry Gallatin during the '65 season, and during the next season, he was replaced in turn by Dick McGuire. McGuire lasted through all of the 1966-67 season, but was replaced during the next season by Holzman.

But through all the changes and the turmoil, the Knicks were improving, to 36-45 in the 1966-67 season and a breakthrough 43-39 the next. They had moved up to third place that season, a heady atmosphere for a Knicks team at that point.

Despite their improvement, though, there was still something missing with the Knicks. It is a delicate task to assemble a basketball team, because all the parts must mesh. It is the ultimate team sport because everybody must play together, offensively and defensively. A team with players who complement each other can sometimes defeat teams of greater individual talent; one example is the Golden State Warriors of 1974-75. A team with players who do not always play together can lose to lesser teams, as happened with some of the Wilt Chamberlain teams in both Philadelphia and Los Angeles.

The Knicks did not quite mesh, and the problem revolved around the center-power forward positions. Reed was doing the best he could at forward, and he was leading his team in both scoring and rebounding. But he was not quick enough to stop the faster forwards, which caused the Knicks some defensive problems.

At center, Bellamy was a puzzlement, as the King of Siam would say. Physically, he had all the ability; he was big, smooth, a good jumper, an excellent shooter. But Bellamy lacked that inner drive that great players all have. Basketball was just a game to him, forgotten—win or lose—as soon as he had showered.

Everyone liked Bellamy. Around the league, players would laugh about his habit of referring to himself in the third person when he was on court, particularly if he had been called for a foul he didn't believe he had committed. ("Referee just won't let Walt do anything in there," he would say.)

But because of his personality, Bellamy never became the player it seemed he was capable of being, and he was never a leader on court. Worst of all, from the Knicks' standpoint, he didn't play the tough defense a team needs from the center. He got his points and his rebounds, but he was never as good a player as his statistics.

Dave DeBusschere, here taking a rebound from the Lakers' Elgin Baylor, is regarded by some as the best defensive forward in NBA history. *(New York Knicks)*

And so the Knicks traded him very early in the 1968-69 season, along with reserve guard Howie Komives, to Detroit for forward Dave DeBusschere. It was a master stroke for the Knicks because all the pieces fell together.

The first thing the trade did for the Knicks was to give them the kind of defensive forward they needed. DeBusschere was easily the best defensive forward in the league; when coaches started voting for an All-NBA defensive team, DeBusschere made it six years in a row.

DeBusschere was a great all-round athlete, good enough to get a $60,000 bonus as a baseball player and to pitch briefly for the Chicago White Sox; he gave up on his dual career because he felt his curve ball wasn't good enough for the major leagues.

He was a natural leader, and the Pistons had made him a player-coach at 24, though he later decided the dual responsibility was too much.

Most of all, he had both mental and physical toughness. He would play so hard that he would come off the court literally drained, and he would drink as much as a six-pack of beer to replenish his lost fluids.

He worked hardest on defense, where he concentrated on denying his man the ball, overplaying him so a pass could not be made. This technique was so successful that a forward playing opposite DeBusschere would go long periods without seeing the ball; it was almost as if the other team was playing four-man basketball.

And yet DeBusschere was quick enough to recover if the other team tried to take advantage of this technique and have his man break for the basket to take a "back door" pass.

If his man did get the ball, DeBusschere tried to cut off his breathing room, crowding him, pushing and shoving as much as he could get away with (which, in the NBA, is considerable). Not surprisingly, he believed firmly in the "no harm, no foul" principle which is the basis for NBA officiating.

"If it were up to me," said DeBusschere when he was playing, "there wouldn't be a foul unless contact were deliberately vicious or unless it seriously affected the play—though I argue this with more conviction when I'm playing defense than when I have the ball myself."

Offensively, DeBusschere did his share, too. He was a good shooter with excellent range, and he made his man work hard at that end of the court—which slowed him down on the other end. Like all the Knicks, DeBusschere was both willing and able to set picks for his teammates to shoot.

DeBusschere's presence also made it possible to return Reed to the middle, where he belonged; and Reed's experience at forward had made him quicker and more mobile than before.

At 6'10", Reed gave away height to many of the centers around the league, but he had the bulk (at 240 pounds) and the strength to stay with the bigger centers, and he was quick enough to give the bigger men fits at the other end of the court.

The Knicks became champions when Walt Bellamy was traded, making room for Willis Reed in the center. *(New York Knicks)*

His strength was legendary. In the NBA, they still talk of the night Reed became enraged and took on virtually the entire Los Angeles team. Apparently he lost his temper because a Laker player jumped on his back.

"Suddenly, Willis totally lost control of himself," said teammate Phil Jackson, who saw the film of the incident. "Anything that moved he hit. After five minutes he had knocked out two Lakers, broken the nose of a third, and downed a fourth. Finally a Knick teammate about his size snuck up behind him and said, 'Take it easy, Willis, it's me!'"

Nobody ever again challenged Willis Reed.

Reed did everything a center is supposed to do. He scored, he rebounded, he blocked shots, he discouraged guards from driving the lane if they had beaten their defensive man outside. With Reed in the middle and DeBusschere at forward, the Knicks won 54 games, ten more than the club record, and lost only 28 in the 1968-69 season.

That was still only good enough for third place in the strong Eastern Division, three games behind champion Baltimore, but in the first round of the playoffs, the Knicks shocked the Bullets by winning four straight.

The Knicks weren't quite there. In the playoffs the team that has been there before is often the team that wins, and nobody had been there more than the Boston Celtics. Although the Celtics had finished only fourth in the regular season, they beat the Knicks in the semifinals for the Eastern Division crown and then took the Lakers in the finals for the NBA championship.

But that was Bill Russell's last season, and when he and Sam Jones retired, the Celtics plummeted to 34-48 the next season. It was a time for a changing of the guard, and the 1969-70 season belonged to the Knicks.

The team that took the floor for the Knicks that year was one of the best in NBA history, and it was also one of the most interesting, consisting of very different personalities who managed to blend into one unit on the court.

At the forward post opposite DeBusschere was Bill Bradley, whose story seemed a combination of those of Frank Merriwell and Jack Armstrong. As a senior at Princeton, Bradley had virtually singlehandedly taken his team to the final four of the NCAA tournament; his teammates were ordinary players. He had been a Rhodes Scholar. He was interested in politics and would, in fact, become a senator from New Jersey when he retired.

Despite his athletic accomplishments, Bradley was not a truly gifted athlete. He admits in his excellent book, *Life On the Run,* that when he leans over to touch his toes, the only part of him that touches the floor is his feet. He was not a good jumper, and at 6'5" was what basketball people call a "Tweener," not big enough for forward and not quick enough for guard.

The Knicks, in fact, weren't sure what they had when Bradley finally joined them, two years after he had been drafted. With his lack of size and jumping ability, they were certain he couldn't play a starting forward, so they tried him first at guard, then as a swing man between guard and forward, while the more talented Russell started at forward.

Bradley wasn't effective as a guard, and being a swing man didn't seem the answer, either. Gradually, the Knicks realized that he could be an effective forward because he was such a smart player. He positioned himself so well defensively that opponents could not take advantage of his relative lack of size. He was an excellent shooter, and he made good use of teammates' screens to get his shots off. He was a very good passer. On another team, with players who relied on their one-on-one games, Bradley would not have been able to play. He could, though, on the team-oriented Knicks.

At one guard position was the well-traveled Dick Barnett, an excellent shooter. At the other was Walt Frazier, on his way—if he wasn't there already—to being the best guard in the game.

Frazier excelled at every aspect of the game. He was an excellent one-on-one player, but he sublimated that part of his game for the good of the team. He ran the team, whipping accurate passes through the tightest defense to his open teammates.

"He owns the ball," said Reed one time. "He just lets us play with it once in a while."

Like DeBusschere and Reed, Frazier was also a great defensive player, making the All-Defensive team four years in a row. That was no accident; he regarded defense as the key to the game. "Offense is inconsistent because it's touch and feel and talent," he said. "Defense, because it mostly means being willing to work hard, is something to rely on night after night, game after game."

Off the court, Frazier became a constant in the New York entertainment diet. Because of his penchant for wearing the wide-brimmed hats that were seen in the movie "Bonnie and Clyde," he acquired the nickname Clyde.

He was a flashy dresser, with a mink coat and a lavish apartment. He drove a Rolls-Royce. At times, he seemed almost a caricature of the noveau riche athlete, spending as fast or faster than he made it.

But appearances were deceiving. Frazier, in fact, was keeping careful track of what he spent. Some of his flashiest accoutrements—such as his mink and sealskin

Walt Frazier became the symbol of the Knicks with his flashy play on the court and his colorful life-style. *(New York Knicks)*

coats—were gifts. He regarded his apartment, and an Atlanta house he had bought, as investments. Even his Rolls-Royce he thought of as an investment, and he had waited two years from the time he first thought of buying it until he thought he had the money to do it.

Frazier had had a spendthrift father who had gone broke, and he had learned a lesson from that. He was determined not to repeat his father's mistake, and he even formed his own investment advice company, to help others as well as himself.

The Knicks were not a deep team that year. Only three reserves got much playing time: Dave Stallworth, making a comeback from his heart attack, Mike Riordan, and Cazzie Russell.

Riodan and Stallworth were all-round players. Russell was the designated shooter, a valued contributor because he could score against anybody and could come off the bench smoking if the Knicks' offense had turned a trifle sluggish.

Unfortunately for Cazzie, his concept of the game started and ended with shooting. At 6'5", though he had great jumping ability, he was never more than an average rebounder.

Worse, defense was never more than a word to Cazzie. The slightest fake had him going in the wrong direction, his man free for an easy basket. With his quickness, he

Cazzie Russell tries to slip one past the outstretched arm of Wilt Chamberlain, but it seems that Wilt is going to block the shot, as Nate Thurmond watches. *(Golden State Warriors; Steve Snodgrass)*

could have been a good defender if he had worked at it, but when Cazzie practiced, it was always on the strong part of his game, shooting.

That, then, was the cast of individuals on the Knicks that season, but this was a team that was far more than the sum of its parts. Red Holzman, who had been a star guard in the early days of the pro game, taught a total-team concept, and he had the perfect team for that style of play.

The Knicks played textbook basketball, the way the game was diagrammed by a coach on a blackboard. They all set screens for each other, they got position for rebounds, they passed the ball until one player had a good shot. They played with a precision that was a joy to watch.

The team was wonderfully balanced. Reed, at 21.7, and Frazier, at 20.9, were the high scorers, but all five starters averaged in double figures, Bradley, DeBusschere and Barnett were all just under 15 points a game. Russell, coming off the bench, scored an average of 11.5 points a game.

The balance showed in their shooting percentages, too. No starter averaged less than 45 percent, nor more than 52; and Russell was an even 50 percent. Because the Knicks were all good shooters and because no one player, or even two, dominated the offense, the other team dared not double-team anybody. And when the game was in the balance in the final seconds of play, any one of the Knicks might be the one to take the game-deciding shot.

Defensively, the Knicks used the same team concept. Reed was the key, because an effective team defense must have an intimidating force in the middle.

Many centers are capable of picking up driving players and blocking shots. Few do, because it means switching off their own men—and if a center switches off and his man gets a pass, it's usually an embarrassingly easy basket.

Reed, though, was an unselfish player. He knew that whatever baskets he gave up because his man was suddenly free would be more than balanced by the times he blocked shots, or forced bad shots or passes.

His dominating presence in the middle enabled guards Frazier and Barnett— particularly Frazier—to take chances on steals out front, just as Bill Russell had done for Bob Cousy.

Meanwhile, all the Knicks were sagging off when the ball was on the other side of the court, plugging the passing lanes, helping out. The important thing, they realized, was how the team did. Perhaps an opposing player would get free more than normal against this type of defense and score 30 points, but his team would get less than its norm and the Knicks would win.

Everything worked right for the Knicks that year. After losing their first game, they then ran off a record 18 straight wins. Eventually they won a club-record 60 games, winning the Eastern Division by four games over the Milwaukee Bucks.

Their fans loved it. Much has been written about New Yorkers and their love and knowledge of basketball, and some of it is understandably exaggeration. As Bradley pointed out in his book, none of the Knicks' starters were from New York that year, and basketball is certainly as hot an item in places like Indiana as it is in New York City.

But there is a special excitement in Madison Square Garden when the Knicks are playing well. That was especially true in the 1969-70 season, because the Knicks were playing the kind of smart, team basketball to which so many of their fans could relate. It was, really, a modern version of the "Jewish game" of the '30s.

In the NBA, though, the season is only the prelude; the playoffs are what counts. A team could finish out of first place in the season and win the playoffs and yet be called the champion, as had happened to the Celtics in the last three of their championships. A team could win in the regular season, but if it lost in the playoffs, it was considered an also-ran.

So the Knicks had to prove themselves all over again in the playoffs. They almost didn't get past the first round. Baltimore took them to a double overtime in the first game before the Knicks won, and it took seven tough games for the Knicks to dispose of the Bullets. The second round was easier, Milwaukee falling in five games, and that set up one of the most dramatic playoff finals in NBA history, with the Los Angeles Lakers.

It had been an interesting and unusual year for the Lakers. Wilt Chamberlain had torn up his knee in the ninth game of the season, rupturing the patella in what was called one of the worst knee injuries ever. It was assumed that Chamberlain would not return to action until the next season.

In the meantime, Jerry West carried the team. He led the league in scoring, 31 points a game, and in steals. He led his team in assists, and played a great defensive game. Some thought he should have been the league's Most Valuable Player, instead of Reed, the players' choice. The Lakers had finished second in the West, two games behind Atlanta.

Amazingly, Wilt returned three games before the end of the season. He had lost some agility, which had never been a particular asset, anyway, and he was rusty from his long layoff, but he was still a powerful presence in the middle, offensively and defensively.

With Wilt, the Lakers beat Phoenix in the first round of the playoffs (after falling behind, 3-1) and then swept four straight from Atlanta to match up with the Knicks.

The first two games were in Madison Square Garden. Their home fans ecstatic, the Knicks won the first game, 124-112, with Reed scoring 37 points, but West's two free throws in the closing seconds gave the Lakers a 105-103 victory in the second game, evening the series.

The third game was one that will be long remembered, a roller coaster ride that left players and fans limp. With 38 seconds left in the game, played in The Forum, West hit a jumper to put the Lakers up, 99-98.

Barnett came back with a field goal that regained the lead for the Knicks with 18 seconds remaining. Then, Wilt was fouled. He missed the first one. But he had always claimed he could make free throws in the clutch, and he hit the second one to tie the score. Only 13 seconds remained.

The Knicks came down and set up DeBusschere for a jumper that put them ahead, 102-100, with only three seconds left. That seemed to be it, and Wilt certainly thought so; he passed the ball in to West and started toward the dressing room.

But West took a couple of dribbles and then, from 55 feet, threw up a prayer. Amazingly, the ball went in. The score was tied, and the game went into overtime.

In the overtime, the Lakers seemed emotionally exhausted, and the Knicks pulled themselves together to win, 111-108. It was a pivotal win, but this series was still far from over.

In the fourth game, Chamberlain out-rebounded Reed, and again the game went into overtime. This time, the Lakers won it, 121-115, and the series was tied again.

There was more drama to come. In the fifth game, the Lakers ahead by ten, Reed tore a muscle in his upper thigh and had to leave the game, which was still in the first quarter. The Knicks seemed doomed, and indeed, the Laker lead climbed as high as 16 points. At halftime, it was still 53-40.

Then, Holzman switched strategies, double-teaming Chamberlain with forwards DeBusschere and Stallworth. The strategy worked. Wilt took only three shots in the second half, and West, incredibly, took only four. The Knicks came back to win, 107-100.

That put the New Yorkers ahead, 3-2, but the party seemed over when the Lakers demolished them in the sixth game at The Forum, 135-113. Chamberlain had 45 points and 27 rebounds, and he was irritated by those who said it was only because Reed wasn't playing. "When my game is going, it goes against anyone," he said.

The Lakers seemed to have a commanding advantage going into the seventh game; if Reed could play at all, he would not be effective, it seemed.

Still, the Knicks had some things going for them. The game would be played in the Garden, and basketball is a game where the home crowd is a very strong factor. Perhaps more important, Chamberlain had never won a seventh game of a playoff final, and he was certain to be thinking about that.

In dramatic effect, the seventh game surpassed anything that had happened before in this remarkable series. The buildup was intense as everybody wondered whether Reed could play at all and, if he did, whether he would be effective.

Reed stayed in the dressing room, undergoing treatment, as his teammates warmed up. The start of the game was delayed a few minutes while he took some last-minute pain-killing injections. When he hobbled out on the court the Garden erupted in sound.

Reed hit his first two shots. As it turned out, those would be his only points of the game. He exerted enough muscle inside to limit Chamberlain to 21, far below Wilt's 45-point outburst of the previous game, but he could not jump or move much, and he was nothing like the dominating player he had been.

It didn't matter. Just the presence of their captain gave the Knicks a psychological boost. Frazier had the game of his life with 36 points and 19 assists, and the Knicks played inspired basketball. They led by 14 at the quarter, 27 at the half and coasted to a 113-99 win for the championship.

Sadly, a series of knee injuries sharply limited Reed's playing time and effectiveness for the rest of his career, which ended in 1974, and the Knicks were not the same team without him. Some measure of what he meant to the team showed in 1973 when, after playing only 30 games during the season, he returned for full-time duty in the playoffs and the Knicks won another championship.

Perhaps if he had stayed healthy the Knicks would have won several. As it is we are left with the memory of one perfectly crafted season. Let's be thankful for that.

16. A Giant by Any Other Name

A basketball underground exists among the game's most fervent fans; it passes along news of hot new stars while they're still in high school, long before the players become known to the general sports public.

That had happened when Wilt Chamberlain was at Overbrook High in Philadelphia. When Wilt was only a sophomore those in the know had already projected him as a future pro star.

So it was that in the early '50s word came along the basketball grapevine that there was a young high school player in Indiana who was going to be the most complete performer yet, a youngster who could score, rebound, and pass the ball, who moved with amazing grace and anticipation and, indeed, was so much better than anybody else on the floor that he appeared to be playing a different game.

The young player was Oscar Robertson, and everything that was predicted for him came true. Robertson got better the further he progressed. As a high school player he led Crispus Attucks High in Indianapolis to 45 straight victories and back-to-back state titles in basketball-mad Indiana. As a collegian, he won three straight national scoring titles and was, naturally, a three-time All-American; his team lost only nine games in three years.

But it was as a pro that Oscar's game really flourished. "I didn't see him play college ball," says Al Attles, who had the unenviable task of defending against Robertson in many pro games, "but I have to think he was one player who was better as a professional than as a college player. The pro game gave him a chance to show a lot more of his individual skills."

What made Oscar so great? Name it. He was, to start with, an excellent shooter. He never seemed to take a bad shot, and he had a superb touch. He could not be handled one-on-one because he had the quickness to take an outside shot or drive, and the size to post his man inside.

His forte was consistency. Night after night he was around 30 points a game, and he did it so smoothly that it always came as a shock to check the stats sheet after a game and see how many points he had scored.

He probably could have scored far more if he'd tried, but he also ran the offense, and ran it as well as anybody ever has. He was both an accurate and imaginative passer, not as flashy perhaps as Bob Cousy had been but just as effective. He was always among the league leaders in assists, a remarkable feat for such a good scorer.

Whether shooting or passing, Robertson operated with a noteworthy economy of movement. "Robertson wastes the least amount of motion of any player I've ever seen," said Red Auerbach. "Every move has a purpose."

Unlike many top offensive stars, Oscar also played well defensively. Built like a tight end at 6'5" and 220, he could play against the biggest guards, and yet, he was as quick as any of the smaller ones.

"And," says Alex Hannum, who regards Robertson as the best player at any position in NBA history, "if his team needed a rebound, Oscar was big enough to go back and get it." Indeed, Oscar led his team in rebounding in his second season.

"You can't stereotype him," said Jack Twyman, a teammate of Robertson's on the Cincinnati Royals. "Whatever is needed at the time, against particular opposition, comes out because he has complete physical control of his body. It's not any one thing; it's his completeness that amazes you."

Attles probably had as much success defending against Robertson as anybody in the league because he played him so tightly. But Attles was always the first to admit that the best he could hope for was to slow Oscar down. Nobody stopped him.

"You'd just try to play position and hope that he was off in his shooting that night," says Attles now.

"The thing that impressed me most was that he always seemed to pace himself. He wouldn't score much early. He'd try to get everybody involved in the game. Late in the game he'd take the ball much more.

"It was really frustrating trying to guard him. He was bigger than most guards, he was so strong and he could go to his left or right. He could go anywhere he wanted.

"It always seemed to me that he pretty much did whatever he wanted to do. And when it got down to the end of the game, if the score was 8-10 points either way, he'd take the ball and just dare you to stop him.

"He had the respect of everybody."

Robertson came to the Royals for the 1960-61 season as a territorial choice. (The Royals, of course, had started their existence in Rochester but had moved after the 1956-57 season because of poor attendance.)

The Royals, who had been the worst team in the NBA the previous season with a 19-56 record, won 14 more games in Oscar's rookie season, a graphic demonstration of how much he meant to the team. The next season, the team finished above .500 (at 43-37) for the first time in eight seasons. That started a run of five straight winning seasons, and the Royals won as many as 55 games in Oscar's fourth season.

There wasn't much doubt who was chiefly responsible. Robertson led the Royals in scoring in each of his nine seasons with the team, scoring more than 30 points a game in six of his first seven seasons. He also led his team in assists each year, and in seven of those years, led the NBA as well.

Oscar Robertson, driving to the basket behind a screen by Lew Alcindor, is considered by most to be the best guard in NBA history. *(Milwaukee Bucks)*

Yet, one thing had eluded Robertson since his college days: a championship. His team had lost in the semifinals of the NCAA tournament in both his junior and senior years at the University of Cincinnati. The Royals had never finished higher than second during his years there, and they had not won in the playoffs, either.

Obviously, that wasn't Robertson's fault. The Royals lacked the one essential ingredient for success: a good big man. It was a tribute to Oscar's skills that they had done as well as they had.

For the 1969-70 season Cousy took over as coach of the Royals and finished at 36-46, fifth in the Eastern Division. Changes would have to be made.

The first was to trade Jerry Lucas to San Francisco; Cousy wanted a running team and Lucas didn't fit that model. The second was to trade Robertson. The primary reason was economic: Robertson's contract was coming up for renewal and the Royals feared they couldn't afford what he would want. Nor was it a healthy emotional situation with the former star guard, Cousy, coaching a present star. Cousy would have been less than human if he hadn't resented the comparisons drawn between him and Robertson, almost invariably in Robertson's favor.

The Royals first tried to trade Oscar to Baltimore during the season, but he exercised a contractual right to veto a trade and stayed with the club. Then, after the season, the Royals traded him to the Milwaukee Bucks.

This time Oscar didn't object because, for the first time in his pro career, he would be teamed with a great center, young Lew Alcindor (as he was then known).

The basketball underground had heard of Alcindor early, too, but by the time he was a senior so had everybody who had any interest in the game. Playing for Power Memorial High in New York City, Alcindor had been more heavily publicized than college All-Americans. He had led his team to 77 straight wins in one stretch, and he was probably the most heavily recruited prep in history, even more than Chamberlain.

Some thought Alcindor could have gone directly to the pros from high school, and they were probably right, but he chose UCLA, a continent away. Eighty reporters attended the press conference at which he announced his decision.

Under coach John Wooden, soon to become a legend in college circles, UCLA was a two-time defending NCAA champion at the time Alcindor made his decision. But the Bruins were to go on to even greater heights with Alcindor.

Because freshmen were not allowed to play varsity ball at the time, Alcindor was limited to freshman competition in his first year. Joining him on that freshmen team were Lucius Allen, Lynn Shackleford, and Ken Heitz, all of whom had been prep stars.

Their first game together was a clash with the UCLA varsity, at that time ranked No. 1 in the country because of their championship of the year before. The freshmen demolished the varsity, 75-60. The UCLA varsity, wrote one reporter, was No. 1 in the country but No. 2 on the campus!

Alcindor hardly broke a sweat in his freshman year. The junior college and freshmen teams the UCLA frosh played that year were badly outclassed, and Alcindor generally came out of the game early, the game already decided.

He and his teammates were just as impressive when they became the UCLA varsity. Alcindor scored 56 points in his first varsity game, against USC. In three years, the Bruins won 88 games and lost only two. UCLA won the national championship three straight years and Alcindor, of course, made All-American all three years.

Teams tried everything to stop him, double- and triple-teaming him. Former Cal coach Pete Newell scoffed at the strategy of having a man "front" Alcindor. "What good does it do to have a man looking at his bellybutton?" asked Newell. That strategy only left another Bruin open. Shackleford, bombing from the corner, benefited the most.

Even the rulesmakers couldn't stop him. In a move that was widely interpreted as anti-black in general and anti-Alcindor in particular, the NCAA banned dunking. It made no difference to Alcindor, the best-shooting big man the game had ever known.

When Alcindor came out of college in 1969, the ABA and NBA were joined in their uneven battle. Where he went was of paramount interest. It had always been assumed that he could make a poor team a winning one, but now there was an added factor: If he signed with an ABA team, he could perhaps help a whole league survive. Knowing he wanted to return to the New York area, the ABA owners agreed to assign his rights to the New Jersey Nets, without bothering about a draft.

Meanwhile, it had to be decided which NBA team could draft Alcindor. Milwaukee and Phoenix had joined the NBA the previous season and, given the choice of culls that expansion teams usually get, had each finished last in their divisions. Phoenix had the worst record in the league, 16-66, to the Bucks' 27-55, but in accordance with NBA rules, the two losers would flip to see who got first pick.

Richard Bloch, president of the Phoenix franchise, had mounted a year-long campaign among his fans to decide what call to make on the coin flip; it had become obvious early that the Suns would be last, and Bloch was understandably trying to distract his fans from dwelling on what was happening on the court.

The fans voted for heads, and Bloch called it that way in the great coin flip. The coin came up tails, and Milwaukee got Alcindor's rights. On such a flimsy basis, pro basketball's future would turn.

But Milwaukee did not have Alcindor yet. Lew announced that he would accept one offer from each league and take the best. He would not negotiate.

The ABA presented him with a $1 million offer. Milwaukee put together a total package valued at $1.4 million. Alcindor, while admitting he would much prefer to play in New York, chose the Milwaukee offer. Then the ABA came back with a better offer, but it was too late.

In his first year, Alcindor averaged 28.3 points a game, second in the NBA only to Jerry West, and finished third in the league in rebounding. He was an easy choice as Rookie of the Year, and his team won a whopping 29 more games than it had the season before. At $1.4 million, the Bucks decided he had come cheap.

More than anything else, Alcindor demonstrated how far the big man had come in basketball. Once it had been assumed that a big man had to be clumsy, but Alcindor was as graceful as a man a foot or more shorter than his advertised 7'2". (Around the NBA, estimates of his height went as high as 7'5".)

Inevitably, he was compared to the dominant big men, Bill Russell and Wilt Chamberlain, but he was a different player from either.

Defensively, he had become an excellent shot-blocker inside, though he did not venture as far out of the middle as Russell had, and players drove the middle at their own risk. He was not as physical as Chamberlain—nobody ever was—but he was more agile than Wilt.

Nobody stops the skyhook of Kareem Abdul-Jabbar, as he is proving against Spencer Haywood. *(Milwaukee Bucks)*

Offensively, he was a good passer, though it took several years to demonstrate that because he seldom had teammates good enough to pass to. But no team wanted to squander his talents by having him pass the ball a lot, because he was a peerless shooter, far better than either Russell or Chamberlain. His specialty became the "sky hook," on which he seemed to be shooting down at the basket. It was a virtually unstoppable shot.

Alcindor's one flaw was that he was not as good a rebounder as he should have been for his size. He was always among the leaders in defensive rebounds but seldom there in offensive rebounds because his shots often took him away from the basket.

In personality, too, Alcindor was different from both Russell and Chamberlain. Russell had used his position to voice what were regarded as militant ideas, though they seem much less strident in today's liberalized atmosphere. Chamberlain was a flamboyant personality, a world-wide celebrity.

Alcindor was much more of a private person than either Russell or Chamberlain. Unlike both of them, he had come from a middle class background and thus had more cultural advantages, and he was more developed socially as a collegian than they had been.

At the same time, he had been more protected in college. UCLA had invoked a rule prohibiting interviews of freshmen athletes, and access to Alcindor was sharply restricted during his varsity competition. For a time it was thought that this was his idea, but it was discovered later that the initiative had come from the UCLA athletic department.

Even as a pro, Alcindor was withdrawn. Sensitive to racial injustices but quiet about them for the most part, he became a Black Muslim. He changed his name to Kareem Abdul-Jabbar and became known by that name publicly after his second season. (In this chapter, which covers his first two years, we will continue to refer to him as Alcindor, the name he then used.)

Nor was he happy living in Milwaukee, a predominantly white city. His social life was very limited, and Milwaukee could not begin to offer the cultural advantages of New York and Los Angeles, the two cities in which Alcindor had spent his life.

On the court, though, the situation was much better. After the normal chaos of the first year, the Bucks had become respectable. Rookie forward Bob Dandridge, a fluid player, provided a complementary scoring punch to Alcindor at one forward. Guard Jon McGlocklin, though slow, was a strong outside shooter. More than anybody else on the team, he benefited from Alcindor's presence; when defense sagged inside on Lew, a quick pass to McGlocklin outside often resulted in two points.

The Bucks finished only four games behind the New York Knicks in Alcindor's rookie season and took care of Philadelphia, 4-1, in the first round of the playoff.

But then the bubble burst. The well-balanced Knicks took them in the second round, 4-1. It was obvious the Bucks still needed one more quality player. Specifically, they needed a guard who could run the offense.

They got him with the Robertson trade. As soon as the trade was announced, basketball fans everywhere looked forward eagerly to seeing Alcindor and Robertson work together the next season.

Nobody was disappointed. Robertson wasn't quite the player at 32 that he had been at 22, but he was still good enough to score more than 19 points a game and direct the offense.

It wasn't, as some have thought in retrospect, strictly a two-man team. The often-underrated Dandridge had an excellent year, averaging 18.4 points a game. McGlocklin contributed 15.8, and the entire starting lineup (Greg Smith played the other forward) averaged in double figures and shot better than 50 percent from the floor.

But there was no question that the team revolved around the young big man, Alcindor, and the veteran playmaker/scorer, Robertson.

Alcindor had added weight and strength, and he was a dominating factor. His 31.7 scoring average and 1063 field goals led the league. He was a close second in field goal percentage, at .577 to Johnny Green's .587; he was fourth in rebounds at an average of 16 a game, and he effectively closed the middle on defense.

Meanwhile, Robertson kept the offense flowing, so defenses could not double and triple-team Alcindor inside. The two were probably the most effective guard-center combination ever.

The season was a cakewalk for the Bucks. They put together two long winning streaks, first taking 16 in a row and then setting a league record with 20. Finishing with 66 wins and only 16 defeats, they were a whopping 15 games ahead of the second place Chicago Bulls in the Midwest Division. It was a season without suspense.

Only one team seemed capable of challenging the Bucks—the defending champion New York Knicks. The Knicks had fallen back somewhat from their great season of the previous year, but they had still finished five games ahead of the 76ers in the East, and they had beaten the Bucks four of the five times they had met during the regular season.

But Willis Reed was again having physical problems, this time with his knee, and he was not the same player in the playoffs that he had been during the regular season. After winning in the first round of the playoffs against the Atlanta Hawks, the Knicks ran into trouble against the Baltimore Bullets.

The Knicks took the first two games of the series, but then Wes Unseld and Gus Johnson took charge on the boards. The Bullets won the next two games to tie the series; the Knicks took a lead with a fifth-game win, and then the Bullets tied it again with a win in the sixth game. In the seventh game, Bill Bradley's jump shot at the buzzer failed, and the Bullets won, 93-91.

Without the Knicks to contend with, the Bucks had no worries. They smashed San Francisco and Los Angeles, by 4-1 scores each time, in the first two rounds of the playoffs. All of their wins came by at least 11 points, and in the fifth game against the Warriors, they won by an incredible 136-86 score.

With Alcindor dominating Unseld, the Bucks swept Baltimore in four games in the finals, by scores of 98-88, 102-83, 107-99, and 118-106.

After only three years, Milwaukee had a champion. More important, Oscar Robertson finally had the championship ring he deserved as the crowning glory for his magnificent career.

17. 33 Straight Wins

Jack Kent Cooke was unhappy. When he had traded for Wilt Chamberlain to go with his two superstars, Jerry West and Elgin Baylor, he had expected to win a championship. Certainly, no other team had three stars of that magnitude. But for one reason or another, Chamberlain's presence hadn't resulted in the championship Cooke wanted by 1971.

The first year Wilt was with the Lakers there had been constant friction between him and coach Butch van Breda Kolff, who seemed determined to prove that he was the boss. That determination got him fired.

Cooke then brought in Joe Mullaney. In the first year Mullaney was there, Wilt tore up his knee early in the season. The second year, Baylor injured his knee and played only two games all season. Both years, the Lakers lost in the playoffs.

Cooke, a self-made millionaire, was not one to sit idly by while fate kicked him in the teeth. He decided he needed a new coach, and he hired Bill Sharman, the former Celtic star who had coached championship teams in the ABL and the ABA, and had just missed another champion with the Warriors in the NBA.

Sharman brought some interesting theories with him. Most important was the fact that he felt the Lakers had to run to win. That ran counter to what was generally thought about the club, with its aging stars; most observers felt the Lakers had to conserve their energy. But Sharman had played on the Celtic team which had set the pattern for fast-break basketball, and he felt it was easier on older players to score a quick basket than to have to work for a harder one.

Two players were most affected by this. One was Baylor, who seriously doubted whether he could play fast-break basketball night after night at his age (37) with his bad knees.

The other player, of course, was Chamberlain, whose double reputation as a "loser" and a player who got coaches fired had been reinforced by his three years with the Lakers.

But Sharman did what Frank McGuire and Alex Hannum had done before him: He sat down and explained to Chamberlain exactly what he wanted from him.

What he wanted, in effect, was for Chamberlain to play "Bill Russell basketball." Chamberlain had always been a superb rebounder, but Sharman wanted him to

Wilt Chamberlain, holding the ball teasingly away from a defender, was a dominant force on championship teams in Philadelphia and Los Angeles, and set scoring records that will probably never be equaled. *(Los Angeles Lakers)*

work hard on getting the outlet pass out quicker to trigger the fast break. Because the Lakers had plenty of good shooters, Sharman told Wilt he didn't have to shoot a lot. He knew that Chamberlain, at 35, could not work hard at both ends of the court, so he emphasized that Chamberlain should play tough defense and loaf, if necessary, on offense.

So, once again, the NBA would see a "new Chamberlain." In reality, of course, what the rest of the league was seeing was simply another facet of the giant. McGuire had wanted him to score 50 points a game, and he had. Hannum had wanted him to pass the ball more to open teammates, and he had done that so well that he had been third in the NBA in assists when the 76ers had won their championship in the 1966-67 season. Now, he would be the defense-rebounding force.

There was one other problem that was not so easy to solve. Sharman believed in light practice sessions the day of the game. Wilt believed in sleeping in, particularly after a game the previous night, because he stiffened up. Grumbling more than a little, he agreed to the practices. He also agreed to tell Sharman when he could not make a practice, so the coach would not be embarrassed by questions from the press. Surprisingly, there would not be many occasions during the season when Wilt missed a practice.

Sharman was a very thorough coach. Among other things, he used game films to prepare his team; that was a common practice in football, but not in basketball. Again, Wilt was skeptical at first but soon saw the value of the films; with Wilt in line, other players swallowed their objections.

The team Sharman inherited was a good one, but one with several question marks. The chief question was age, with Baylor at 37, Chamberlain at 35, and West at 33.

The second question was depth. The Lakers' reserves were strictly journeymen. Any injuries which caused Sharman to use a reserve for an extended period of time would cripple the team.

So it was with some trepidation that Sharman started the season. The Lakers opened with four straight wins on the road, which buoyed his spirits, but then West hurt his ankle; Jerry missed five games, and the Lakers lost three of them, including their home opener. That was obviously exactly what Sharman feared.

Nine games into the season, it was painfully obvious that Baylor could no longer make it as a front-line player. Sharman went to him and said he would have to go with young Jim McMillian as the starter. Baylor decided that, instead of suffering the humiliation of being benched, he would retire. "I'll always feel bad about that," said Sharman, but he had no choice.

Baylor's retirement solidified the team. Elgin had been a great player, maybe the best forward ever, but age and knee injuries had robbed him of his great skills. McMillian was nowhere near as good a player as Baylor had been in his prime, but he was considerably better than Baylor at 37.

Emotionally, his retirement probably helped, too. Chamberlain and Baylor had never gotten along. Elgin had been the accepted team leader since his rookie year, the star player and a leader off the court, too. When Wilt arrived, Baylor's position changed. Baylor had always been a joke teller, but Wilt didn't laugh at Elgin's jokes; in turn, Baylor showed very little respect for Chamberlain.

Baylor had been the team captain, too. Because of his long service with the team, West could have had the honor when Elgin left, but he told Sharman to let Wilt have it. No doubt that contributed to bringing the team together.

Then the team started to win. It was a perfectly balanced team. McMillian, only 6'5", was very quick and an excellent shooter; at the other forward, Happy Hairston played tough defense and rebounded. Gail Goodrich at one guard was a remarkable shooter. Goodrich was not a strong defender, partially because he was only 6'1", and he was not a playmaker. On this team he didn't have to be, because West was a tremendous defensive player and a fine playmaker, in addition to being able to put the ball in the hoop as consistently as any guard who ever played the game. With Goodrich at the other guard, West didn't have to score quite so much, so he could work even harder on the other aspects of his game.

Meanwhile, Chamberlain was playing magnificently in the role Sharman had assigned him. He was blocking the middle against everybody, which minimized Goodrich's defensive weakness. He was rebounding and firing the ball out quickly so the Laker fast break could get moving. He had settled so comfortably into his new role, in fact, that he wound up taking fewer shots than any of the other Laker starters that season, a trend that continued in the playoffs. That was a complete turnaround from the days when he had taken most of his team's shots.

The wins started coming, eight, nine, ten in a row. Nobody thought much about it, including the team. "I don't remember anybody getting excited until we hit 14 or 15," says Sharman.

And still the wins kept coming. "When we got up to 18, we started to feel a little pressure," says Sharman, "but it was a good feeling. The record at the time was 20, and they really wanted it, especially West and Chamberlain, because they had such great pride. I never had to give them any pep talks."

The twentieth was a big game, an overtime game in which they beat Phoenix to tie the record. "That was one of the few close games," says Sharman. "One of the most remarkable things to me about that streak was the fact there weren't many close games."

In the next game, the Lakers beat Atlanta to set an NBA record. "Then, everybody started looking for things to keep it going," says Sharman. In the major American sports, the winning record was 26, set by the 1916 New York Giants in baseball. (Ironically, the Giants didn't even win a pennant that season.)

The Lakers surpassed that record on December 22, and they kept going until the streak had reached 33. Finally, in a nationally televised game in Milwaukee, they lost.

For more than two months, from November 5 to January 7, the Lakers had been undefeated. Perhaps the most incredible aspect of the streak was that 16 of the victories came on the road. The home court advantage in basketball is often figured at 5-10 points, and it may be even more. The home crowd can intimidate both players and officials. But nobody intimidated the Lakers.

In the understandable letdown immediately following the streak the Lakers lost four of six. It was their only slump of the year. They went on to win a record 69 games, losing only 13, for a winning percentage of .841, another record.

Their accomplishment almost defied belief. To put it into perspective, think of it this way: If you subtract that great winning streak, they still won nearly three-quarters of the remaining games, 36 of 49! If, instead of winning 33 straight, they had won only 16 of the 33, they still would have won in their division by a game over the second-place Warriors. As it was, they finished 18 games ahead of the Warriors, though the San Francisco team had a quite creditable winning percentage of .622, with 20 more wins than losses.

Everybody contributed. All the starters scored in double figures. Goodrich was actually the leading scorer, averaging 25.9 points a game; West was a bare tenth of a point back. McMillian chipped in nearly 19 a game.

Chamberlain scored only 14.8 points a game but led the league with 65 percent from the floor. Wilt also led the league with 19.2 rebounds a game, and Hairston just missed the top ten with 13.1 a game. West led the league in assists.

"That team could beat you any way," notes Sharman, "on defense, on offense, on rebounding. Defensively, West had a greater season than any guard I've ever seen, and Wilt did a great job of controlling the middle."

It was also a lucky team. The early injury to West was the only serious one a Laker starter suffered, and Jerry didn't miss another game after he recovered from that injury. Chamberlain and Goodrich played all 82 games; Hairston and McMillian each played in 80.

Sharman had convinced Chamberlain that he could use a little rest, but Wilt still averaged about 42 minutes a game, and only Boston's John Havlicek and Milwaukee's Kareem Abdul-Jabbar (as Lew Alcindor now called himself) played more minutes.

The Lakers weren't deep, but they did get some help off the bench from guard Flynn Robinson, who averaged nearly ten points in the 64 games he played, center-forward Leroy Ellis and forward-guard Pat Riley.

Was this the greatest team ever? Most observers give a slight edge to the 1966-67 Philadelphia 76ers, who had nearly the same record (68-13) against what seemed to be tougher competition.

Still, as Sharman notes, "How can you vote against a team that wins 33 straight?"

The consistency that carried the Lakers to 33 straight was the key to their season-long success. One indication of that: The team scored 100 or more points in 81 of its 82 games.

The Lakers couldn't even stop themselves. In March, their division title long since a mere formality, all the Lakers were invited by Chamberlain to a party at his palatial new home. The party lasted all night.

The next night, the Lakers won their game by nearly 40 points.

As dominating as the Lakers had been during the regular season, however, they still had to prove themselves in the playoffs, and there were some anxious moments.

The Lakers took Chicago out in four straight in the first round of the playoffs, but they were hurting, literally. An old fracture had separated in Chamberlain's right hand, and he had played with it taped because he didn't want to either miss any games or play with a cast. He also had a fracture in the middle of his left hand, and he further hurt that hand when he banged it on a rim.

Meanwhile, Hairston had a sore foot, McMillian a bruised thigh, and West a twisted back, though they all played. Sharman had strained his vocal cords—an ailment he suffered in other critical moments, too—and could barely talk.

In the opener of the second round against Milwaukee, at home, they were embarrassed, 93-72. West made only four of 19 shots, and Chamberlain was outscored by Abdul-Jabbar, 33-10, though he outrebounded him, 24-18.

The Lakers came back to win two tight ones, 135-134 and 108-105; in the second game, Wilt clinched the win with two free throws in the closing seconds.

The Bucks tied the series at 2-2 with another lopsided win, 114-88, but that turned out to be their last shot. The Lakers won the next two from the defending champions to advance to the finals against New York.

Again, the Lakers were shocked in the opener, as the Knicks took a surprisingly easy 114-92 win. But it became obvious quickly that the Knicks' win was a fluke. With Willis Reed again sidelined because of a knee injury, the Knicks had nobody to bother Chamberlain in the middle, and that was the difference as the Lakers won four straight to take the title. Only one game was really close, the fourth game which went to overtime before the Lakers won, 116-111.

One of the marks of a great team is its ability to win even on bad nights, and the Lakers had certainly proved their greatness in the playoffs. Not one of them had played as well as during the regular season; West, especially, was off with a 38 percent shooting percentage that was far below his norm. Yet, the Lakers had lost only three games in three rounds, and they were champions.

Not since 1965, when the Boston Celtics had won, had an NBA champion repeated, and no team would win back-to-back titles in the '70s decade.

Why? There were a number of reasons. The league was becoming better balanced. One team might dominate one year when everything went right, as the Lakers had done, but it could not continue its domination past a year. Physically, the game had become more demanding because of a longer schedule and more travel; players seemed to be injured more. Psychologically, it was more difficult to sustain success than to achieve it the first time.

All these factors affected the Lakers as they failed to defend their title.

Emotionally, they started to come apart even while they were celebrating victory. The Players' Association had voted that the coaches' bonus should come from management, not out of the players' playoff money, so the Lakers did not vote any money to the coaches; the players' shares came to about $15,000.

Management first said it would not pay the coaches either, though Cooke later relented. Chamberlain, never one to avoid controversy, spoke up against Cooke. He also wanted to renegotiate his contract (he was on the last year of a two-year contract). Cooke didn't want to, and his wishes prevailed over the long and acrimonious summer. It wasn't a good omen for the season to come.

Still, the team played well that season, winning 60 games against 22 losses and taking another divisional title. Considering all their problems, they may even have played better than they had the year before. "All our luck turned around that year," says Sharman. The year before, the Lakers had escaped serious injuries. This time, Hairston tore up a knee and played only 28 games. West missed 13 games with a torn hamstring, and was later injured during the playoffs, too.

The team was in turmoil all season, with players coming and going. Forwards Bill Bridges (who filled the gap caused by Hairston's injury), Mel Counts, and Bill Turner joined the team.

Meanwhile, Ellis, Robinson, and John Trapp were traded away. Rookie seven-foot center Roger Brown jumped to the ABA, after playing in just one game for the Lakers.

Chamberlain again led the league in rebounding and made almost a fetish of not shooting. In 82 games, he took only 586 shots. "He used to take that many in a game," quipped one observer. Five of his teammates took more shots. Playing little more than half as many minutes as Wilt, reserve Keith Erickson took 110 more shots, and Erickson was never considered a gunner.

In the playoffs, the Lakers struggled by Chicago in seven games and beat the Warriors four out of five, including an astounding 56-point victory (126-70) in the third game. That put them in the final against New York for the third time in four years.

This time it was the Knicks' turn again; they won in five games. After the fifth game, Chamberlain went into the Knicks' dressing room to congratulate the winners. When he came out, he was face to face with Bill Russell, working as a TV commentator. The two did not speak.

That, as it turned out, was Chamberlain's last pro basketball game, though that would not become evident for some time. Wilt was jumping to the ABA.

The new league had first approached Chamberlain in 1968, when he was still with Philadelphia. The ABA presented him with a tentative contract for $1.5 million over five years to play for the Los Angeles Stars.

The story broke before Wilt signed a contract, however, and Cooke and Philadelphia owner Irv Kosloff reached agreement on trading Wilt to the Lakers. Cooke offered Wilt enough for him to turn his back on the ABA.

The next year the ABA tried again. The idea was to have West and Chamberlain play for an L.A. team that would be coached by Baylor. Chamberlain did not want to play for Baylor, and both he and West declined the ABA offer.

By 1973 Wilt was disenchanted with Cooke and the Lakers—a natural turn of events for Chamberlain, who seldom remained contented for very long—and the ABA had another, much better offer ready. This one was for $1.9 million spread over three years, for Wilt to play and coach. His team would be the San Diego Conquistadors.

The deal was typical of the crazy moves that were being made, particularly by the ABA, at this stage of the "war." The Conquistadors were playing in a 3200-seat arena because owner Dr. Leonard Bloom could not reach terms with Peter Graham, proprietor of the much larger San Diego Arena. If the Conquistadors (or the Qs, as they were known in San Diego) filled their tiny arena for each game, that still wouldn't pay Chamberlain's salary.

But Bloom believed that, with Chamberlain, he would have a powerful enough attraction that he could get the voters to approve the building of a new arena.

Perhaps Bloom's gamble would have paid off—if Wilt had played. He didn't. Bloom had thought that Chamberlain was free to play, but the Lakers sued to make Wilt their (playing) property for his option year. The court ruled in the Lakers' favor, a ruling which was consistent with other such cases prior to that.

So Chamberlain was strictly a coach. For Bloom, it was a tragic situation, but for the rest of the basketball world it was hilarious. Chamberlain scheduled practices he didn't show up for. He was late for the first game the Qs played, and assistant Stan Albeck had to coach the team until he showed up. He lived in Los Angeles between games. When interviews were scheduled with him, he failed to appear. One can only imagine what a blistering critique Chamberlain the player would have had of Chamberlain the coach.

After one season Wilt was gone, leaving the franchise in shambles. The bond issue for a new arena failed to pass, and Bloom reportedly lost $1 million in the one disastrous season.

There was one interesting sidelight to the legal battle between Wilt and the Lakers. When testimony was being given, Wilt's salary was brought out. It was higher than West's, although Jerry had been told by Cooke that he was the highest-paid Laker. The enraged West quit the team.

And the Lakers, without first Chamberlain and then West, would not win another title until the next decade. But for one shining season, they were the most successful—and maybe the best—team in NBA history.

18. The Mountain Man Takes Command

Though basketball men admire any player with special talents, there is nothing quite like the excitement they feel when a quality big man becomes available. That had last happened in 1969 when Lew Alcindor graduated from UCLA. Now, in 1974, UCLA had another outstanding center who had completed his college career, Bill Walton, and the pros could hardly wait.

Walton hadn't been pursued by college recruiters with anything like the zeal with which they had recruited Alcindor and Wilt Chamberlain because Bill had played for a suburban high school in the San Diego area, an area not generally known for its basketball excellence. It was almost inevitable that he would go to UCLA—his brother, Bruce, had played football there, he liked the southern California beach-oriented life and UCLA was, of course, both a fine school and a basketball power—but it had not been particularly big news.

But Walton had bloomed as a collegian. He had far surpassed the college accomplishments of Chamberlain, whose college career was punctuated with disappointments. More significant, he had even surpassed the accomplishments of Bill Russell and Alcindor, who had had magnificent college careers.

The Walton-led Bruins had won an incredible 88 consecutive games before finally being beaten by Notre Dame in Bill's senior year, a defeat the Bruins avenged later that season. That demolished the old record of 55 set by Russell's USF team, a record which had stood for nearly two decades.

Walton himself was named the outstanding college player for all three of his seasons. Though he did not seek individual honors or go after individual records, he could be awesome when he turned it on. In the NCAA finals against Memphis State in his junior year, he hit 21 of 22 field goal attempts and finished with 44 points, the final two coming on free throws.

The only disappointment of his collegiate career was the fact that the Bruins were narrowly beaten in the NCAA finals of his senior year, preventing him from matching the three straight titles Alcindor's team had garnered.

Though he was often compared to Alcindor because the two were both great centers on great UCLA teams, Walton was truly unlike any center who had played before, a big man with the enthusiasm and many of the skills of a much smaller player.

He was smaller than Alcindor. In fact, throughout his career, Walton was listed at 6'11", though he was probably seven feet; he perceived, accurately enough, that seven-foot players were thought of as "freaks" by basketball fans. Yet, he was a much more physical player than Alcindor, and a better rebounder.

He was a good shooter but not in the class of Alcindor, who could be devastating; Lew had once scored 61 points against Washington State, when the Cougars were foolish enough to try one-on-one coverage, a mistake no college team made after that.

Both men were intimidators on defense, probably second only to Russell in collegiate history as shot-blockers. Alcindor did it more gracefully but Walton might have been a shade more frightening.

Two things set Walton apart from other big men. One was the completeness of his game. Every other big man had had one weakness; Walton really had none. He could do it all—shoot, rebound, play tough defense, pass the ball, even dribble it when necessary.

He had some outstanding players as teammates on the UCLA team, particularly Keith (Silk) Wilkes (known as Jamaal Wilkes after his rookie year in the pros), who became an outstanding pro and played on championship teams with the Warriors and Lakers.

But Walton made his team better than its individual parts, as he would later do in one memorable year as a pro. He was surely the best-passing big man ever, and teams could not sag onto him as they had with Alcindor because he would immediately whip a pass to an open teammate.

One player in particular benefited from Walton's style—guard Greg Lee. Sometimes, Lee would loft a pass high to the basket, and Walton would soar up and put it in. Other times, Walton would return the favor, zipping a pass to Lee for a jump shot from outside.

For all his teammates, Walton's style provided a great morale boost. It is easy for a really good big man to score a lot of points, and there is always the temptation to build an offense around the center. That has obviously happened with Chamberlain, Alcindor/Abdul-Jabbar, and George Mikan.

But nobody really likes to be a spear-carrier, even if that style is successful. The beauty of Walton's play was that everybody on the team was involved. Only occasionally—as in that Memphis State game, where Walton was playing at the absolute peak of his game and it made no sense to do otherwise—did the Bruins really play to Walton offensively. Every player got his share of shots; indeed, Walton often passed up shots to dish off to a teammate.

With all that, too, he brought an unparalleled enthusiasm to the court, particularly in the most important games. He loved playing basketball. In contrast to Alcindor, who had played virtually without expression, Walton played with a full range of emotions, openly displayed. His enthusiasm was contagious, and it made the Bruins a joy to watch. Earlier Bruin teams had reflected the personality of coach John Wooden and seemed machine-like in their precision. This team reflected Walton's personality; the Bruins seemed to enjoy playing the game.

Walton had one other point in his favor: He was a white star in a game dominated by blacks. Indeed, many basketball people thought his third Player-of-the-Year award had come more because he was white than because of his playing ability. David Thompson, a black forward from North Carolina State, had had a better season, but the votes didn't go that way.

Walton himself deplored the fact that he was regarded as the "white hope" of the game.

"I think the [world's] biggest problem is racism," he told Bud Furillo of the *Los Angeles Herald-Examiner* in an interview during his senior year. "People can't accept the fact that some people are black, some yellow, some brown, white, and red. The whites have gotten it into their heads that, because they're white, they're right. They think that everybody else is wrong. You can't exist that way. You have to look at everybody as individuals.

Bill Walton, shown in one of his too-frequent healthy moments, was a dominating force until injuries cut him down. *(San Diego Clippers)*

"I think color has a lot to do with interest in me. It's been so long since there's been a white player who makes people say, 'This player's good.' You have to realize that people who support basketball are white, upper-middle class. So the white fans dig on me because I'm white."

Walton was right, though pro teams would certainly have been very interested in him whatever the color of his skin. There seemed no question he could be an outstanding pro.

The Philadelphia 76ers had even tried to get him to turn pro after his junior year. The 76ers, because their record had been the worst in the NBA that season, had the first draft choice that year. But Walton was determined to play his full college career, and the disappointed 76ers drafted guard Doug Collins instead.

If anything, Walton's market value was even higher after his senior year, and he had two leagues bidding for his services.

The San Diego Conquistadores owned the ABA rights to Walton. San Diego owner Dr. Leonard Bloom, who had just finished a disastrous year with Chamberlain coaching but not playing, now hoped Walton could save the franchise.

Bloom would get help from other ABA owners. Knowing how much Walton could mean for the league's survival, other owners pooled their resources so Bloom could make a substantial offer.

Rumors proliferated. Because Walton so seldom spoke to the press much of what was written and said about him was conjecture, often fueled by his advisor, Sam Gilbert.

It was assumed, though Walton never said so publicly, that he wanted to stay in the Southern California area, and thus would be receptive to an offer to play in his home town.

That left NBA owners with a decision to make: Should they change the draft procedures and assign his rights to the Los Angeles Lakers, who theoretically would have a better chance of signing him, or should they follow normal procedures?

The league had made no concessions to Alcindor when he had graduated, though he wanted to play in either New York or Los Angeles. Following that precedent, no concessions were made to Walton, either, and he was drafted by the Portland TrailBlazers.

Rainy Portland seemed to be no place for a southern California beach boy, and the ABA offer was apparently higher, too; the figures, strictly unofficial, which were reported at the time were a $2.5 million offer from San Diego, $1.9 from Portland.

Nevertheless, Walton chose the TrailBlazers because he wanted to prove himself against the best competition available. Though the ABA had improved enough to be very close to the NBA in the eyes of many impartial observers, it was still perceived as a minor league, without television coverage, by most of the nation's basketball fans. Walton didn't want to be part of a sideshow.

It is an axiom in the NBA that a really good big man can be an important factor virtually from the start of his pro career. George Mikan and Bill Russell had led their teams to championships in their rookie years. Wilt Chamberlain had been the NBA scoring champ as a rookie. Lew Alcindor had turned a doormat into a strong contender as a rookie; in his second year, the Bucks were champions.

Many expected the same thing to happen with Walton and Portland. It didn't, for a number of reasons.

Though the TrailBlazers had been a bad team, they had two individual stars, guard Geoff Petrie and forward Sidney Wicks. Petrie had scored more than 20 points a game in three of his four pro seasons. Wicks, who had led UCLA to a championship when Walton was a freshman and ineligible for varsity competition, had averaged more than 20 points a game in each of his three NBA seasons, and he was also a strong rebounder.

Though basketball is a five-man game, a lot of championships have been won by teams with only three outstanding players: at center, forward, and guard. The TrailBlazers seemed to have an ideal combination.

There was one exception to this ideal: Petrie and Wicks disliked each other and would seldom even pass each other the ball. The TrailBlazers were split by this animosity; worse, the split was often along racial lines; Petrie was white and Wicks was black.

Walton was infuriated by this. His whole concept of basketball was as a team game, with everybody participating. Now, he was playing on a team which made a mockery of that concept.

That was problem No. 1. An even bigger problem, though, was Walton's physical condition. At UCLA he had been bothered by tendinitis, a condition which doctors thought would disappear as he got older. As a pro, though, his physical problems got worse, not better.

From the start, the Portland management was concerned because Walton was a self-proclaimed vegetarian. His weight had fallen from 235 to 214 pounds, and the TrailBlazers worried that he would be unable to match up with NBA centers physically.

Walton had adopted a rigid vegetarian diet as a senior at UCLA and would not eat meat, fish, poultry, or dairy products. Nor would he eat or drink anything containing additives or preservatives. At his most extreme, he even ruled out tap water.

"Most people in this country are junk food addicts," he told Ralph Barbieri in a startling article for *Sport* Magazine. "Most junk foods are loaded with sugar, which has a very damaging effect on the body. A lot of friends of mine have had a real tough time trying to cut sugar out of their diets. Tests have been conducted that show that the reason for this is that sugar itself is definitely physically addictive.

"Also, most of the meat that is eaten contains poisons that are present because the animals have been shot up with steroids and other crap, force fed and then brutally killed. A lot of other foods contain poisons as a result of having been processed and refined, which means that nutrition is taken out and restricting chemicals are put in.

"I believe that continually taking these poisons into our bodies over long periods of time can eventually cause cancer and premature death."

It didn't help Walton's cause, though, when he continually developed physical problems as a rookie that kept him out of games. The worst was a bone spur on his heel, a very painful injury but one that others have played on. Walton would not, though he was accused of malingering.

Thus Walton played only 35 games as a rookie, and averaged less than 13 points a game when he did play. The TrailBlazers improved, but only to 38-44; they were a badly beaten third in the NBA's Pacific Division.

Despite his problems, Walton was optimistic about the future. "I am looking forward to a long career in the NBA," he said after the season. "I love basketball. I love to play it, and I plan to play it for a long time. I think I can help the Portland TrailBlazers."

For a time, though, it seemed he would never have a chance to prove that last statement because it seemed that his Portland career would quickly end, and all because of statements he made at a press conference in San Francisco.

Walton had always been outspoken and a political activist. At UCLA he had answered the phone by saying, "Impeach Nixon!" He had campaigned for the United Farm Workers, hardly a position that endeared him with the whites who were his greatest fans as a basketball player. But that was nothing compared to the criticism he got when he publicly condemned the FBI.

Walton had been living in Portland with Jack Scott, who was working on a book on Bill. Scott and his wife, Micki, had moved out before the FBI came across information which seemed to indicate that the Scotts had transported Patty Hearst and friends across the country.

Trying to find out where the Scotts were, the FBI had questioned Walton at the office of his attorney, Charles Garry (who had also been the attorney for the Black Panthers). Later, Walton complained that the FBI was still harassing him.

Finally, Walton appeared with the Scotts at a press conference in San Francisco in which all three accused the FBI of "harassment." Walton referred to the FBI as "the enemy" and spoke of "our rejection of the United States government."

A few days later, Walton said he had been referring to the "trends, practices, and activities of the recent [Nixon administration] government," not to the Constitution. But the damage had been done.

Walton was reprimanded in newspaper editorials and columns. The Portland management issued a statement deploring what Walton had said. NBA commissioner J. Walter Kennedy said, "Thinking people everywhere will agree with these [the Portland management's] sentiments."

Portland fans wrote complaining letters by the thousands, many of them including threats not to buy tickets if Walton remained with the club. It was assumed that Walton would have to be traded to a more cosmopolitan area—New York, Los Angeles, San Francisco—where his views and lifestyle would be more easily accommodated than in conservative Portland.

He wasn't traded. He improved as a second-year player, pushing his scoring average to 16.1 points a game, but injuries still plagued him. He played only 51 of the team's 82 games, and the TrailBlazers actually slipped one game to a 37-45 record and fell into the division cellar.

Something obviously had to be done. To their credit, the Portland executives realized that the real problem was not with Walton, and they started to build a team around him. Wicks was sold to Boston, and Petrie was traded to Atlanta, a deal that resulted in the TrailBlazers getting the rights to Maurice Lucas in the ABA dispersal draft. Physically and emotionally the TrailBlazers were much better off, because they were rid of the Wicks-Petrie conflict that had torn the team apart.

The TrailBlazers also had a new coach, Jack Ramsey, long considered one of the top tacticians in the NBA. Ramsey, who replaced Len Wilkens, taught a style of play that best suited Walton's talents, with an emphasis on defense and a team-oriented offense.

Maurice Lucas, driving for the basket here, teamed with Bill Walton during Portland's championship season, but when Walton was hurt, Lucas' effectiveness was diminished, and he was eventually traded to New Jersey. (New Jersey Nets)

Now, the TrailBlazers were finally set. Lucas was the ideal power forward. He had the size (6'9") and strength to play the strongest forwards on defense, and he was known around the league as an "enforcer" type. He was a good rebounder, and he and Walton were the most effective pair of rebounders in the league. He was also a fine shooter.

Lucas's presence also made it possible for Ramsey to make a starting forward out of Bob Gross, who had been a reserve the previous season. A skinny 6'7", Gross was not a good rebounder, but with Walton and Lucas in the lineup he no longer had to be. Now he could concentrate on his shooting; he was a great threat operating out of the corner and taking pressure off Walton and Lucas inside.

The key guard was Lionel Hollins. A disappointment as a rookie the year before, Hollings was over his first-year jitters and ready to take charge. He was very fast and a very good shooter. Adept at penetration, he was very effective working the give-and-go with Walton.

Ramsey also got maximum mileage out of his other guards, Johnny Davis, Herman Gilliam, and Dave Twardzik. All had specific qualities which helped the team. Gilliam was an excellent shooter, Davis a good playmaker. Twardzik was ... well, it's difficult to describe exactly what he was. Another benefit from the ABA dispersal draft, Twardzik had no big reputation like Lucas. He was too small and too slow, but he somehow got the job done with sheer determination, and he became an important part of the team.

The TrailBlazers were a well-meshed team that year, with players having complementary skills which covered up for individual weaknesses. And they had Bill Walton playing at the top of his game. Still bothered by injuries, Walton missed 17 games, but in the 65 he played, he was magnificent. He led the league in rebounding, he shot accurately, he closed down the middle on defense and he made the offense go with his remarkable passing.

Lucas actually led the team in scoring that year, averaging 20.6 points a game, but there was no question that Walton was the player his teammates looked for when they needed a big basket; Bill averaged 18.6 points a game on 53 percent shooting.

Because Walton missed so many games, Portland finished second to Los Angeles in the Pacific Division, the Lakers finishing at 53-29 and the TrailBlazers at 49-33. But that was just a prelude, anyway, to the NBA's real season: the playoffs.

The divisional champions got a bye in the first round, so the Lakers watched while Portland disposed of the Chicago Bulls, 2-1, and the Golden State Warriors took Detroit by the same tally.

In the semifinals the Lakers beat the Warriors in a series which followed form exactly: Each of the seven games was won by the home team, and the Lakers prevailed because four of the games were played at The Forum.

Meanwhile, the TrailBlazers were having a somewhat easier time in beating

Denver, 4-2, which set up a Portland-Los Angeles series for the conference championship and a matchup between the two great former UCLA centers, Walton and Kareem Abdul-Jabbar. It was an uneven confrontation, though, and despite the fact that the Lakers had had a better season record, Portland had a clear team edge.

Jabbar had had another of his routinely great years, averaging more than 26 points a game. But in contrast to the TrailBlazers' great balance, he was one of only three Lakers to average more than ten points a game; Cazzie Russell and Lucius Allen were the others. Nor could the Lakers, as a team, play defense as well as the TrailBlazers.

Still, nobody could have anticipated the result of the series: Portland swept through the Lakers in four straight. Walton was magnificent, but so was the rest of the team; the TrailBlazers were reaching their peak at precisely the right time.

Afterward, Jabbar was bitter because so many saw the Portland win as a triumph for Walton, too. In fact, Jabbar played throughout the series, but his teammates simply did not measure up. The Walton-Jabbar matchup was pretty much a draw, but the Portland team was far better than the Lakers as a whole.

Meanwhile, in the Eastern conference, the Philadelphia 76ers had followed form to beat Boston, 4-3, and Houston, 4-2, for the conference championship; during the regular season, the 76ers had finished first in their division with a 50-32 record, which was also the best overall for the conference.

Seldom has an NBA finals provided a more interesting matchup than that year. On one hand, there were the TrailBlazers, a very well balanced team. On the other were the 76ers, a collection of immensely talented individuals who sometimes played as if they had never been introduced to one another.

Individually, the 76ers could do it all. Julius Erving, the celebrated Dr. J, was playing his first year in the NBA and convincing even the most skeptical that everything that had been said about him in the ABA was, if anything, an understatement. Erving swooped and soared for his points, an average of 21.6 a game.

At the other forward was George McGinnis, the Indiana strongboy who had left college after two years to play in the ABA. McGinnis played like a raging bull. Defensively, he often looked as if he were going for the pass of the cape; he often was faked completely out of a play. But he more than made up for his defensive deficiencies with his offensive play. With his great strength, he was unstoppable when he drove to the basket; prudent defenders got out of the way. He was also a superb rebounder.

At guard the 76ers had Doug Collins, a superb offensive player who—at 6'6"—often just jumped above his man to score. The other guard was Lloyd Free, self-proclaimed "All World" and "Prince of Mid-Air." Later in his career, the gifted Free became a fine all-round player. At that stage, he was primarily a shooter, and he was not adverse to letting it fly from well beyond the top of the free throw circle.

Perhaps the most spectacular player of all time — Julius Erving, the fabled Dr. J —goes up for one of his many varieties of dunks. (*Philadelphia 76ers*)

(above) Darryl Dawkins, who went directly to the NBA from high school, became known for his backboard-breaking dunks, but he also had a great soft touch on other shots. (*Philadelphia 76ers*)

(left) Two great young centers, Houston's Moses Malone (*right*) and Darryl Dawkins of Philadelphia battled under the boards as 76ers Maurice Cheeks (No. 1) and Caldwell Jones watched. (*Houston Rockets*)

Julius Erving comes over the top to block this shot by James Silas, who formed one of the league's most explosive backcourts with George (Iceman) Gervin in San Antonio. *(San Antonio Spurs)*

(above) Lloyd (World) Free got the reputation of being strictly a gunner with Philadelphia and San Diego, but he became a team leader when traded to the Golden State Warriors. *(Golden State Warriors)*

(right) The easy way to score: George McGinnis shoves Cedric Maxwell away with one hand while shooting with the other. *(Indiana Pacers)*

At center, coach Gene Shue alternated three players, Caldwell Jones, Harvey Catchings, and Darryl Dawkins. Jones and Catchings were tall and slim; Dawkins was simply immense. Dawkins had gone directly from high school to the 76ers and now, in his second year, he was still a boy, emotionally. But physically, he looked like a two-story building going up for a jump shot.

With this collection of talent Shue did little more than throw out the ball for practice. There was no attempt to install real team discipline, and it probably would have been a failure if Shue had tried it.

Around the league the 76ers were regarded with a mixture of awe and hilarity. They drew large crowds wherever they played, and they were often billed as a circus would be.

The basic problem was that only one basketball could be used. Both guards, Collins and Free, were great shooters; both forwards, Erving and McGinnis, had the ability to score 30 points a night. To keep the situation from complete chaos, Erving tried to subordinate his talents to the team, which probably hurt both him and the team.

Still, with all their problems, the 76ers looked like the next NBA champion when they took the first two games of the playoffs, both in Philadelphia.

Then the momentum changed completely. The TrailBlazers came home to their friendly fans, who had coined the word "Blazermania" to describe their crazed affection for the team, and blitzed the 76ers twice, 129-107 and 130-98. The series shifted back to Philadelphia for the fifth game, but Portland won that one, too, 110-104.

The sixth game was on a Sunday in Portland. The TrailBlazers almost ran away with it early, leading by 67-55 at halftime, but Erving, displaying all his incredible talents, scored 40 points to keep the 76ers in it.

With just five seconds to go, Portland led by two, 109-107. If the 76ers could tie the game, it would go into overtime. If they could win it then, they could go back to Philadelphia for the seventh game.

It seemed to make sense to go to Erving. Instead, McGinnis threw up a brick—as he had through most of the series. It bounced off, Walton got the rebound, fired it out to Davis, who dribbled away the remaining time. Portland was the NBA champion, the first team ever to win four straight after losing the first two games of the finals.

It was a magnificent game for Walton, who had 20 points, 23 rebounds, seven assists, and eight blocked shots. It was an equally magnificent series, and he was named the Most Valuable Player.

"I've never coached a better player," said Ramsey. "I've never coached a better competitor. I've never coached a better person than Bill Walton."

"They played team ball," said Portland owner Larry Weinberg. "They played unselfish ball. They are the embodiment of what is best in professional basketball."

(below) Bob Gross, shown scoring against Indiana, was a key man when Portland won an NBA championship. *(Portland Trail Blazers)*

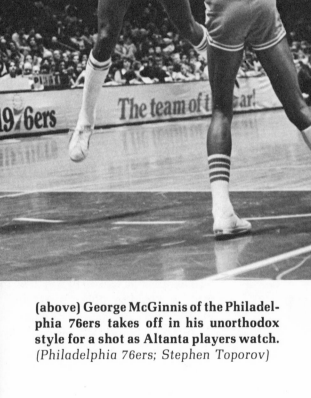

(above) George McGinnis of the Philadelphia 76ers takes off in his unorthodox style for a shot as Altanta players watch. *(Philadelphia 76ers; Stephen Toporov)*

Tributes came, too, from the Philadelphia side. "Bill Walton is the best player for a big man who has ever played the game of basketball," said Shue. "We couldn't contain him. He dominated the middle and that threw us out of our game."

Shue paused for breath and then added. "He doesn't have any weaknesses. You can't shut him off. He can score when he has to, but he is above all else a team player. He makes the players around him so much better."

The TrailBlazers had looked so good, had played together so well, there was talk of a dynasty building. But, as has happened so frequently in recent years, it all started to unravel the very next season. Though the TrailBlazers won the Pacific Division title, Walton was hurt late in the year. Without him in the playoffs, Portland went down, 4-2, to Seattle in the second round, after an opening round bye.

Walton missed the entire 1978-79 season because of the injury to his foot, and there were charges that he had been forced to play when hurt, which had further damaged his foot. He announced that, with his contract up at the end of the season, he would not return to Portland.

That created a great bidding war, of course, because Walton had proved how much he could mean to a team. Every club but one insisted that he undergo a physical examination by the team doctor before he signed.

The one exception was the San Diego Clippers, who were willing to take the word of Walton's agent and doctor, Dr. Ernest Vandeweghe, a former NBA player himself who had a son playing at UCLA. On Vandeweghe's opinion, the Clippers signed Walton to a multiyear contract at a reported $900,000 a year.

Walton played only 14 games for the Clippers in the 1979-80 season, though the injury that sidelined him this time was different from the one he had suffered in Portland. The next year, he went down before the opening game of the regular season.

Thus, it seemed that the rest of Walton's career would be more likely to be discussed in the pages of a medical journal than the *NBA Guide.*

He would be robbed of any chance to be compared with the all-time greats because he had only one season in which he played as much as three-quarters of a season. As fans, we would be robbed of a chance to see more of one of the best and most exciting players who ever played the game.

And everybody is left with one glorious season and a long period of conjecture on what might have been . . . if Walton could only have stayed healthy.

19. Three-Point Range

Since the start of basketball there has been an almost constant tinkering with the rules, trying to bring the game into balance. Most of the changes have been gradual ones, the result of evolution, such as the gradual widening of the free-throw lanes, in an attempt (mostly futile) to minimize the influence of the big men on the game.

Only two changes in NBA history have been truly radical. One, of course, was the 24-second clock, which changed the game—and probably saved pro basketball.

The other was adopted before the start of the 1979-80 season: the three-point field goal for shots made from beyond a line that was 23 feet, 9 inches from the goal at the center and 22 feet in the corners.

The origin of the three-point field goal was nearly two decades before the NBA experiment. Abe Saperstein, founder of the American Basketball League, had proposed it in 1960. It was not enough to save the ABL, which needed good players more than rule changes.

When the American Basketball Association began, it, too, adopted the three-point rule, and the three-point basket became a staple of ABA games.

Louie Dampier, a guard who played in the league from its start to finish, was probably the best known of the three-point shooters, though it was Les Selvage who held the individual game record. On February 15, 1968, playing for the Anaheim Amigos, Selvage hit ten three-pointers on an incredible 26 attempts, also a record.

The fact that both the ABL and ABA had used the three-pointer probably delayed its acceptance by the NBA because it was associated with failure and thought of as a gimmick.

When the NBA Board of Governors (owners) decided to try it before the 1979-80 season, it was strictly experimental. Many thought, in fact, that it would be discarded after a year.

Gene Shue, then the coach of the San Diego Clippers, had been the one who proposed the rule. "At the time I seemed to be the only person who thought it would be good for basketball."

After it had been adopted, Shue hit 14 in a row beyond the arc in a practice session to demonstrate how easy the shot was—at least in practice, with no opponent guarding him and no game pressure.

Brian Taylor of San Diego shoots one of the 90 three-point field goals he made to lead the NBA in the 1979-80 season. *(San Diego Clippers)*

Many who had been in the ABA and liked what they had seen of the three-point play also supported it. They argued that it opened the game up somewhat, easing the congestion around the basket.

The three-point play also added a little strategy to the game. A team trailing by six points in the last couple of minutes, for instance, could gamble on catching up by hitting two such shots, instead of trying for more certain two-pointers.

Those arguments probably wouldn't have been persuasive to the old-line NBA owners, however, except for one thing: TV ratings had been declining and there was pressure on owners to spice up the game, make it more attractive. The three-point play, which fans certainly liked, was one way of doing that.

Not surprisingly, Shue's Clippers tried three-point plays more frequently and more by design than any other club. Shue set up plays to allow his long-distance bombers, Brian Taylor and Freeman Williams, to fire away.

The strategy was successful. Taylor led the league with 90 three-pointers, and also had the league high of 239 attempts. Williams hit on 42, of 128 attempts.

In percentage, Taylor ranked fifth in the league with .377 and Williams tenth with .328. There are two interesting notes about those statistics. The first is that those percentages would have been considered adequate—and in Taylor's case, more than adequate—for all kinds of shots by guards in the early days of the NBA, when a 40 percent accuracy figure was considered extraordinary.

A more relevant consideration was that three-point statistics were deceiving; because a player got half again as many points for hitting a three-pointer, his percentage was really the equivalent of a half-again figure.

Thus, Taylor's equivalent percentage was an excellent .566, and Williams' .492.

Even more startling was the percentage of Seattle's Fred Brown. The three-point play was made for Brown; he had made a career of firing away from such great distances that he was nicknamed "Downtown," that presumably being the area from which he shot.

Brown hit 39 of 88 shots, for a percentage of .443; his equivalent figure was .665. Or, looking at it another way, Brown averaged more points per attempt on his three-pointers than did Cedric Maxwell, whose field goal percentage of .609 on regular shots led the league.

The long-distance bombing of Taylor and Williams, though effective and spectacular, didn't make much difference to the Clippers, who finished a badly beaten fifth in the Pacific Division. Nor did Brown's three-pointers make a lot of difference to Seattle because he tried them relatively few times, only slightly more than one a game, averaging less than one successful shot every other game.

One team did benefit greatly from the play, though: the Boston Celtics. Ironically, Boston general manager Red Auerbach had been one of the most vehement opponents of the shot before the season. He changed his tune quickly when he saw how it helped his team.

The Celtics, as always, relied on their fast break, but when that fast break was stopped, they had some problems. They lacked the big man—like Kareem Abdul-Jabbar—who could always score inside. Their center, Dave Cowens, though one of the best in the league, was undersized at 6'8". Cowens preferred to move out for a jump shot, or drive to the basket if his man came out on him.

But the Celtics also had two excellent long shots—guard Chris Ford and rookie forward Larry Bird. When their fast break was stopped and it appeared their offense might be stagnating outside, the Celtics could always flip the ball out to Ford in front or Bird in the corners.

For the season, Ford was second in accuracy with a .427 mark and Bird third at .406, both marks, remember, corresponding to better than 60 percent accuracy on regular field goal attempts. In three-pointers made, Ford and Bird ranked third and fifth, respectively.

That, in turn, opened up the inside more for Cowens and strong forward Maxwell, who both had good season. The Celtics went on to a 61-21 record that was the best in the league, though they disappointed in the playoffs.

No one player, though, enjoyed the three-point play more than the peripatetic Rick Barry, now playing for the Houston Rockets, the fifth city in which he had played during his long and distinguished, if controversial, career.

Rick Barry shows his remarkable body control as he slips past the guard of Bob Love for a basket against Chicago. (Golden State Warriors)

Barry was no stranger to the three-point play. In the 1971-72 season, he had made 73 of them while leading the ABA in scoring with a 31.5 average, the only player to win scoring titles in both the ABA and NBA.

Barry had gone from there back to the Golden State Warriors and had led the Warriors to a championship in 1974-75. His contribution that year is often overlooked (indeed, in a miscarriage of justice, he did not even win the MVP award that season), but he virtually carried the Warriors, a young team with no other established stars. He led his team both in scoring, with 30.6 points a game, and assists, with 6.2. He ran the offense because the Warriors had nobody who really qualified as a point guard, and he got the clutch baskets.

"I never saw a player have the year Rick had in '74-75," said Bill Walton years later. "It's easy for a center to dominate the game because of his size, and fairly easy for a guard, because he has the ball. It's usually impossible for a forward to dominate, but Rick did that year."

But Barry was as temperamental as he was talented. Like many great stars before him, he was not willing to accept a lesser role as his skills diminished with age. He often acted as if he, and not Al Attles, were the coach of the team, ordering teammates around. Not surprisingly, his teammates resented that, and the Warriors started to go downhill with Barry.

In 1978, Barry's contract was up. Warrior owner Franklin Mieuli made Rick a generous offer, but Houston surpassed it, apparently offering Barry $500,000 a year for two years and throwing in a house.

Barry signed with Houston, giving the standard athlete's line that he had to look out for his family. Before his Houston contract was up, he was divorced from his wife, Pam.

Before he left, some of Rick's teammates threw a party for him; the cynical thought it was to make sure he would leave. No tears were shed at his departure.

The deal turned out to be a disastrous one for the Rockets, who had to surrender point guard John Lucas and $100,000 as compensation under the ruling of NBA commissioner Larry O'Brien.

Barry's great skills had been eroded by time, and his new teammates were no fonder of him than his old ones. *Houston Post* writer Tommy Bonk noted that in one five-game stretch, when Barry passed the ball, he never got a return shot.

After that first season, Bonk wrote: "Rick Barry, you should retire. You are on the wrong team at the wrong time. You have been a great player, but you aren't any more. Unless you want to watch Robert Reid take away most of your playing time next year, settle up the final year of your contract."

Barry did not take that advice. He didn't want to turn his back on a half-million, for which he can hardly be blamed. He didn't play much in the 1979-80 season, and when he played, he hardly looked like the great star he had been.

But he could still shoot. Barry had come full circle as an offensive player. As a rookie, he couldn't shoot at all from outside but he was a great driving forward and he got a lot of points inside. As the years (and knee operations) piled up, he became more and more reluctant to drive; by the end of his career, he almost never did. But he'd worked on his outside shooting so faithfully that he had become an excellent shooter, even from the three-point range. Make that, especially from that range.

On February 6, 1980, playing against the New Jersey Nets, Barry hit seven three-pointers. That record didn't last long. Three nights later, he sank eight of the shots against Utah. He got all his 24 points that night on three-pointers.

Barry had been given the option by Houston coach Del Harris to go for a three-pointer when the opportunity was right. Harris hoped to force defensive changes that way. "They can't drop off and double up on (center) Moses Malone and that helps us," said Barry.

Rick's three-pointers were crucial early in the game; he hit two straight early in the second period to give the Rockets a 38-30 lead. Later, the Rockets started moving away from the Nets, eventually winning by 117-95, and Barry's shooting became more an exhibition than an important part of the game.

"After I hit the first seven, I started thinking about breaking my record," he said. "The game was out of reach, and I wanted to do it for the fans. When the shot went in I was thrilled for the crowd, because they were loving it so much. We're here to please the fans and they've responded to it."

Barry's eight successful three-pointers came on 12 attempts, and that climaxed an incredible week for him. Including seven-of-ten against New Jersey, he was 16-for-28 on three-pointers.

For his exploits, Barry was named NBA Player of the Week. It was the last significant honor he received in his career. His contract was up at the end of the season, but Houston made no attempt to re-sign him. Nor did any other clubs, though he was a free agent. Though Barry still wanted to play—and talked wildly of a "conspiracy" against him because nobody would sign him—his career was over. Finally accepting that, he took a route familiar to many former jocks—becoming a TV color man.

Moses Malone of the Houston Rockets soared above the crowd to score. Teammate Rick Barry watched on the left. (Houston Rockets)

After its first season, the three-point rule still drew mixed reviews from those in the game.

One fear had been dispelled: that it would create specialists. Unlike baseball, with its designated hitter rule, or football, where a player can do nothing else but punt or place kick, basketball cannot accommodate specialists well. Every player must play both offense and defense. A player whose sole value is shooting from the three-point range would be a liability to a club.

Some coaches had been converted from skepticism to approval. One such was Portland's Jack Ramsey, though he had been burned by the play. In one Portland-Kansas City game, the TrailBlazers were ahead by nine points with about a minute and a half to play. Kansas City guard Otis Birdsong hit three straight three-pointers to tie the score. "In previous years that game would have been put away," noted Ramsay.

"I believe it (the rule) has been beneficial," he added. "It introduced a strategic factor, and the fans like it."

John MacLeod of the Phoenix Suns had been strongly opposed to the rule when it had been adopted, but he, too, had changed his mind.

"It does add excitement," he said, "and it certainly has altered last-minute strategy for coaches. The three-point goal has forced defenders to come out and to respect the ability of outside shooters."

In general, a coach's opinion depended on the type of club he had. Paul Westhead of the champion Los Angeles Lakers virtually ignored it, for good reason.

"Our whole style has been to avoid that kind of play," he said. "We run the fast break and like to work the ball in to Kareem. If you'll notice, he hasn't tried too many three-point skyhooks lately."

Westhead, though, admitted it made a difference when the other team had the ball. "We've felt the impact more on the defensive side, in guarding against the last-second shot that could tie or win a game."

Billy Cunningham, coach of the Philadelphia 76ers, was another who had his team try three-pointers only in desperation, but he admitted that was only because of the kind of players he had.

"We don't have a Chris Ford. If we did, I'd certainly work his skills into our offense. We're basically an inside-oriented team. That's where our strength lies, with people like Dr. J., Caldwell Jones, and Darryl Dawkins."

Most of the doubters had come around. There was very little talk that the rule should be abandoned; the Warriors' Franklin Mieuli was the only owner who still opposed it outright, perhaps because his team of the previous year had had trouble hitting from ten feet, let alone 23.

Those who were still skeptical of the rule mostly proposed modifications in it.

Some thought, for instance, that it might be best to limit its use to the last two minutes of a game, when a trailing team would use it to catch up.

But the NBA Board of Governors had the final word: With hardly any discussion or dissent, they voted to make the rule permanent for the 1980-81 season.

20. Who's the Best: Magic or Bird?

Because pro basketball depends on colleges for virtually all its players, it is an exciting moment when a star collegian turns pro. There is always the question whether he will succeed or fail as he moves on to the higher competition.

Some players step into the pro ranks without hesitation: Oscar Robertson, Wilt Chamberlain, Elgin Baylor, Kareem Abdul-Jabbar, and Marques Johnson were all stars from game one. Others, like Jerry West, develop more slowly but become stars.

Some, though, never become the stars in the NBA that they were in college. In recent years, such players as Rick Mount, Ernie DiGregorio, Scott May, and Rickey Green, though all played pro for a time, were disappointments.

So there's always a little apprehension mixed in with the excitement when a team drafts a college star. Will he become an outstanding pro, or will some weaknesses which were not obvious in college show up when he plays professionally?

Some years, too, produce more outstanding rookies than others. Robertson and West turned pro the same year, for instance. In 1977, Johnson, Walter Davis, and Bernard King were all rookies, and at the same position, forward.

The 1979-80 season was another like that. Oddly, the 1979 draft was considered a bad one by most in the NBA because there was no depth; teams picking beyond about the tenth selection in the first round were in trouble.

But the quality at the top was amazing. Forwards Calvin Natt and David Greenwood, both of whom made the All-Rookie team, looked like they'd be around for a long time. Greg Kelser, though slower developing, seemed a potential star for Detroit. But three rookies stood out above the others, making this one of the great rookie years in NBA history.

The first, and least-publicized (though he played in New York, the media center) was center Bill Cartwright, a cherubic-faced giant who was selected by the Knicks.

Cartwright had been a high school senior the same year that Darryl Dawkins had been, a continent away—Dawkins in the east and Cartwright in the west.

At the time, Dawkins had been considered the more advanced of the two. At 6'11", Dawkins was somewhat shorter than Cartwright, who was at least 7 feet, but he was heavier, stronger, and a better jumper.

Dawkins chose to turn pro immediately, with the Philadelphia 76ers. His progress since then had been spotty, largely because he didn't get much playing time in his first

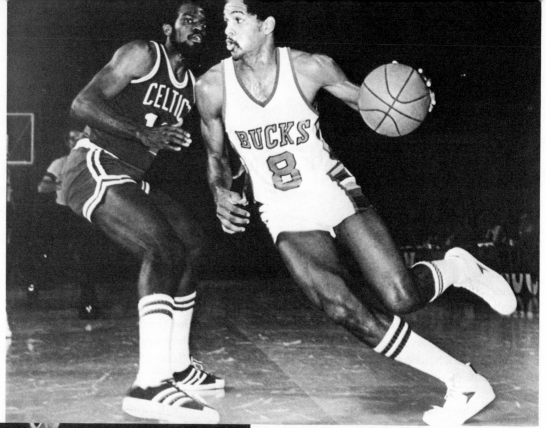

(above) Marques Johnson, driving against the Celtics' Sidney Wicks, was an outstanding rookie and an even better player in subsequent seasons for the Milwaukee Bucks. *(Milwaukee Bucks)*

(left) Walter Davis, showing his great body control in this action against the Cleveland Cavaliers, helped Phoenix improve when he shifted from forward to guard. *(Phoenix Suns)*

two years. By his fifth pro year—and Cartwright's rookie year—he was still known more for his backboard-shattering dunks than for all-round excellence.

Cartwright had chosen to go to the University of San Francisco, the same school that had produced Bill Russell. He arrived in the same class with forward James Hardy and forward/guard Winfred Boynes. All three had been high school All-Americans, and it was assumed they would bring at least one NCAA title to USF, and probably more.

That never materialized. The Dons had some great moments—including a 29-game winning streak when the three were sophomores—but they never got beyond the opening round of the NCAA tournament.

Hardy and Boynes turned pro after their junior years, going to New Orleans and New Jersey, respectively. Both failed. Boynes was too small to play forward and not a good enough ballhandler to play guard, and New Jersey surrendered him to Dallas in the expansion draft in 1980. The moody Hardy was inconsistent, and he was cut by the Jazz (by then in Salt Lake City) in 1980.

Meanwhile, Cartwright continued to improve. As a freshman he was a good shooter and nothing else. He was not a good passer because, in high school, he was supposed to shoot, not pass. Playing for the first time against players near his size, he was pushed around constantly. He was neither a good rebounder nor a good defender.

But he worked to better himself. He worked on weights to build up his strength, and he practiced constantly. By the time he was a senior he led the nation in rebounding, played good defense, and was a virtually unstoppable scorer inside.

Still, there were many who doubted he'd be a good pro. Noting the similarity in physique and shooting ability with one of the great pro disappointments of recent years, some called him "a fat Jim McDaniel." That assessment ignored the fact that Cartwright had the desire to succeed that McDaniel had lacked.

The Knicks drafted him on the first round but he was expected only to be the backup to Marvin Webster, whom the Knicks had signed as a free agent the year before in an expensive deal that had cost them a first-round draft choice and forward Lonnie Shelton. Cartwright was expected to learn his trade slowly.

But Webster was hurt when training camp came around, and he remained on the injured list well into the season. The Knicks had to use Cartwright, and what seemed like a bad break turned into a good one.

Cartwright scored 22 points in his first game, and that was an accurate indication of what his season would be like. He averaged 21.7 points a game and would have been a shoo-in for Rookie of the Year honors most years. In this season, though, he wasn't even close, because Larry Bird and Magic Johnson were both rookies.

Bill Cartwright gave the Knicks the outstanding center they'd been looking for as a rookie in the 1979-80 season.
(New York Knicks)

Larry Bird was a contradiction, a white player from the country who played like a black player from the city. A marvelously accurate shooter from the outside, Bird was an even better passer. Before he played a minute as a pro, basketball people were calling him the best passing forward ever to play the game, better even than Rick Barry.

Bird had had an interesting career even before he turned pro. He had started his collegiate career at Indiana University but quit after his freshman year because the school was too big for him. He went home to French Lick, Indiana, and drove a truck for a year before resuming his college career at much smaller Indiana State.

At Indiana State he had been virtually a one-man team and got the Sycamores to the NCAA finals, where they had lost to Michigan State. Bird did everything for his team. At 6′9″, he was big enough to rebound well; he could score from inside and outside; and, of course, he often set up teammates for baskets with his sharp passing. He was the best all-round college player since Bill Bradley.

He also had an enormous negotiating edge because he was a fifth-year player. The NBA at the time had a rule, since dropped, that a team could draft a player whose class had graduated and retain the rights to that player even if he returned to play one more year of college ball.

The Celtics had drafted Bird after what would have been his senior year if he hadn't dropped out of school. He returned to Indiana State to play one more year. The Celtics then had from the end of the college season to the May draft to sign Bird; if they didn't, he would go back into the draft pool and other clubs would have a chance to draft him.

The once-proud Celtics had finished a sad 29-53, dead last in their division, in the 1978-79 season. They needed Bird badly, and Bird's agent, Bob Woolf, knew it. The Celtics finally got Bird, but only after agreeing to a five-year, $3.25 million package.

As great a player as Bird had been in college, there were some who wondered how good a pro he'd be. One of the questions about him was his speed and quickness; the other was personal.

Bird wasn't fast, and he could be burned defensively by a quicker man. In college, his coach, Bill Hodges, had usually assigned Bird to the opposing forward who was the weaker offensive player. That's a strategy most coaches of one-star teams use (Elgin Baylor at Seattle is a classic example) because they don't want that star fouling out.

In the NCAA finals, Hodges had assigned Bird to Michigan State's Greg Kelser, who repeatedly went around Bird for his shot. That seemed to affect Bird's offense, too; he shot only seven for 21 from the floor. Would that be a pattern in his pro career?

A more serious question was his personality. Bird admitted he felt uncomfortable in the city. "I hate to hear people say, 'There goes Larry Bird' when I go into a restaurant or theater," he said, shortly after signing with the Celtics. "People treat me different here."

At Indiana State he had been shielded by his coach. Bird would not give interviews. His reason? He didn't want to take away publicity from his teammates.

As a pro he consented to interviews, but that didn't mean he had to like it. "I wouldn't go out of my way to give an interview," he admitted. "That's more information, more recognition, more times my name gets in the paper. I don't want that. I don't understand why people want to talk to me."

There were some who thought Bird simply wouldn't be able to adjust to the big city life, that the pressures would force him to quit.

There was a precedent from another sport. In the '50s, the Baltimore Orioles had signed a young pitcher named Bruce Swango out of high school to a large bonus contract, but Swango had to quit—after accepting the bonus money, of course—because he couldn't pitch in front of crowds. They made him too nervous.

Bird, though, could play in front of crowds. In social circumstances people made him very nervous; in athletic situations they inspired him to play better.

"I'm not a good practice player, never have been," he said. "I think I'm a fan player. I move faster, better. I react to the roar of the crowd. I have to have a crowd to play before."

Larry Bird, a great shooter and perhaps the best passing forward ever, was named Rookie of the Year in a tight battle with Magic Johnson.
(Boston Celtics)

Though he scored only a disappointing—to him—14 points in his opening game, the doubts about Bird were quickly dispelled. He played marvelously, at least as well as he had in college.

He averaged 21.3 points a game and nearly 10.5 rebounds, an excellent figure for a forward. He fit perfectly into the Celtics' style of play, which had always featured quick and accurate passing, and he averaged nearly five assists a game.

Defensively, he was adequate, aided by the fact that his running mate at forward, Cedric Maxwell, always took the stronger offensive forward.

Bird wasn't the only change the Celtics made that year. They had signed M. L. Carr as a free agent, and Carr became the sixth man the Celtics have always had in their good years, coming off the bench to swing between guard and forward.

Guard Tiny Archibald, who had been plagued by injuries, came back to have an excellent year, scoring well and running the offense. Ford became an unexpectedly strong asset because of his ability to hit three-pointers.

But there was no question that Bird was the most important difference between the team that had won 29 games the season before and the team that won 61 in 1979-80, a whopping 32-game improvement that made the Celtics the winningest team in the league.

Bird made the All-Rookie team, of course. He even made the first-string All-NBA team. And yet, there was a running debate all season whether he or Earvin (Magic) Johnson was the best rookie.

Physically, Johnson was unlike any player the NBA had ever seen. At 6'9", he played guard—but he could swing into a forward spot or even into the pivot when the Lakers wanted him there. At one critical point in the season the pivot is exactly where they wanted him and he responded in brilliant fashion (but more about that later).

Johnson had played only two years of college ball, leading Michigan State to the NCAA championship his sophomore year. He turned pro after that season because it seemed his market value would never be higher, and perhaps also because there was nothing more he could learn from college players.

Though he was only 20, normally conservative basketball men were lavishing extravagant praise on Johnson. At 6'9", he overpowered smaller guards and yet he had as much quickness as those three-quarters of a foot shorter. Defensively, he smothered opponents with his long arms and flicked the ball away with his quick hands. His ballhandling was so astounding that it had earned him his nickname. He needed to work on his jump shot, but those who had watched him closely knew that he had no trouble shooting when his team needed points. It was only in lopsided games that he lost interest and shot sloppily.

To make it even better, Johnson's personality was a match for his ability. He bubbled. Unlike Bird, he had no trouble talking to the press, or to anybody else. His effervescence spread to his teammates. Even Kareem Abdul-Jabbar, who had been so aloof over the years, became more enthusiastic with the arrival of Johnson.

Statistics alone don't measure the value of a player like Magic, but his were all good. He was third on his team in scoring, averaging 18 points a game, second to Jabbar in rebounds, second to Norm Nixon in assists—figures which were a tribute to his all-round game. He converted 53 percent of his field goal attempts and 81 percent of his free throws, which answered the questions about his shooting ability.

He, too, made the All-Rookie team, and he seemed on his way to a long and exciting career (though there would be some questions when a knee injury which required an operation sidelined him early in the next season).

So, who was the best rookie? The vote, taken right after the end of the regular season, favored Bird by a surprisingly lopsided 63-3 margin. One can only guess what went on the minds of the voters, but it seems reasonable to assume that the vote was actually much closer than that, that a lot of the voters thought a long time before they decided Bird had had the better season.

The Celtics nearly made a clean sweep of the postseason honors, with Bill Fitch honored as Coach of the Year and Red Auerbach as General Manager of the Year.

Very soon, events would make a mockery of those awards.

21. A Championship That Ended a Friendship

It had been a year to remember in Los Angeles basketball circles, and not just because of Magic Johnson. There were so many bizarre happenings, in fact, that Magic's play—which would have been the headliner almost anywhere else—was almost a sideshow.

First, Jerry Buss had bought the club from Jack Kent Cooke. The deal was the biggest financial transaction in sports history. In addition to the Lakers, Buss had bought the Kings hockey team, the 17,505-seat Forum and even 13,000 acres in the Sierra. The deal totaled $67.5 million, part of it Buss's individual purchase and part of it a partnership deal with his real estate firm, Mariani-Buss Associates.

Cooke, a self-made millionaire, had made more than a few waves in Los Angeles sports in the 17 years he had owned the Lakers. Among other things, he had built The Forum because of a disagreement with the management of the Sports Arena, adjacent to the Los Angeles Coliseum and USC campus.

But alongside Buss, Cooke seemed pure vanilla, as straightforward as a Cincinnati businessman.

Buss is a man of such complexities that he seems almost fictional. It is hard to believe that he can really exist, a wheeler-dealer who was once a chemistry professor at USC.

Before that, he had earned his Ph.D. in physical chemistry at USC when he was 24. His doctoral dissertation was entitled, "The Bond Dissociation Energy of Toluene."

Buss—still known as Dr. Buss to his real estate associates—did not linger long in the academic world. He soon got into real estate and became a multimillionaire long before he purchased the Lakers, etc., at the age of 46.

He is a collector—of rare coins, rare stamps, and pretty girls. He consumes so conspicuously as to be almost a parody of a rich man, from his Bel Air mansion to a $127,500 Rolls Royce Camargue.

Yet, he is also an intellectual, reading the *Iliad,* Camus, and Sartre—along with such more pedestrian volumes as Irving Wallace's *The Nympho and Other Maniacs* and *Baldness: Is It Necessary?*

Buss first got involved in professional sports with the Los Angeles Strings of World Team Tennis. (He and his associates also controlled three other franchises in the league, and when they folded the four teams, the league folded, too.)

Colorful and controversial owner Jerry Buss of the Lakers brought a fresh approach to promoting his team. *(Los Angeles Lakers)*

At first, the Strings played at the Sports Arena, but Buss had problems with the management and moved his team's matches to The Forum when Cooke gave him a reduced rent. "It wasn't charity," says Buss. "He made money on the Strings."

Buss signed Chris Evert and Ilie Nastase for the Strings and did well, but it still wasn't the big leagues. He wanted a team that would be on the front page of the *Los Angeles Times* sports section day after day. The Dodgers and Rams weren't for sale, but the Lakers were. Cooke and Buss got along because they were both grand thinkers, and when the 66-year-old Cooke decided he wanted to sell, Buss was there.

Buss has made some interesting changes in the Lakers' (and The Forum) operation, and some of his ideas are certain to be incorporated into future franchises.

Since he owns The Forum, in which there are sports or entertainment events 220 to 240 days a year, he has sold year-round tickets for choice seats. People can buy a seat location that entitles them to see everything that is staged in the arena.

He has a variable-ticket-price system, keeping some tickets low enough so that anybody can afford them while pricing the very best seats very high, because he has discovered—as have some other owners—that some people will pay virtually any price for the best seats. In fact, when Buss first took over, he raised the price of courtside seats (sold only on a season ticket basis) from $20 a game to $60, so he could get some cancellations and have seats available for himself and his friends. There were no cancellations, and Buss does not sit at courtside.

He is a firm believer that stars sell tickets, and to prove his point he renegotiated Kareem Abdul-Jabbar's contract up to $1 million a year; it was Buss's idea, not Jabbar's, though Kareem didn't complain.

(That was just the beginning for Buss. He later upgraded salaries for all the Laker stars, and in June of 1981 stunned the rest of the NBA by signing Magic Johnson to a 25-year, $25 million contract.)

Jerry West had grown tired of coaching, so Buss moved him into the front office and brought in Jack McKinney, who had been an assistant at Portland, as head coach. McKinney then persuaded Buss to hire Paul Westhead as an assistant.

It seemed an ideal situation for McKinney. Abdul-Jabbar had recommended McKinney's hiring to Buss, and Kareem seemed more eager than he had in years. McKinney had persuaded Buss to trade for strong forward/center Jim Chones, who would make an important contribution to the Lakers that season.

McKinney had liked what he had seen of rookie guard Mike Cooper, a relatively unknown player who came on to give the Lakers great flexibility because he could play either guard or forward. Magic Johnson, of course, was bringing his special talents and exuberance to the club. Veterans Jamaal Wilkes and Norm Nixon were solid players.

The talent seemed to be there, and so was the coaching. The Lakers were sharp, well-drilled, and hustling in their first 13 games, nine of which they won. A championship certainly seemed possible.

Then, on November 8, the Lakers had a day off. Westhead, McKinney's best friend, called him to see if he wanted to play tennis. McKinney did, and he set out for the courts at Westhead's condominium on his son's bicycle, because his wife had the car.

Coming down a hill to an intersection in Palos Verdes, a plush suburb south of Los Angeles, McKinney hit the brakes. The bike stopped abruptly, and McKinney was thrown over, landing on his head.

The collision knocked him unconscious. When ambulance attendants answered the emergency call from a passing motorist they thought McKinney was certain to die. He was rushed to the hospital and placed in the intensive care unit, suffering from severe head injuries, a facial fracture, and a fractured elbow.

McKinney's condition was so serious that only members of his family visited him—and Westhead, who was described to the hospital personnel as Jack's brother. "Jack has been like a brother to me," said Westhead at the time.

It was three weeks before McKinney could go home, and his recovery was painful and slow. His mental faculties were diminished, his reflexes impaired, his balance unsteady.

In his absence, Westhead took over the team, though he made a point of saying he was only the caretaker. His system was McKinney's system. And the Lakers kept winning.

By the end of January, McKinney felt he had recovered enough to take over the team. Buss, though, decided it would be better to wait until the season was over, and McKinney spent the rest of the season scouting, under the assumption that he would return as coach for the next season.

The Lakers kept winning, and winning, and winning. It was a finely-balanced team, with no real weaknesses and one great strength: shooting. The Lakers set an NBA record with a team shooting percentage of .537.

And, of course, they had the superstar, Kareem Abdul-Jabbar, finally living up to his reputation as potentially the best big man ever to play the game.

Finally? Kareem could insist, with considerable logic, that he was playing no better than he always had. It was the team that was better and, thus, made him look better.

After the auspicious beginning of his pro career—an NBA championship in his second season—Kareem's professional life had been marked by disappointment and his personal life by tragedy.

In 1973, seven members of a group called the Hanafi—with which Kareem had been affiliated after his conversion to the Muslim religion—were murdered in a Washington, D.C., house that had been bought for them by Jabbar.

Because Kareem was thought to be a target, too (it was believed the murder had been committed by rival Black Muslims), he was accompanied by a bodyguard for several weeks.

In 1977, the Hanafi group, led by Jabbar's Muslim mentor, Khalifa Hamaass Abdul Khaalis, invaded three Washington, D.C., buildings, including the national headquarters of B'nai B'rith. They held 132 hostages for 38 hours; at the end, one was dead and seven were wounded. Khaalis was jailed, and members of the Jewish Defense League allegedly threatened to kidnap Jabbar.

Though Kareem was never physically harmed as a result of these events, the mental trauma resulted in a series of migraine headaches, and the headaches also hit him when his marriage started breaking up.

Under the circumstances it was remarkable that Jabbar played so well so consistently, earning MVP awards in 1971, '72, '74, '76 and '77, equaling Bill Russell's total of five.

But his teams didn't win after that championship in Milwaukee, and Jabbar got the blame.

Because of their obvious physical advantage, much is expected of talented big men like Russell, Chamberlain, and Jabbar. Perhaps too much. Because he was surrounded by generally inferior talent, Jabbar could not carry his team to victory. So, while players were voting him the best in the league in five years, fans and press were calling him a disappointment.

Before the 1975-76 season the Bucks traded Jabbar to the Lakers for three young players, Dave Meyer, Brian Winters, and Junior Bridgeman. It was a trade forced on Milwaukee because Jabbar had announced that he wanted out.

Adrian Dantley fires against the Lakers as Kareem Abdul-Jabbar leaps to try to block the shot. Dantley became the NBA's leading scorer in the 1980-81 season. *(Utah Jazz)*

Jabbar had what he thought was his best year, averaging 27.7 points a game and leading the league with 16.9 rebounds and 4.12 blocked shots a game. But his team finished at 40-42.

In the 1976-77 season, the Lakers finished first but lost strong forward Kermit Washington and their best guard, Lucius Allen, before the playoffs. Portland beat the Lakers four straight.

"We were playing, more or less, with four guards and me," said Kareem to John Papanek in a *Sports Illustrated* article. "Don Ford was out-rebounded by Maurice Lucas something like 45-12. Yet everything written said that Walton had outplayed me. Walton played a great series. I played a great series. The TrailBlazers played a great series. The Lakers played a poor one."

Los Angeles fans blamed Jabbar for the team's failures. The press accused him of loafing. But in 1979-80, there was a miraculous turnaround.

Part of it was caused by Magic Johnson. "He creates things for us the way nobody ever has for this team," said Jabbar.

Johnson's personality also seemed to bring a spark into Kareem's play; Jabbar was playing with an emotion and joy that he had seldom demonstrated before.

Johnson also took the pressure off Jabbar. "Early in the season," said Westhead, "everything was Magic this and Magic that. People sort of forgot about Kareem. In a way that was good, because, before long, everybody realized that Magic or no Magic, this team is nothing without Kareem."

The Laker team was playing with a cohesiveness and unity it hadn't had in years. Kareem was having one of his best years, scoring nearly 25 points a game, leading the club in rebounds and blocking almost 3.5 shots a game—and demonstrating a passing ability he had seldom had the chance to use before.

The Los Angeles fans, heretofore known more for walking out on tie games with two minutes to play than for their basketball knowledge, were appreciative of the change in the team. No longer were they riding Jabbar.

One game more than any other showed the difference in Kareem—and in the fans—a mid-February contest against Houston. A migraine headache, brought on, some thought, by his pending divorce suit, forced Kareem to his bed.

The pain, he later said, was so bad he was crying. Naturally, he couldn't make it to The Forum for the start of the game, and he was not expected to play at all. The Lakers stayed barely ahead of Houston until midway through the third period.

Then, Jabbar suddenly appeared, and the fans gave him a standing ovation. He quickly blocked five Houston shots and hit six of the seven he took, and the Lakers won, 110-102.

"Bringing in Kareem is like wheeling out nuclear weapons," said Houston coach Del Harris.

Asked if Jabbar were better then Houston's Moses Malone, Rick Barry said, "What kind of ridiculous question is that? Kareem is probably the best athlete in the world."

In the context of the season, the game was meaningless; had the Lakers lost, it would have made no difference in the final standings.

Why, then, had Kareem bothered, with all the pain he was suffering? "These guys are my teammates," he said, "but they are also my friends. They needed me."

Jabbar continued to play well for the rest of the season, and the Lakers won their division with a 60-22 record; in the league, only Boston's 61-21 was better.

Once again, he was considered the best by those writing about the games. "I view that with total cynicism," he said of the change in attitude.

Of more importance was the fact that he won the MVP honor for the sixth time, more than any NBA player ever had. In all sports, only Gordie Howe had ever won six MVP awards in the same league. (Howe, in addition to his six NHL awards, also had won one MVP award in the WHA.)

Along with fellow divisional champions Milwaukee, Atlanta, and Boston, the

Lakers got a bye in the first round of the playoffs, and then easily handled Phoenix, 4-1, in the Western conference semifinals.

In the conference finals, the Lakers met the defending champion Seattle Super-Sonics. The Sonics had been the NBA's most consistently successful team over the past three seasons, winning one championship and finishing as the runnerup the season before.

But they were no longer the same team that had been so successful. Internal rivalries, centering around guard Dennis Johnson, had broken up the unity of the team. Johnson would be traded for Phoenix's Paul Westphal in a blockbuster trade after the season.

The Sonics had enough left to edge the Lakers, 108-107, in the first game of the series at The Forum, but the Lakers then reeled off four straight wins to advance into the NBA championship series.

It had been assumed that the Lakers would meet Boston there, and it would have been an especially interesting matchup because of the star rookies, Magic Johnson for the Lakers and Larry Bird for the Celtics.

But the Celtics, after blanking Houston, 4-0, in the Eastern conference semifinals, were manhandled by the Philadelphia 76ers in the conference finals, 4-1. The 76ers, starting 6'11" Darryl Dawkins and Caldwell Jones and coming in with 6'10" Steve Mix and 6'9" Bobby Jones, had simply overpowered the smaller Celtics.

Ironically, the Celtics' general manager and former coach, Red Auerbach, had long preached the value of the big man. In the off-season he would move quickly to rectify his team's shortcomings, trading for seven-foot Robert Parish and drafting 6'11" Kevin McHale. But that was too late to save them in the 1980 playoffs.

The 76ers' size didn't scare the Lakers, though. The Lakers had the tallest man on the court in Jabbar, a 6'11" strong forward in the underrated Jim Chones, and the largest guard in history in Johnson. In every game of the final series, the Lakers out-rebound the 76ers.

For the first five games Jabbar was dominant, averaging 33.4 points a game.

In the first game, he scored 33 points, got 14 rebounds, blocked six shots, and passed off for five baskets. He thoroughly intimidated Dawkins, who played listlessly before fouling out after only playing 18 minutes. The Lakers won, 109-102.

Jabbar got 38 points and another 14 rebounds in the second game, but this time Dawkins, over his first-game jitters, got 25 and Julius Erving and Maurice Cheeks each chipped in 23, as the 76ers evened the series at one apiece.

For the third game the series shifted to Philadelphia, but it made no difference to Jabbar, who got 33 points, another 14 rebounds, and blocked four more shots to lead the Lakers to a 111-101 win. But in the fourth game, Jabbar slipped to 23 points and 11 rebounds. Dawkins got 26, and the 76ers won, 105-102, to even the series, which returned to Los Angeles for the fifth game.

In the fifth game, the Lakers were holding a narrow edge when Jabbar twisted his ankle badly with three minutes and 58 seconds remaining in the fourth quarter. The Laker fans moaned as he was helped off the court and into the dressing room.

Surprisingly, the Lakers were able to extend their lead while Kareem was out of the game. As often happens when a star leaves the game, the other team got anxious. The 76ers tried to exploit Jabbar's loss and wound up pressing, forcing shots and passes. The Lakers moved to an 81-73 lead after three quarters.

Nobody thought they could hold that lead without Jabbar, though, and when he came back out of the dressing room and limped back onto the court early in the fourth quarter, the fans in The Forum went wild.

Jabbar seemed hardly able to move on his bad ankle, but his pride drove him on to a fantastic display. He scored 14 of his team's 27 points in the fourth quarter—finishing with a game and series high of 40 points—and the Lakers pulled it out, 108-103.

After the game, though, the Lakers' celebration was muted because it was feared their big man wouldn't be able to play until the next season.

Kareem Abdul-Jabbar re-affirmed his dominance as the Lakers won a championship. *(Los Angeles Lakers)*

Jamaal Wilkes, coming from behind the basket to score against San Antonio, was so smooth a player that his contributions were often underrated.
(*Los Angeles Lakers*)

At first, it was thought Kareem's ankle might be broken, but X-rays showed that it was merely a bad sprain. That was no real consolation; sprains can be a long time healing, especially one as bad as he had suffered.

Jabbar would stay behind in Los Angeles for treatment while his teammates went to Philadelphia for the sixth game. Everybody conceded that game to the 76ers, of course, and Laker fans could only hope that Jabbar would be recovered enough to play in the seventh game on Sunday afternoon.

What followed was one of the most amazing games in NBA playoff history. The Lakers baffled and shocked the 76ers, not only winning but maintaining control of the game all the way. By the end, they were breezing.

With Jabbar out, it had been expected that Westhead would go with Chones at center because Chones had played most of his career at that position. Instead, Westhead put Magic Johnson there. It was an inspired decision.

With Magic in the pivot the Lakers changed their style, running more and using fewer set plays off the center, perhaps no more than half a dozen. "Magic is pretty observant," said Westhead. "He knows what everybody else is supposed to be doing."

Without Kareem, Magic decided, "I'd take things into my own hands. I got the green light to do *my* thing." That meant doing everything, and doing it well.

There was no aspect of the game he didn't dominate. He whirled, jumped, and moved for 42 points, high for the game and the series, shooting 14 of 23 from the floor and a perfect 14-for-14 from the free-throw line. Not bad for a player who wasn't supposed to be a good shooter, remember?

He got a game-high 15 rebounds (as he and Jabbar had both done, incidentally, in the fifth game). He dished out seven assists.

Magic wasn't the only Laker who turned it on. Forward Jamaal Wilkes decided that, to help compensate for the loss of Jabbar's points, "I was going to shoot until my arm fell off." Wilkes had had problems with his shooting earlier in the series, but he hit a career-high 37 points in this game, 16 of them in the third quarter, when the Lakers scored 33 points.

But it was really Magic's game. He completely befuddled the 76ers, and he inspired his teammates to play at an emotional level that pros seldom reach.

"It's hard to put a label on what he does, but he's a monster of a player," said the disappointed Erving after the game. "He keeps coming at you. It's really hard to imagine what he'll be like once he gets a couple of years under his belt."

The Lakers came out firing, to a 7-0 lead on two Wilkes' jumpers and a three-point play by Chones.

"If we had jumped out early, it would have been a different story," said Erving, who scored 27 points, "but we were just pussyfooting around."

The 76ers did come back to go ahead, 16-15, as Erving scored four baskets, but it was 32-29 Lakers at the quarter. At the half, it was 60-60, but the Lakers stormed to a 93-83 lead at the end of three quarters.

Philadelphia wasn't dead yet. Playing their best stretch of defense during the game, they crept to within two points, at 97-95, on a Bobby Jones' tip-in with seven minutes to go. With five minutes left the Lakers still held on to that two-point margin, 103-101.

In a Los Angeles hospital bed, Jabbar was watching on television, more nervous by far than if he'd been playing. With the Lakers' lead at two, "That was very serious nervous time," he said. "I think that's when I started biting the pillow."

The Lakers quickly relaxed Jabbar and all their fans. A Johnson tip-in and a Wilkes' three-point play off a drive pushed the lead to seven points. Then, Norm Nixon stole an Erving pass at midcourt and fed Magic for the basket. Fouled by Erving on the play, Johnson converted the free throw to make it 111-103 with just 2:22 left, and the Lakers were on their way to the 123-107 final.

"Everybody thought we were going to roll over," said Magic after the game. "Everybody thought we were going to fade. We didn't. We fooled all y'all."

For his efforts Johnson was named the MVP of the series. Losing, he said, had never crossed his mind. "I knew we were going to win, because I've always won."

Indeed he had. Three years before, it had been the Michigan state high school championship. One year before, he had carried Michigan State to the NCAA title. Now, he had led the Lakers to the NBA championship. The basketball world was his, and he was only 20.

Inevitably, Magic's great performance led many to say and write that he, not Larry Bird, should have been Rookie of the Year. That only proved how important it is to have the voting on regular season awards done before votes can be influenced by the emotion of postseason play.

On the record, Bird had had a better rookie season. He deserved the award he had gotten. But it was becoming clear that Magic was improving at a much more dramatic rate than Bird. The Celtics' rookie was a very good, solid player, but Magic . . . well, Magic could do things nobody else had ever done.

One man could not share in the Lakers' happiness—Jack McKinney, who had started the season as the Lakers' coach but was fired during the final playoff series. As usual in this kind of situation, there are two versions of what happened, the one by McKinney and the one by club owner Jerry Buss.

McKinney says that when he first proposed that he return to coach the Lakers in late January, Buss said he wanted to wait a little longer—but that the understanding was that McKinney would return sometime during the season.

By mid-February, the team was playing very well, obviously on its way to the playoffs. McKinney and Buss met again. "We decided it wouldn't be a good time to make a change," said McKinney in an interview with Richard O'Connor for *Sports Illustrated*. "Personally, I felt it would be unfair to both Paul and the players. So, the plan was that I could continue scouting, and after the season, Paul and I would go away and resolve the situation."

After the fourth game of the championship series, McKinney had returned from Philadelphia to meet his wife in Portland, where she had been visiting. They drove back to Los Angeles. On the way, says McKinney, he phoned home and was told by his son that the news on the radio was that he'd been fired. "So I'm out," said McKinney. "Just like that."

Buss's version is less dramatic. He contends that he had called McKinney and said he wanted to meet when McKinney returned from Philadelphia. "I guess some reporters must have asked him why, and he said, 'I think I'm getting fired.'

"Next thing you know, I'm deluged with calls: 'Is Jack McKinney getting fired?'

(left) Jack McKinney, talking during a timeout, started the 1979-80 season as head coach of the Lakers but was critically injured in an accident and wound up as coach of the Indiana Pacers for the next season. *(Indiana Pacers)*

(right) Paul Westhead, McKinney's best friend and hand-picked assistant, took over when McKinney was injured and coached the Lakers to a championship. *(Los Angeles Lakers)*

Now what could I say? Say no, and then 10 days later maybe fire Jack? I would have lost all credibility."

Immediately after the playoffs, Buss announced that Westhead was being signed to a four-year, $1.1 million contract, easily the most lucrative contract in NBA coaching history. (Ironically, Westhead was fired in November 1981.)

Buss probably could have handled the situation more tactfully, but it's hard to see how he could have made any other decision than the one he did. Though it may have been McKinney's team, Westhead had done an excellent job of coaching it to a championship, and he certainly deserved the chance to return.

The decision plunged McKinney into deep depression. Eventually, he was convinced that he was too young to give up on his career. In the bitter aftermath, McKinney would not talk to Buss, nor to Westhead, who had been his closest friend.

There was one final touch of irony: McKinney got back into NBA coaching by accepting an offer with the Indiana Pacers, owned by Sam Nassi, a friend and business associate of Buss. A coincidence? Nassi insisted Buss had had nothing to do with it, but few believed that, which was a fitting end to a year nobody believed.

22. Order on the Court: The Little Men Whose Word Is Law

On playgrounds and in gyms all over the country, basketball players choose up sides and play the game without referees. Fouls are called by the players, and the fouled team gets the ball out of bounds.

There are those in the NBA who sometimes wish their game was that simple. It is not, of course. In the NBA, referees are not only required; they are a very important part of the game.

Night after night, fans walk out of arenas muttering that the game was decided by the referees, and the fans are often right.

It is safe to say that calls made by NBA referees decide far more games than those made by NFL officials or umpires in the American and National baseball leagues. Disputed calls which decide games are so rare in both football and baseball that they rate headlines. In the NBA they are routine, and not because the officiating is worse. The nature of the game makes it inevitable.

Many NBA games are so close that one critical call can swing a game. Even in lopsided contexts, a call early, when the score is close, can affect the momentum of the game.

The one problem which has never been fully solved in basketball is to define exactly what a foul is and how much a player and a team should be penalized for fouling.

For instance, if you watch a college and a pro game on consecutive nights, you will see a great difference in interpretation of fouls. College officials are much quicker to call fouls because of body contact; in the pros, refs tend to allow a lot on contact if it doesn't seem to affect the play. That's one important reason why few officials work both pro and college games.

For both colleges and pros, rules changes have been frequent. One primary concern has been how to penalize a team which fouls more frequently than the other team. In college, when a team has more than six defensive fouls in a half (offensive fouls are not counted in the team total in this category), the other team is in a "bonus" situation, and gets an extra free throw. In the NBA, that situation is created with a team's fifth defensive foul in a quarter.

But even then, college and pro rulemakers differ on how the rule is administered. In college, a player in a bonus situation gets one-and-one; if he makes the first shot, he gets an additional one.

The pros decided (correctly, I think) that this can actually penalize the fouled team, because a player could (and often does) miss the first shot, and his team loses the ball because the defending (fouling) team gets the rebound. So, in the NBA, a player gets one *plus* a penalty, which means that he gets two shots even if he misses the first. In the case of a shooting foul, he gets three shots to make two points; if he makes the first two shots, of course, he doesn't get the third.

Early critics of the game said it was a parade from one foul line to the other. NBA rulemakers have tried to eliminate some of that by ruling that nonshooting fouls result only in the fouled team getting the ball out of bounds, until the seventh team foul of a quarter, and that offensive fouls never result in free throws.

That has speeded up the game, but free-throw shooting is still a very important part of the game. It is not at all uncommon in the NBA for one team to score more field goals, yet lose, because the other team scored more free throws.

The various rules changes have been made to try to eliminate the possibility that a team can gain an advantage in fouling. But there are still times when a team will deliberately foul. For instance, coaches will sometimes tell their teams to "take a foul" in the closing seconds of a quarter; if the defensive team is not over its foul limit for the quarter, it can then force the offensive team to use up valuable time in taking the ball out of bounds, instead of driving to the basket.

Calvin Murphy, shooting a jump shot against the Lakers' Michael Cooper, was thought too small at 5′ 10″, but he continued shooting over bigger men, and in the 1980-81 season, he set an NBA record by hitting 78 consecutive free throws. (Houston Rockets)

Some players, too, virtually invite fouls because of their weakness in free-throw shooting. It was foolish, for instance, to let Wilt Chamberlain have an unobstructed shot at a field goal which he would probably make; fouled, he might very well miss both free throws.

One other aspect of basketball fouls is paramount: the player limit. After six fouls, a player is out of an NBA game.

Some sort of limit on fouls is necessary; otherwise, the game would be much rougher than it is. But having a limit also affects the outcome of a game, and not only because a player may have to leave. If a player picks up his third foul early in the second quarter, for instance, a coach will take him out for the rest of the half; if he picks up his fourth early in the third quarter, he will usually be taken out for the rest of that quarter. Thus, even if a player doesn't foul out, his playing time can be severely restricted, which punishes his team.

Again, Chamberlain figures in this, in a perverse way. It was one of Wilt's proudest boasts that he never fouled out of a game. But there were many games in which he played cautiously once he got his fifth foul, which meant that he was not the force he would normally be. There are also many games in which he committed what would otherwise have been his sixth foul—but no referee wanted to be the first to foul out Wilt Chamberlain.

The problems of officiating in pro basketball will probably never be solved. Indeed, they have even been getting worse. Here are what seem to be the most serious problems:

Body contact. Officially, basketball is a noncontact sport, but nobody who has ever sat behind the basket at a pro game would ever believe that. There is an incredible amount of contact and collision under the boards, and there is lesser contact elsewhere on the floor.

Obviously, the referees cannot call a foul every time two players bump. The whistles would be going so frequently it would sound like a parakeet convention, and the game would be ruined.

So, what do you call? The NBA philosophy has generally been to call only those fouls which affect the play. Officially, that's known as "no harm, no foul." The cynical amend that to "no blood, no foul."

Sometimes, the NBA will crack down for a time on specific types of fouls. One such example is the practice of "hand-checking" by defensive players, who put a hand on their offensive man to keep him from getting away. This practice, annoying to the offensive player, can cause flareups later in the game. So, periodically, the NBA will instruct its referees to call fouls for hand-checking. The practice will cease for 2 to 3 weeks, at which time officials will forget about it and everybody goes back to hand-checking, just as before.

Speed. The big speedup in the game, of course, came with the installation of the

24-second clock. But even since then the game has been getting faster and faster because the players are much better athletes.

"I think it's a much tougher game to officiate now than it used to be," says Norm Drucker, NBA supervisor of officials, who officiated at pro basketball games from 1953 to 1977. "The game used to be more physical; now it's faster, and it's harder to see what is happening."

Size. NBA players are so tall and jump so well that much of the game is played at or above the level of the rim. An official is several feet below. From his perspective, it becomes extremely difficult to make goal-tending calls, for instance.

Movement. The difficulty in officiating varies in direct relationship to the movement of the game. Baseball, for instance, is the easiest game to officiate in because the umpire can set himself in anticipation of almost every call he makes. The home-plate umpire, for instance, is in position for every pitch; a first-base umpire is right by the bag to make the call on the runner.

Football is somewhat more difficult, though many calls (such as offsides) are made by an official who is set in position for the call. It is significant that the controversial calls in football are usually those on which an official is moving and cannot anticipate, as in pass-interference penalties.

John Havlicek, showing the determination that marked his great career, goes after a loose ball as referee Darrell Garretson watches. *(Boston Celtics)*

In basketball, the referee is always moving, and he can almost never anticipate what is going to happen. (Indeed, an official who tries to anticipate always gets himself in big trouble, because he will think he sees something which doesn't happen.) The basketball official has to be prepared for almost anything to happen, and he has to watch several things at once, including such things as whether the player with the ball is traveling and whether an offensive player is in the lane more than three seconds—in addition to determining which of ten players may be doing something which should be called a foul.

Crowd intimidation. Because basketball is played in a closed arena with fans sitting as close as a few feet from the sidelines, fans are much more a part of the game.

NBA fans are the most knowledgeable of any following the major sports. Certainly, they are among the most vocal, constantly advising refs that they are blowing calls that should be made for the home team.

Occasionally, refs will get irritated enough to talk back to fans, which is a serious mistake. Usually, the fans only mutter under their breaths as they approach the scorer's table during a time out.

If it stopped there it would be all right, but it often gets uglier, especially in the important games. Officials may have to be escorted in and out of an arena by police, to keep irate fans away. In one playoff game, for instance, a fan came running onto the court, abusing referee Richie Powers. He picked the wrong man. The combative Powers belted him.

Some officials are bothered more by home town fans than others. Consciously or unconsciously, these referees become "homers." The close call always goes to the home team, and that's one important reason why teams win so much more frequently at home than on the road in the NBA.

But at least one other official has gone the other way. Through the years, visiting teams were very happy to walk on the floor and find Earl Strom as one of the officials. Strom was known as a referee who would defy the home crowd; if there were any question which way a call should go, he allegedly would always make it for the visiting team.

Coach and player intimidation. Coaches in the NBA spend much of their time stalking up and down the sidelines, yelling abuse at referees. It is a typical sight in the NBA to see a referee point to a coach and signal a technical foul. Technicals result in free throws for the other team, of course, and sometimes in the ejection of a coach, but coaches often feel the risk of a technical foul is less important than the chance that a referee might be coerced into making a critical call in favor of the coach's team.

Coaches, at least, are some distance from the officials, and only some of them are big enough to be physically intimidating. Players can be much more intimidating because they are on court, towering over an official. A referee certainly has to be concerned about that, though the best ones train themselves to ignore it.

The distressing fact is that some of the best players in the NBA over the years have been official-baiters. Rick Barry is one example. It's probably fair to say that Barry was never whistled for a foul which he admitted to; conversely, there were thousands of times when Barry whined, begged, and howled about calls he didn't get.

One San Francisco television station trained its cameras on Barry for part of a game and came up with a three-minute segment which did nothing but show Barry grimacing, clutching his hair, and gesticulating wildly about calls (and non-calls) to which he objected.

Barry's routine got so far out of hand that it actually worked to his disadvantage. Though it is axiomatic in the NBA that the superstars get the benefit of the doubt on foul calls, Barry found late in his career that he was fouled repeatedly without getting a call; since he was the best free-throw shooter in the game, that was critical to both him and the team he was playing for. There is no doubt that officials were determined not to give him anything. On an objective basis, that is not good officiating; on the human level, I can neither blame the officials nor sympathize with Barry.

Another superstar who detracted from his reputation with his referee-baiting was Oscar Robertson. Like Barry, Oscar spent much of his time complaining about calls and trying to coerce officials. Al Attles, who is otherwise an extravagant admirer of Robertson's, remembers one of the worst examples.

"We [Warriors] were playing Cincinnati," says Attles, "in one of the very early nationally televised games.

"For some reason I don't remember, the telecast didn't actually pick up the game until we had played about five minutes. In the first couple of minutes of the game, Oscar had said something that got him a technical. Well, once the game came on TV, he cursed the officials and complained for the whole game. I never saw such abuse. But he knew they wouldn't dare give him another technical and eject him from the game, because he was the big star and they needed him on television."

In recent years, the NBA has taken significant steps both to upgrade the quality of officiating and the support the officials get, both of which are important. No sport can be taken seriously unless its officials get backing from the league, and in any sport, officials command more respect from players, coaches, and fans when there is a constant effort to improve the quality of the officiating.

During the 1978-79 season there was an experiment with three referees that seemed to work out well. Before it was implemented, some feared that having a third official would mean more fouls, but in fact, there was no significant difference in the amount of fouls called.

Having a third official cut down on the amount of territory each one had to cover. That particularly helped weaker officials. The one disadvantage seemed to be that the lead official had less responsibility, and the lead officials seemed reluctant to overrule bad calls by other members of the crew. But that seems to be a problem that could be worked out.

The experiment was discontinued after one year because of the cost, but even when it was dropped, there was considerable sentiment to retain the three-referee program. It seems almost certain that three refs will be a standard for future NBA games.

Meanwhile, the program for selecting NBA referees has become much more organized, and the standards more consistent than they were in the early years of the league.

The NBA runs a summer camp for men who want to become NBA officials. In rare cases, these officials go directly into the NBA. Usually, they are assigned to the Continental Basketball League, which serves as a training ground for officials just as it does for players. An official who looks good in the CBL is brought up to the NBA when there is an opening.

What is the NBA looking for in a referee?

"We're looking for very fine judgment," says Drucker, "and a man who is in good physical shape, so he can take the rigors of pro basketball.

"We also do psychological testing now, because a referee needs a certain kind of makeup. He must have drive, have a good reaction to stress, and emotional stability."

Once in the league, referees are observed by representatives of the NBA office. The observers never announce their presence in advance, and the notes they take can determine what games the officials at that particular game will work in the future, and even if they will work in the NBA in the future. At the end of each season, Drucker and his assistants evaluate all officials, and sometimes officials are not rehired because their work has not been up to standard.

Early in the NBA's history, referees were part-time workers, with full-time jobs elsewhere. Now, says Drucker, they are all full-time during the NBA season, though some men work at other jobs in the off-season. The difference between then and now is money: NBA officials now earn between $25,000 and $60,000 a season, depending on length of service and the number of games worked.

"The more experienced officials usually work a full 82-game schedule," says Drucker. "Some of our younger ones will only work 62 games. Too much exposure can ruin a young referee."

This standardized system would have amazed the referees from the early days of the NBA, when the game and the structure of the league were much more haphazard.

The most famous of the early referees was Pat Kennedy, who worked on every level, from high school up through the pros. In his way, he helped legitimitize the NBA, because he was the first well-known referee to move from the college game to the pros.

Kennedy was a highly competent referee from the technical standpoint, but

Pat Kennedy was the first flamboyant referee in the NBA, setting a pattern for others to follow. *(Hall of Fame)*

what made him famous was his showmanship. When he called a foul, he would sprint over to the offender and scream at him: "No-o-o-o, no-o-o-o-o, no-o-o-o!" Sometimes, he would even shout, "I caught you this time!"

Flamboyant is probably too mild a word to describe Kennedy. He never simply called a foul. He would leap, spin, point, and use whatever other forms of body language he thought of. He even had different styles with his whistle, sometimes blowing long blasts, and other times a series of staccato bursts.

He became almost a bigger show than the players, and his appearance often brought forth additional newspaper columns or mentions on radio and, at the very end of his career, TV. All of that helped attract additional fans to a sport which was still struggling.

Kennedy ended his career traveling with the Harlem Globetrotters and burlesquing his style (and, not incidentally, earning more money than he had as a serious referee). But his contribution to the NBA was a considerable and lasting one.

Sid Borgia was another referee from the early days who was known as a strong personality. Borgia was a very decisive referee who never backed down on a call. Predictably, when those calls went against the home team, neither fans nor players nor writers liked it. The headline SID BORGIA DOES IT AGAIN was seen more than once over a story of a losing game.

But Borgia, and his colleagues, had to be firm. In those days, particularly, officiating could be a nasty business. Though the crowds weren't quite so unruly as those in the early part of the century (when games were literally played in a cage), they were much less disciplined than the crowds of today. That was especially true in the smaller cities, where fans tended to be more involved with their teams.

"It was an entirely different game when I worked," said Borgia. "There was no money in it and you had to be hungry and crazy to do it.

"Fans who came to a game took a personal dislike to any referee. In the smaller towns, they considered their teams their personal babies."

Some nights were worse than others. Borgia remembered one in Syracuse when he and John Nucatola (later to be the supervisor of officials just before Drucker) officiated a game between the Nets and the New York Knicks.

Six policemen had to escort Borgia and Nucatola to the dressing room after the Nets had lost, to protect the referees from irate fans. The refs stayed there until the fans cleared out of the arena, and then police took them directly to the train station. They didn't even dare return to the hotel to get their clothes!

Another time, again in Syracuse, a fan questioned Borgia's courage, which was stupid if nothing else; courage was something Borgia, and all the early refs, had to have in abundance. When Borgia yelled back, the fan came out of the stands. Borgia hit him, and the fan eventually sued; the $35,000 case was settled out of court for $500, Borgia said later.

The trend in recent years has been to less colorful officials. "We've taken the view that people come to see the game, not the officials," says Drucker. "Basketball officials come to be known, anyway."

Especially if the home team loses.

Bob Leonard of the Indiana Pacers showed what emotions a coach goes through. *(Indiana Pacers)*

23. What a Difference a Coach Makes

Critics of pro basketball often say that, because of the 24-second clock, it really makes little or no difference who coaches the teams because the strategy is all the same: one-on-one.

It is true that the strategic potential is more limited in the NBA than in collegiate ball. Teams cannot stall or go into the four-corners offense (for which some of us say: Hallelujah!).

Theoretically, NBA teams cannot play zone defense, though it is difficult to tell the difference between the collapsing and switching man-to-man defenses used in the NBA and a straight zone defense; and a center like Kareem Abdul-Jabbar plays so close to the defensive basket at all times that a three-foot string attached between Jabbar and the basket would never be broken.

It is also true that there are owners—though fewer in number than they used to be—who regard coaches as expendable, like a Kleenex.

But coaches do make a difference; Lenny Wilkens turned the Seattle franchise from an also-ran into a champion, for instance. And there is often a considerable difference in the style of teams, even within the tight framework of the 24-second clock.

A Dick Motta-coached team, for instance, bears little resemblance to those coached by Red Auerbach disciples. When John Macleod came to the Phoenix Suns, he brought with him a collegiate style which featured a lot of ball movement.

Dick Motta, one of the first college coaches to become successful in the pros, won a championship in Washington and then went on to the expansion Dallas Mavericks. *(Dallas Mavericks)*

At a time when other coaches were relying on 7 or 8 players, Al Attles won a championship with the Golden State Warriors by using the talents of 11 players; only the twelfth player, Steve Bracey, saw limited action. Attles resolutely talked in terms of playing time, not starting, and there were many times when reserves got more time in a game than the starters. Two reserves—shot-blocking center George Johnson and guard Phil Smith, who played great defense as well as offense—were as valuable as the players starting ahead of them.

Some coaches, too, are winners wherever they go. Alex Hannum won NBA championships at St. Louis and Philadelphia, and an ABA championship at Oakland. Bill Sharman was a winner at San Francisco in the NBA, coached an ABA champion at Utah, and then jumped back to the NBA to coach a record-setting champion in Los Angeles.

Yes, coaches do make a difference.

Who has been the best coach in the NBA? There's not much argument there. Red Auerbach, who coached all but two of the Boston Celtics' teams that won 11 NBA championships in 13 years, was the choice of the media panel that selected the NBA's all-time bests at the thirty-fifth anniversary time, and that finding is supported by other coaches.

Auerbach's influence on the game is as important as his long winning streak. His emphasis on rebounding and the fast break, for instance, has been copied by most coaches since. A surprising number of former Celtics players have become coaches— Sharman, Tom Heinsohn, K. C. Jones, Bob Cousy, Bill Russell, Don Nelson.

Ironically, Auerbach had a lot of problems early in his career, some of his own making but most due to circumstances. In his first year with the Washington Caps, for instance, his team won 17 straight at the start of the season and won its division by 14 games. But in the first round of the playoffs, the Caps lost to the Chicago Stags.

"Red didn't know how to substitute in those days," says Fred Scolari, a guard on that team. "He played the starters so long, we were all exhausted by the end of the season."

At Boston, Auerbach put in his fast break, but he lacked the rebounding he needed to make that strategy most effective. The Celtics scored a lot of points, but too often they gave up more. "It was common knowledge around the league that he was on the verge of getting fired before he got Russell," says Hannum.

Fortunately for Auerbach, he got Russell. And fortunately for the rest of us, too, because those great Celtic teams live on in the memory.

It's difficult to get Auerbach to talk about his coaching methods; having spent a lifetime building a reputation for rudeness, he is reluctant to blow it. But those who have played for or coached against him say there is no particular secret to his success.

"He was really a stickler on physical conditioning," notes Sharman. "When he was coaching, there was no restriction (as there is now) on when veterans could report, and we would be there 7 or 8 weeks before the season started.

(above) Red Auerback, with the inevitable victory cigar, is generally regarded as the NBA's top coach of all time. *(Boston Celtics)*

(left) Lenny Wilkens changed the Sonics from a 5-17 team into a championship one. *(Seattle SuperSonics)*

"Then we'd play 18 to 20 exhibitions, and when the season started, we were really in mid-season shape.

"He really advocated the fast break, even before Bill Russell was there, but he didn't believe in a lot of set plays." (So limited, in fact, that one time when Auerbach was coaching an all-star team on tour, Oscar Robertson called out the Celtic plays by number.)

"Red was not a good individual teacher because he didn't have the background. He didn't give us much individual instruction for that reason.

"But he was a very good psychologist. You know, when you play 100 games a season, it's awfully difficult to think of something (as a coach) to say before about the ninetieth game. But Red was always able to make a game special."

Sharman adds that Auerbach became very good at what had been his weakness— making substitutions. "He's very intelligent and he studied the game, so he knew just when to make changes."

Russell, in *Second Wind,* remembered that Auerbach was so dedicated to winning that he made it very uncomfortable to be around him when the team didn't win.

One thing that bothered Russell as a player, though, was the way Auerbach yelled, seemingly indiscriminately, at two players, Satch Sanders and Don Nelson.

When Russell succeeded Auerbach as coach of the Celtics he was determined that he wouldn't yell at Sanders and Nelson without cause, and for a long time, he didn't. Then he noticed that Sanders and Nelson didn't seem to be playing very well; for long periods of time they would contribute so little they were almost invisible on the court.

Finally, wrote Russell, he realized what Auerbach had been doing. "Then it dawned on me that it didn't matter so much why I yelled at Satch and Nelson; I just had to do it regularly, at certain intervals, the way you take vitamin pills. . . . I found myself thinking, 'Okay, it's seven-twenty. Time to yell at Satch and Nelson.' "

With that, Russell realized what a great motivator Auerbach had been. Red had known exactly which players needed to be bullied and which encouraged, and those who needed to be left alone. He had been solicitous of those on the bench because they weren't getting the attention from fans and media that the starters were.

It is easy to underestimate the value of a coach like Auerbach to a team like the Celtics. Certainly, the Celtics had great talent: At one point, for instance, Cousy, Sharman, Sam Jones, and K. C. Jones were all available for the backcourt.

But it takes the right kind of coach to get the most out of that kind of talent. Auerbach was especially good in that he impressed on each player the importance of playing his role: Russell was the defender and rebounder, for instance, Cousy the playmaker, Sharman and Sam Jones the shooters. If each did his job the team would win.

Even more remarkable was the selling job Auerbach did on players like Frank Ramsey and John Havlicek—and on the media, too. There were times when lesser players were starting ahead of Ramsey and Havlicek, but those two men never complained because Auerbach made them realize how important they were coming off the bench as the "sixth man."

And like Frank Sinatra, Auerbach did it his own way. He often seemed arrogant in his dealings with others, including his trademark of a "victory cigar" that he would light on the bench when the game was safely won. He seemed to take special delight in rubbing it in against Fred Schaus, the Laker coach at a period when the Celtics so often beat the Lakers in the NBA finals.

But there is more to the coach than that, as Hannum learned during one of the bleakest periods of his life. "That year in San Francisco when we had traded Wilt and won only 17 games," says Alex, "the Celtics came to town and, of course, beat us. After the game, Red made a point of coming over to me and telling me not to get my dauber down, that better times were ahead. He had sympathy for me in that position, and I always appreciated that."

All good coaches have one thing in common: They know how to motivate players. Beyond that, their methods often differ. Here, in their own words, are some explanations of coaching philosophies.

Bill Sharman followed his playing success by becoming a championship coach in two pro leagues. *(Los Angeles Lakers)*

Bill Sharman:

I've always felt a coach and his players have to be very dedicated. It's important to work hard to get physical conditioning, and it's equally important to have the right mental approach. I always wanted to be prepared for any situation, because I've found that the more you work at it, the luckier you get.

My thoughts on physical conditioning came a lot from Auerbach, of course. I feel that a basketball player has to be in better shape than anybody, besides boxers—and even a boxer only has to prepare for 4 or 5 fights a year. A basketball player has to play for six months.

Conditioning affects everything a player does—running, jumping, quickness, and, especially, shooting. When a player is tired, that's when he loses his shooting touch.

I've never had too many plays. There aren't many secret plays in basketball. If somebody comes up with a backdoor play that's successful, every coach steals it.

I believe in looking first for the fast break; that's another thing I got from Red Auerbach. The fast break is the most productive type of offense. There are times when you don't want to fast-break—if the other team is much better, you might not want them to have the ball too much—but generally, the fast break comes first.

It's very important to know how to motivate players. When I was coaching the Warriors, for instance, I never had to say anything to get Rick Barry up. If anything, he was almost too charged up, so I'd try to calm him down a little. Other guys were more lackadaisical, so I'd have to work on them. Other guys might respond better if you gave them specific responsibilities.

Alex Hannum

I always felt I had the best possible background for coaching because I had been exposed to different styles.

I was born and raised on the West Coast, and I went to college at USC where Sam Barry coached the slow-down game with a lot of set plays. Sam never went to the fast break.

When I played pro ball, at Syracuse and Rochester, I was on teams which were dominated by the East Coast give-and-go philosophy, playing with guys like Al Cervi, Bob Davies, Bobby Wanzer, and Red Holzman.

That was a guard-dominated game. They could shoot two-handed set shots from outside, and they were deadly from out there. If you let them shoot, they'd hit 50 to 60 percent, so, of course, you couldn't let them shoot.

That was the basis of their game. It all started from the outside. The threat of their shooting would draw the defense out, and then they'd work the give-and-go to get shots inside. That was directly contrary to what I'd been taught before.

And, of course, I was exposed to fast-break basketball, especially in my later years in the pros.

When I started coaching, my style was a combination of these three things. I used the give-and-go, and there was a lot of the Sam Barry influence, too. For instance, I had a double-pick down low that was a direct steal from Sam.

But I differed from Sam in that I believed in running, too. If you don't run, I think you're throwing away two-thirds of your potential offense.

Red Holzman:

There never really was a time when I thought I'd be a coach. When you're young you always think you can play 40 years. It isn't until you're near the end of your career that you realize it isn't going to happen.

I studied basketball a lot when I was playing, and then, when I became a coach, I discovered I was dealing with an entirely different concept. I always thought of myself as a good team player, but I basically was concerned with what I was doing.

Red Holzman was a star player in the early years of the NBA and then became one of its most successful coaches. *(New York Knicks)*

When you're playing you're not thinking about 11 guys. When you start coaching, you have to be concerned with what everybody can do.

I've changed some in dealing with players, but it's mostly been because of the players. When I started coaching the Knicks, for instance, the team was way down and I had to emphasize discipline. After awhile, when the guys were veterans and team-minded, I didn't have to concern myself with that so much.

The Knicks' teams of the early '70s were a lot similar to the Rochester teams I played on, so that probably made it easier for me as a coach. We had a lot of guys with smarts. Plus, we had a lot of guys who could handle and pass the ball, which you don't always have. And they knew they had to play team ball, because there weren't many of them who could go off and do much on their own. That was the reason we were good.

The biggest difference I've noticed is that we have much more one-on-one today, and that's something I've had to adjust to. I think it's fine, if it's done within the team framework. It's exciting and certainly productive. The players have such great talent and shooting abilities, it's best to take advantage of them.

Coaching has changed a lot in the NBA in the last 15 or 20 years, and nothing is more reflective of the change than the way coaches are hired.

"Typically, in my day," says Holzman, "the coach would get fired during the season and the owner would go to the oldest player on the team and make him the player-coach. If he did well for the rest of the season, he'd be named the coach for the next season."

That was how Holzman got his first job. At the tail end of his playing career he was picked up by the then Milwaukee Hawks, owned by Ben Kerner. During the 1953-54 season, Kerner decided coach Fuzzy Levane wasn't his man, and elevated Holzman.

That was also how Holzman lost his first job. In 1957, with the Hawks struggling after a move to St. Louis, Kerner fired Holzman and moved up guard Slater Martin. But that didn't last long. After five games, Hannum took over.

"Slater never wanted to coach," says Hannum. "He agreed to only if I would figure out the strategy and make substitutions from the bench. We were rooming together at the time so it was no problem to work together.

"But after five games, Slater went to Kerner and told him he was quitting if he had to keep coaching. He intimidated Kerner and forced him to hire me. But I was the guy they least needed on the floor by then, so it was easy for them to move me up."

It wasn't always done that casually, but the general feeling in the NBA at that time was that coaches should be former NBA players—though the most successful of all, Auerbach, had never played in the league.

The watershed period was probably the 1955-56 season. At that time the nine coaches in the league were Auerbach and eight former players—Hannum, Dolph Schayes, Harry Gallatin, Paul Seymour, Jack McMahon, Fred Schaus, Richie Guerin, and Dave DeBusschere. With the Knicks, Gallatin was replaced in early season by Dick McGuire—another player.

The next year, when Schaus decided to concentrate on general manager duties at Los Angeles, he recommended that Princeton coach Butch van Breda Kolff be hired as coach. When van Breda Kolff took his team to a 52-30 season, a 15½-game improvement over the prior Laker season, it opened a few eyes.

"I had seen Bill's teams play and was very impressed," Schaus later told Bob Ryan of the *Boston Globe*. "He was a good teacher of fundamentals, and yet his teams were loose. He knew how to use his teams' strengths and cover up his weaknesses, which is a lot of what pro coaching is all about, in my opinion.

"The basic problem in the league as I saw it was that very talented players were coming into the league lacking fundamentals. It was evident that more teaching would have to be done, so the place to look was the colleges."

Nobody became more committed to the idea of hiring college coaches than Jerry Colangelo. While working for the Chicago Bulls, Colangelo "discovered" Dick Motta, then coaching Weber State. He recommended Motta highly to Dick Klein, the Chicago owner, and Klein eventually hired Motta.

By that time, Colangelo had become the general manager of the Phoenix franchise. In 1970, he hired Cotton Fitzsimmons out of the college ranks; in 1973, he hired John MacLeod from Oklahoma.

"My theory was that teaching was paramount," said Colangelo. "The game was going to get more sophisticated. But a lot of people in the NBA were resentful of the college people at first. They felt it was an intrusion on the fraternity."

More and more, owners and general managers agreed with Colangelo. By the 1980-81 season there were 14 former college coaches and only nine former NBA players coaching NBA teams, and even those nine often had former college coaches as assistants.

The change was inevitable because of a shift of emphasis on what the coaches needed. When there were few teams in the league, ex-players could reasonably be expected to know what most players in the league could or could not do. The most important part of a coach's job was relating to the players, and it was expected that an ex-player could do that better than anybody who had not played in the league.

But with the rapid expansion of the league, nobody could be expected to know every player. The unbalanced schedule made it possible in some cases for two teams to play each other once early in the season and again late in the season, by which time a lot of changes could be made.

So it was important that coaches be able to scout other teams and use more sophisticated information, such as films. NBA teams are now nearly as advanced in film techniques as NFL teams. Films are broken down so coaches can get tendencies, both of teams and individual players.

Probably the first to use film extensively was Sharman, when he was coaching the Warriors in the mid-'60s. He was convinced that films were the way to go, but he met with considerable resistance from some of his players.

"After awhile," he remembers, "when the lights were turned off, some players would close their eyes and doze off. They didn't think the films were important.

"Bill Bertka, my assistant and chief scout, and I talked over this problem, and Bertka came up with a solution: He spliced shots of nude Playboy bunnies in between the basketball action.

"That got the players' attention very quickly, and I felt we got much better results from the films after that."

Coaching has changed, too, because the players have changed, physically and emotionally.

Physically, players run much faster and jump much higher than they did in the early years of the league, and that has changed the entire concept of the game. Now, the game is played much of the time above the level of the basket and, as Hannum notes, there is no longer a need for players to work for two-on-one situations. Because of the jump shot, says Hannum, "a player knows he can come down one-on-five and get a shot off."

Rapidly escalating salaries and expansion of the NBA, which has created many more playing positions, have made players much more independent. The general atmosphere of the times, too, has made players more likely to question a coaching directive, which some coaches find hard to deal with.

And yet, the good coaches survive, whatever the conditions. If anybody would seem to be of the old school, for instance, it would be Red Holzman, the patriarch, whose playing and coaching careers have spanned the dramatically different eras in the NBA. But Red has had no trouble adjusting, and his Knicks are definitely on the rise.

What is his secret? Though he has had to change his approach toward much of the game, Holzman still believes in one thing: "If you treat everybody fairly, you'll be all right."

At bottom, that's what coaching is all about.

24. The Big Trade

Pro basketball teams have never been reluctant to trade star players. Wilt Chamberlain was traded twice, first by San Francisco and then by Philadelphia. Kareem Abdul-Jabbar went from Milwaukee to Los Angeles in his prime. Oscar Robertson moved from Cincinnati to Milwaukee, helping to bring a championship to the Bucks.

But typically, the big basketball trades have been forced. The star either wanted to leave (Jabbar, Robertson, and Chamberlain the second time) or the team trading him could no longer afford him (Chamberlain the first time). Usually, the trades have involved a star on one end and a bunch of lesser players and/or draft choices at the other.

That's why the Dennis Johnson for Paul Westphal trade before the start of the 1980-81 season was such a stunner. This time, a trade was star-for-star, and at the same position of guard. Neither team involved in the trade was looking to the future; each thought it was gaining something for the present in the trade. And though Johnson and Westphal played the same position, they were very different players: Westphal was a great shooter, Johnson a defensive specialist.

The background of the trade was fascinating, not least because the teams involved—Seattle and Phoenix—were both expansion teams which had traveled vastly different routes.

The Sonics had been formed for the 1967-68 season, which they finished in typical fashion for an expansion team: a record of 23-59. The Sonics gradually improved, to a high-water mark of 47-35 for the 1971-72 season; but the next season, they plunged to a 26-56 mark, hardly better than their first year.

Owner Sam Schulman was willing to try almost anything to bring a winner to Seattle. When Spencer Haywood decided, after starring in the 1968 Olympics, that he was ready to turn pro after his sophomore season, Schulman broke the NBA rule which prohibited signing players until their college class had graduated. When NBA commissioner J. Walter Kennedy tried to enforce the rule, Schulman took him to court, suing the entire NBA, to keep Haywood.

Then, for the 1973-74 season, Schulman brought in Bill Russell as the coach-general manager at a salary that, though undisclosed, was high enough to make Russell blink. After retiring as player-coach of the Boston Celtics, Russell had said he would never coach again, but Schulman's offer changed his mind.

Russell coached the Sonics for four years, but he was unable to bring the dramatic turnaround for which he and Schulman had both hoped. His second and third season were the best—both 43-39 and good for second place in the division. But in his fourth season, the Sonics slipped back to 40-42 for a fourth-place finish, and Russell and Schulman parted by mutual (dis)agreement. Overall, Russell's Sonics teams had lost four more games than they had won.

Bob Hopkins took over as coach at the start of the 1977-78 season, and the team seemed to be disintegrating: The Sonics won only five of their first 22 games.

At that point, Schulman realized something drastic had to be done, and he brought Lenny Wilkens back as a coach. Wilkens had coached the team for two years previously, when he was also a player, and had the 47-35 mark that was still the best in Seattle's history at that point. Then he had gone on to Portland as a player-coach for one season and then simply a coach for another.

Except for his second season at Seattle, Wilkens' coaching record had not been startling: He was 38-44 in his first season at Seattle, 38-44 and 37-45 in two seasons at Portland. But he was learning his trade, and he was ready to apply what he had learned when he took over for Hopkins.

He effected what could nearly be called a miracle. From the point he took over, the Sonics were a startling 42-18. Overall, their 47-35 record was good for third place in the division and a spot in the playoffs.

Wilkens did it by emphasizing the team aspect of basketball. Each player had his role. He got excellent rebounding out of Marvin Webster, Jack Sikma, and Paul Silas; Webster became an effective shot-blocker, earning the nickname "The Human Eraser," and Silas was as good as any defensive forward in the league.

In the backcourt, Johnson played superb defense and acted as the playmaker, leaving Gus Williams free to gamble for steals and to use his incredible speed for fast-break getaways.

With their combination of the Webster-Silas-Sikma rebounding and Williams' speed, the Sonics excelled at what coaches like to call the "transition game," turning defense into a fast-break offense instantly.

By the time the playoffs started, the Sonics were the hottest team in the league, and they sailed through three rounds of the playoffs. Los Angeles fell, 2-1, in the opening round; division champ Portland, whose 58-24 record had been the league's best in regular season play, was dispatched, 4-2, in the conference semifinals, and Denver fell by the same 4-2 result in the Western Conference finals.

It seemed the Sonics were going all the way when they took a 3-2 lead in the NBA championship series against a Washington Bullets team that had managed only a 44-38 record in regular season play and hardly seemed to belong in the finals.

But then Bullets' coach Dick Motta told everybody, "The opera isn't over until the fat lady sings." Nobody knew what Motta meant by that remark—the evidence

Lonnie Shelton was part of the compensation package awarded Seattle by NBA commissioner Larry O'Brien when Marvin Webster played out his option and went to New York. *(Seattle SuperSonics)*

suggests that Motta didn't know, either—but if he were suggesting that the result was not a foregone conclusion, he was exactly right.

The Bullets evened the series by a smashing 117-82 win at home and, though the final game was scheduled for Seattle before the Sonics' adoring fans, that loss seemed to take something out of the Sonics. In that final game, they bowed to the Bullets, 105-99.

No matter. The Sonics knew they'd be back, and indeed they were, the very next year.

But first, there was one big change in the lineup. Webster had played out his option and, unable to get what he wanted financially in Seattle, signed with the New York Knicks.

When the Sonics and Knicks were unable to come to agreement on compensation for Webster, NBA commissioner Larry O'Brien ruled that the Knicks would have to surrender power forward Lonnie Shelton and a first-round draft choice.

The course of events was disastrous for the Knicks, because Webster, away from the superior supporting cast he'd had in Seattle, proved to be no more than an average center in New York; he averaged only 11.3 points a game in 60 games. The next season, he missed all but 20 games because of injury.

To replace Webster, the Sonics made a deal with Denver for Tom LaGarde, who had backed up Dan Issel as a rookie the previous season. With LaGarde at center, the Sonics won 18 of their first 23 games.

Then LaGarde was injured, and Wilkens moved Sikma to the post. Sikma had played center in college and had originally been viewed as a center prospect for the pros, until he was moved to power forward. He had some expected problems returning to the pivot, but he played better and better as the season progressed, and the Sonics finished 52-30, to win in their division. With Sikma settling in at center and the muscular Shelton at power forward, there was no question that this was the best Sonics team yet.

Because they were division champions, the Sonics were able to bypass the first round of the playoffs, and then they blitzed Los Angeles, 4-1, in the conference semifinals. The conference finals were more difficult; they had to come back from a 3-2 deficit to win the final two games and down the Phoenix Suns.

Meanwhile, the Bullets had come through the Eastern half of the playoffs, beating Atlanta and San Antonio by the same 4-3 tally, and were once again poised to meet the Sonics in the championship series. It was logical to expect a Bullets' win, especially since the Bullets' season record of 54-28 had been the best in the league.

But this series was completely different from the previous year's. The Bullets won the first game, but then the Sonics swept through the next four for the title.

The key game was the fourth, which the Sonics won in overtime at Seattle, 114-112. Then, they closed out the series with a 97-93 win on the Bullets' home court, and there was no more talk of the fat lady.

Jack Sikma, driving for a basket against Detroit, became the center around which the great Seattle teams were built. *(Seattle SuperSonics)*

Sikma was a big factor in the Sonics' dominance, blocking 16 shots in the five games and sweeping the boards with ferocity. But the key to the Seattle win was Johnson.

Johnson had been an unknown when he was taken on in the second round of the 1976 college draft. He had played his college ball at Pepperdine, a small college in the Los Angeles area, and seemed to lack the shooting skills necessary for success in the NBA.

But nobody could question his defensive skills. Johnson's defensive ability kept him in the league and earned him recognition on the all-defensive NBA team by his second season.

For the NBA championship, Wilkens made a daring move, putting Johnson on Washington's smooth small forward, Bob Dandridge. Johnson gave away two inches in height (6'4" to 6'6") to Dandridge, but he had the quickness to stay with Dandridge and probably a touch more strength. Dandridge's quickness had been something the slower Seattle forwards had had trouble with the previous year, but Johnson markedly reduced his effectiveness in this series, enough to turn the balance of superiority from the Bullets to the Sonics.

Meanwhile, Johnson was also running the offense for Seattle, and he did his twin jobs so well that he was named the series Most Valuable Player. More important, he got the ultimate tribute: Teams started looking in the draft for a "Dennis Johnson-type guard."

Not since the Boston Celtic team of the 1968-69 season had a team repeated as NBA champion, but the Sonics seemed to be in an excellent position to break the string of one-time championships. The team was basically a young one, and it seemed it would improve for at least a couple of years before it started to decline.

And, indeed, the Sonics posted their best season record ever in the 1979-80 season, winning 56 and losing only 26. But that record was good only for second place behind the Lakers in the Pacific Division.

Worse, there were disquieting reports coming from the team. Players were complaining that Johnson was suddenly more interested in getting his own shots than in passing the ball. His assist total actually went up, from 280 to 332—but so did his shots, from 1110 to 1361. On the team, only Gus Williams took more shots, and Johnson's shooting percentage of .422 was the ninth-best on the team.

The Sonics battled their way through the first two rounds of the playoffs, but then bowed meekly to the Lakers, 4-1, in the Western Conference finals, winning only the first game.

The magic was gone, and Wilkens made it clear that he thought he knew why: Lenny called Johnson's attitude a "cancer" on the club. It was obvious Johnson would have to be traded.

At the same time, Phoenix was ready to trade Westphal, partly because Westphal himself wanted out and partly because the Suns' management had decided they wanted to change the makeup of the team.

The Suns had been one of the solid teams in the league, finishing with records of 49-33, 50-32, and 55-27 for the last three seasons.

Westphal had been a very important part of that success. Since coming to Phoenix in a trade with Boston for Charlie Scott (one that Red Auerbach would like to forget), Paul had been a consistent scoring machine, averaging more than 20 points a game for his five seasons in Phoenix.

When he had come out of college, Westphal had been compared by some to Jerry West. Offensively, he was close. He has an excellent shooting touch (overall, in his five seasons with the Suns, he hit on more than 50 percent of his field goal attempts), and a variety of moves to get open.

West, though, played superlative defense. Westphal at times hardly seems to play any defense at all, leaving his man early to get the jump on the fast break.

Nonetheless, because of his offensive ability, Westphal had been valuable to the Suns and had made his mark on the All-Star team. But he was chafing at Phoenix coach John MacLeod's system of limiting time played. He had averaged only slightly more than 30 minutes a game (Johnson, by comparison, had logged almost 300 more playing minutes in the 1979-80 season), and he felt his effectiveness was limited by his relative lack of playing time.

At the same time, the Suns wanted to make their team stronger. With a slender 6'9" center, Alvan Adams, a non-rebounding forward in Walter Davis, and a guard like Westphal, who did not play as tough as might be expected with his 6'4" size, the Suns got pushed around a lot. They had out-rebounded only one team in the league: the 24-58 Utah Jazz.

As the first move to change their style of play, the Suns wanted Johnson. So, the deal was struck, All-Star for All-Star. The results, for the first year, have been drastically different.

Many wondered how the Sonics would be able to function with two high-scoring, weak-defense guards, Westphal and Williams. That was never put to the test. Williams didn't report, on the advice of agent Howard Slusher, and Westphal was injured early in the season. Also troubled by other injuries, the Sonics fell out of contention early.

Meanwhile, the trade was working out magnificently for Phoenix. Johnson was playing extremely well, back to his form of the Seattle championship year, giving the Sonics the backcourt defense and playmaking they needed.

His presence as a playmaking guard made it possible for the Suns to switch Davis to the backcourt. In turn, Jeff Cook—a center in college—moved to forward to team with Adams and "Truck" Robinson. Suddenly, a team that had been nearly the worst rebounding team in the league became one of the best.

Dennis Johnson, in a characteristic cheeks-blown-out shot, drives for the basket against Kansas City. Johnson made Phoenix a big winner in the controversial Johnson-Paul Westphal trade. *(Phoenix Suns)*

"We just got tired of being the bangees and wanted to be the bangers for awhile," said Phoenix general manager Jerry Colangelo.

The move to the backcourt was not greeted with whole-hearted enthusiasm by Davis, understandably. He had been the NBA Rookie of the Year as a small forward in 1977-78, and had been an All-Star in each of his first three seasons in the league. He had averaged 23.1 points a game, with a variety of virtually unstoppable shots. Players with those credentials don't often have to make a position switch in mid-career.

The Suns knew all this, and it was not a decision that was made overnight. "I think we were more worried about how it would affect Walter psychologically than we were about the physical aspect," said Colangelo. "Athletically, Walter is superb, with exceptional skills.

"We felt it wasn't a matter of whether he would make it but when. Walter is a perfectionist who attained a high level of performance at forward.

"We were concerned about how he would handle making inevitable mistakes."

Davis, indeed, had troubles in early season. He forced passes into the wrong areas, and he sometimes took the wrong shots. But by mid-season, he was adjusting quite well.

"I've resigned myself to being more patient," he said. "My problem has been comparing my performance at guard to how I played as a forward. I realize now that was wrong.

"Now that I feel a little more comfortable back there, I think I'm playing better. I'm going to the baseline more and getting the shots I like."

There was one aspect of the switch that had helped Davis. At forward, he had been weak defensively, because he lacked the size and strength to handle many of the league's forwards. That problem no longer existed in the backcourt.

"I think it's much easier to defend guards than it was forwards," said Davis. "Forwards spend most of their time posting each other up. At guard, you're further from the basket, so you can gamble more. I just try to stay down, keep my knees bent, maintain position and play as hard as possible.

"There's still physical contact outside, but not as severe. I think officials let more contact go on inside, largely because it's so obvious outside. I was always getting banged around and held as a forward. Now, at least, I'm a big guard and I get to on little guys."

said he also got a lot of help from Johnson. "Dennis talks a lot. Most good e players do, because communication is the key to good defense.

"Dennis has been in the league for awhile and he's played against most of the guards. He sits down before games and tells me how to play my opponents. He tells me their strengths, their weaknesses. He's just been a tremendous help."

With the acquisition of Johnson and the switch of Davis as the key moves, the Suns moved to a divisional championship. And so, for the first year at least, the standings after the Big Trade were Phoenix 1, Seattle 0.

25. The Ticket to Better Basketball

The previous chapters in this book have detailed the high moments of pro basketball, but there are some low ones, too. The game's popularity, on a steady ascent for two decades, has leveled off, and there is no question that the sport faces some serious problems.

One of them, oddly, is the fact that the players are so good. It is exciting to watch a player like Julius Erving make plays that were unthinkable years ago. (One example, from a 1981 game: Erving blocked a shot by New Jersey's Mike O'Koren with his right hand, cupping the ball between his hand and wrist. Gaining control of it he fired a pass downcourt to a teammate for a layup.) But at the same time, players have been unwilling or unable to learn some of the basic moves of the game, offensively and defensively.

"I call it more of an art form today than a game," says former coach Alex Hannum. "When Dr. J comes down and makes one of his great plays, it's almost as if the defense applauds him. Then, somebody on the other team will come down and do his thing."

Al Attles has noticed much the same thing. "Because they're such good shooters," says Attles, "they've never really learned to work the ball down low or set picks—things that we just took for granted when we were growing up.

"And when I mention blocking out on rebounds, they don't know what I'm talking about. They feel they don't have to worry about getting position for rebounds because they can use their great jumping ability to beat somebody else to the ball. But, of course, if they don't have position, they have to jump over somebody's back to get the ball, and that's a foul.

"I know what happens. It used to be that you had to do things the coach's way in high school or you didn't make the team. Now these kids come along who are so talented that the coach doesn't dare kick them off the team. He knows that even if they don't do everything he wants them to do they'll still be great players for him. So, players come to the pros without the fundamentals they used to have."

With the new style of play has also come a different attitude. Listen, for instance, to these remarks from a coach who had just been fired:

"All they talk about in coaching today is how you motivate the players. Why do you have to motivate players? Shouldn't they motivate themselves? Isn't the chance to play with the best in the profession motivation enough?

"I came in during the early days of the NBA. We didn't make the money the players make today, and we didn't have the comforts or the prominence. We played basketball because we loved it or because it was what we did best and could make a living at it.

"We weren't as good as the players that have come along since, but we gave it a hell of a lot more. The coaches I played under—Al Cervi, Alex Hannum, Dolph Schayes, Paul Seymour—didn't have to motivate players. We lived and talked basketball all the time.

"Today, I don't think half the players know who they're playing that night until they look at the tickets they leave at the box office for their friends. They know the latest dance steps, but they don't know the plays. The more money they make, the less they care about it."

A recent gripe? Not at all. That was Johnny Kerr, after he'd been fired by the Phoenix Suns in 1970.

This problem obviously has been a long time building. Hannum could see it when he agreed to take over the Denver Nuggets in 1971—but only if he could be coach, general manager, and president of the team.

"I wasn't eager to leave the West Coast," says Hannum, "but I felt the Denver club eventually would be a profitable one, because there had to be a merger [of the NBA and ABA]. The only way I would come in, though, was if I had complete control.

"In the evolution of the game, we've seen the agents get involved. We've seen players who always want more money, and players who are interested in their individual play, not the team. Unless I had the hammer of being able to say a guy was gone if he didn't play, I didn't think I could handle the situation."

Hannum, remember, is a guy who once challenged Wilt Chamberlain to a fight, so he is not one to back down from a challenge. But the modern player was too much for him, even in 1971.

Denver owner William Ringsby was willing to give Hannum that kind of authority, but Ringsby couldn't stay the distance. The club was losing $400,000 a year, and Ringsby broke that down into the 40 Denver home games.

Ringsby told Hannum, "I figure every time I come to a game I'm paying $10,000 for my ticket, win or lose. That takes a lot of the enjoyment out of it." Soon after that, Ringsby sold the club, and when Hannum's three-year contract expired, the new owners didn't renew it.

Since then, the situation has gotten worse. The long NBA-ABA war turned basketball into a seller's market for the first time. The players were able to get contracts that are simply unbelievable by earlier standards. More important, they have (through the Players' Association) been able to force concessions from the owners on a lot of issues—option clauses, free agency, restrictions on training camp time, fines.

It has been routine to see top draft choices unable to report to training camp on time because their agents have been unable to reach a salary agreement with the teams that drafted them.

In 1981 we saw one player, Gus Williams of Seattle, sitting out a year because of a contract squabble between the Sonics and Williams' agent, Howard Slusher. Even more extreme in its way was the situation between the Golden State Warriors and guard John Lucas.

Lucas missed four games and several practices, without excuses, during the first half of the season. He also missed the team flight to one game. Yet, the Warriors could fine him no more than a game's pay (which he forfeited by not appearing, anyway) because of the agreement with the Players' Association. And they could not suspend Lucas because the clause allowing that had been taken out of his original contract signed with the Houston Rockets, and assumed by the Warriors.

At the same time these player problems were building, a lot of teams were struggling. Though owners were often able to stay afloat because the value of their franchises increased dramatically (enabling them to borrow against that value for operating expenses in some cases), box office problems had caused a lot of franchise movement, which hurt the league's image.

Television ratings were down, and there was even talk that CBS might not renew its contract. Everybody in the NBA knew how important television money is; the lack of it had caused the ABA's demise.

These problems of players and management are intertwined. So are the solutions. Here are some of the changes I'd like to see made, not necessarily in order of importance:

1) NBA owners and the Players' Association should work together to restore more control of the game to owners and coaches. Though it may please an individual player to be able to thumb his nose at management, players have a big stake in the game's stability.

Within that framework, some specific changes could be worked. Owners and general managers must have more authority to fine players, to prevent a repeat of situations like the one with the Warriors and Lucas.

More time should be allowed for training camps; teams simply don't have the time to get into proper condition and coaches don't have the time to fully judge rookies in the present atmosphere.

Along with that, there should be a rule which says that players who aren't signed before the opening of training camp cannot play that season, which would put more pressure on both agents and club managements to reach an agreement. When a player reports late he's unable to get into playing condition fast enough to do his best, which cheats both club managements and fans.

A team salary limit should be implemented. That would circumvent anti-trust statutes because individuals would not be limited, but it would also prevent the richer clubs from buying too many high-priced stars (as the Philadelphia 76ers did with Julius Erving and George McGinnis, for instance) because one superstar would automatically mean less money for the rest of the team.

Individual salaries would still remain at a high level, but this kind of limitation would force some leveling off, and it should also help competitive balance.

2) Owners should put more money and effort into marketing studies and their implementation.

Traditionally, basketball has been the city sport, but the inner city populations are dwindling; between 1975 and 1979, the inner cities in the major metropolitan areas lost a population of six million. The NBA has to learn how to deal with the shifting population, and how to extend its appeal to the suburban areas.

At the same time, the NBA has to learn how to appeal to women. Surveys have shown that women are more likely to buy tickets to pro basketball games than to the other team sports, but NBA teams have scheduled a minimum of promotions that appeal to women.

3) More money should be put into scouting and coaching. As we have seen in the previous chapter, coaching has become much more sophisticated in recent years, and that is a trend that must be accelerated. Precisely because players are coming into the pros without fundamental skills, more assistants are needed for solid individual coaching. Money spent on additional coaches and scouts will probably show more improvement in the game than that put into larger player salaries.

4) The schedule should be changed, probably to something like a January-July time frame. This idea has been promoted for years by veteran sportswriter Leonard Koppett, a man who has often been ahead of his times.

It makes no sense for the NBA to fight the double-barreled competition of the NFL races and Christmas for the first part of its schedule.

By starting in January, the NBA could get up a good momentum before the Super Bowl, and it would then have a 2½-month stretch before baseball started its regular season.

Basketball was developed as a game to be played indoors in the winter, but that's no reason it should be confined to the winter; playoffs, of course, have already extended into June in recent years.

5) NBA teams should borrow shamelessly from the NFL's "communistic" theories of revenue sharing.

Traditionally in the NBA, home teams have kept all the gate receipts. This has contributed to the feeling rampant in the NBA: Every man for himself.

In truth, the NBA, like all professional sports leagues, is more of a cooperative venture than a competitive one. The league is only as strong as its weakest link.

In a regular business, it is to the advantage of a company to get as big a share of the market as possible. But in sports, if one team is dominant year after year, even the dominant team's attendance will drop after awhile. The attraction of a game is its unpredictability.

To help balance the economics (and, hopefully, the competitive aspect), teams should put in a gate-sharing plan, perhaps 60-40 as it is in the NFL, perhaps even 50-50.

Even under that system, the richer clubs in the more populous areas would have a built-in edge. If, for instance, the Knicks sold out every game in 20,000-seat Madison Square Garden, they'd get half of that revenue for 80 games; other teams would share only for the few games they played in New York.

But at least that plan would even out the revenues somewhat, and some of the clubs that are struggling now would have a better chance of staying in business.

6) Finally, and most important, the league must adopt a comprehensive television policy. Again, the example of the NFL, which shares almost all TV revenues, is instructive.

The NBA does have a league-wide policy on nationally televised games, but otherwise, television policy has been chaotic. Unlike the NFL, which has network telecasts on every regular season game, only a few NBA games are on the network. So teams work out their own local contracts, and those revenues can obviously vary greatly from New York to Denver.

League owners need to sit down and devise a way of controlling and sharing those revenues, and they need to decide how much basketball should be on network television and how much on the burgeoning cable networks.

Basketball has great potential as a televised sport, because it is played in a confined area, which enables most of the action to be shown with one shot. Its potential has not always been exploited, but there is no reason it can't be.

Because pro basketball is relatively new, it doesn't have the traditions of football, let alone baseball. But the very lack of tradition also makes it easier to change.

How quickly and how completely NBA owners make changes will determine the future of the sport. Without significant change, the sport will not advance and may even regress.

Even with all its problems, pro basketball is a great sport, played by athletes with exciting skills. But with the right kind of change, it could be even better.

Statistics

Collecting pro basketball statistics can be a tricky business. Some categories—such as blocked shots and steals—have only been established in recent years; even rebounding was not recognized as a statistical category in the early years.

Statistic keeping can vary greatly from city to city in the NBA. Nobody has satisfactorily defined what constitutes an assist, for instance, and assist totals have varied widely from city to city, from game to game and from season to season. Thus, the record book says that neither Bob Cousy nor Oscar Robertson ever had a season in which their passes led to as many scores as in Kevin Porter's best, but it would be difficult to convince anyone who saw all three play.

Finally, many players played in both the NBA and the ABA, but the NBA doesn't recognize ABA statistics. So, players like Julius Erving, Rick Barry, and Artis Gilmore have lost many points and rebounds, which distorts the overall statistical table.

Nonetheless, I have done my best to collect statistics and season records which reflect how teams and individuals have done in the four primary professional leagues: the NBA, ABA, BAA, and NBL.

N B L

Standings

Team	W	L	Pct.	GB
1937-38				
Eastern Division				
Akron Firestone	14	4	.778	—
Akron Goodyear	13	5	.722	1
Pittsburgh	8	5	.615	3.5
Buffalo	3	6	.333	6.5
Warren	3	9	.250	8
Columbus	1	12	.091	10.5
Western Division				
Oshkosh	12	2	.857	—
Whiting	12	3	.800	0.5
Fort Wayne	13	7	.650	2
Indianapolis	4	9	.308	7.5
Cincinnati	3	7	.300	7
Kankakee	3	11	.214	9
Dayton	2	11	.154	9.5
1938-39				
Eastern Division				
Akron Firestone	24	3	.889	—
Akron Goodyear	14	14	.500	10.5
Cleveland	14	14	.500	10.5
Pittsburgh	13	14	.481	11
Western Division				
Oshkosh	17	11	.607	—
Indianapolis	13	13	.500	3
Sheboygan	11	17	.393	6
Hammond	4	24	.143	13

Team	W	L	Pct.	GB
1939-40				
Eastern Division				
Akron Firestone	18	9	.667	—
Detroit	17	10	.630	1
Akron Goodyear	14	14	.500	4.5
Indianapolis	9	19	.321	9.5
Western Division				
Oshkosh	15	13	.536	—
Sheboygan	15	13	.536	—
Chicago	14	14	.500	1
Hammond	9	19	.321	6
1940-41				
Oshkosh	18	6	.750	—
Sheboygan	13	11	.542	5
Akron Firestone	13	11	.542	5
Detroit	12	12	.500	6
Chicago	11	13	.458	7
Akron Goodyear	11	13	.458	7
Hammond	6	18	.250	12
1941-42				
Oshkosh	20	4	.833	—
Fort Wayne	15	9	.625	5
Akron Goodyear	15	9	.625	5
Indianapolis	12	11	.522	7.5
Sheboygan	10	14	.417	10
Chicago	8	15	.348	11.5
Toledo	3	21	.125	17

1942-43

Fort Wayne

Zollner Pistons	17 6	.739	—
Sheboygan Redskins	12 11	.522	5
Oshkosh All-Stars	11 12	.478	6
Chicago Studebakers	8 15	.348	9

Toledo Jim White

Chevrolets	0 4	.000	7.5

1943-44

Fort Wayne

Zollner Pistons	18 4	.818	—
Sheboygan Redskins	14 8	.636	4
Oshkosh All-Stars	7 15	.318	11

Cleveland Chase

Brass	3 15	.167	13

1944-45

Eastern Division

Fort Wayne	25 5	.833	—
Cleveland	13 17	.433	12
Pittsburgh	7 23	.233	18

Western Division

Sheboygan	19 11	.633	—
Chicago	14 16	.467	5
Oshkosh	12 18	.400	7

1945-46

Eastern Division

Fort Wayne	26 8	.765	—
Rochester	24 10	.706	2
Youngstown	13 20	.394	12.5
Cleveland	4 29	.121	21.5

Western Division

Sheboygan	21 13	.618	—
Oshkosh	19 15	.559	2
Chicago	17 17	.500	4
Indianapolis	10 22	.313	10

1946-47

Eastern Division

Rochester	31 13	.705	—
Fort Wayne	25 19	.568	6
Toledo	21 23	.477	10
Syracuse	21 23	.477	10
Tri-Cities	19 25	.432	12
Youngstown	12 32	.273	19

Western Division

Oshkosh	28 16	.636	—
Indianapolis	27 17	.614	1
Chicago	26 18	.591	2
Sheboygan	26 18	.591	2
Anderson	24 20	.545	4
Detroit	4 40	.091	24

1947-48

Eastern Division

Rochester	44 16	.733	—
Anderson	42 18	.700	2
Fort Wayne	40 20	.667	4
Syracuse	24 36	.400	20
Toledo	22 37	.373	21.5
Flint	8 52	.133	36

Western Division

Minneapolis	43 17	.717	—
Tri-Cities	30 30	.500	13
Oshkosh	29 31	.483	14
Indianapolis	24 35	.407	18.5
Sheboygan	23 37	.383	20

1948-49

Eastern Division

Anderson	49 15	.766	—
Syracuse	40 23	.635	8.5
Hammond	21 41	.339	17
Dayton	14 26	.350	30.5
Detroit	2 17	.105	

Western Division

Oshkosh	37 27	.578	—
Tri-Cities	36 28	.563	1
Sheboygan	35 29	.547	2
Waterloo	30 32	.484	6
Denver	18 44	.290	18

B A A

Standings

Team	W	L	Pct.	GB

1946-47

Eastern Division

Washington Capitols	49	11	.817	—
Philadelphia Warriors	35	25	.583	14
N.Y. Knickbockers	33	27	.550	16
Prov. Steamrollers	28	32	.467	21
Toronto Huskies	22	38	.367	27
Boston Celtics	22	38	.367	27

Western Division

Chicago Stags	39	22	.639	—
St. Louis Bombers	38	23	.623	1
Cleveland Rebels	30	30	.500	8.5
Detroit Falcons	20	40	.333	18.5
Pittsburgh Ironmen	15	45	.250	23.5

1947-48

Eastern Division

Philadelphia Warriors	27	21	.563	—
N.Y. Knickbockers	26	22	.542	1
Boston Celtics	20	28	.417	7
Prov. Steamrollers	6	42	.125	21

Western Division

St. Louis Bombers	29	19	.604	—
Baltimore Bullets	28	20	.583	1
Chicago Stags	28	20	.583	1
Washington Capitols	28	20	.583	1

1948-49

Eastern Division

Washington Capitols	38	22	.633	—
N.Y. Knickerbockers	32	28	.533	6
Baltimore Bullets	29	31	.483	9
Phil. Warriors	28	32	.467	10
Boston Celtics	25	35	.417	13
Prov. Steamrollers	12	48	.200	26

Western Division

Rochester Royals	45	15	.750	—
Minneapolis Lakers	44	16	.733	1
Chicago Stags	38	22	.633	7
St. Louis Bombers	29	31	.483	16
Fort Wayne Zollner Pistons	22	38	.367	23
Indianapolis Jets	18	42	.300	27

A B A

Standings

Team	W	L	Pct.	GB

1967-68

Eastern Division

Pittsburgh Pipers	54	24	.692	—
Minnesota Muskies	50	28	.641	4
Indiana Pacers	38	40	.487	16
Kentucky Colonels	36	42	.462	18
N.J. Americans	36	42	.462	18

Western Division

New Orleans Buccaneers	48	30	.615	—
Dallas Chaparrals	46	32	.590	2
Denver Rockets	45	33	.577	3
Houston Mavericks	29	49	.372	19
Anaheim Amigos	25	53	.321	23
Oakland Oaks	22	56	.282	26

1968-69

Eastern Division

Indiana Pacers	44	34	.564	—
Miami Floridians	43	35	.551	1
Kentucky Colonels	42	36	.538	2
Minnesota Pipers	36	42	.462	8
New York Nets	17	61	.218	27

Western Division

Oakland Oaks	60	18	.769	—
New Orleans Buccaneers	46	32	.590	14
Denver Rockets	44	34	.564	16
Dallas Chaparrals	41	37	.526	19
Los Angeles Stars	33	45	.423	27
Houston Mavericks	23	55	.295	37

1969-70

Eastern Division

Indiana Pacers	59	25	.702	—
Kentucky Colonels	45	39	.536	14
Carolina Cougars	42	42	.500	17
New York Nets	39	45	.464	20
Pittsburgh Pipers	29	55	.345	30
Miami Floridians	23	61	.274	36

Western Division

Denver Rockets	51	33	.607	—
Dallas Chaparrals	45	39	.536	6
Washington Capitols	44	40	.524	7
Los Angeles Stars	43	41	.512	8
New Orleans Buccaneers	42	42	.500	9

1970-71

Eastern Division

Virginia Squires	55	29	.655	—
Kentucky Colonels	44	40	.524	11
New York Nets	40	44	.476	15
Floridians	37	47	.440	18
Pittsburgh Condors	36	48	.429	19
Carolina Cougars	34	50	.405	21

Western Division

Indiana Pacers	58	26	.690	—
Utah Stars	57	27	.679	1
Memphis Pros	41	43	.488	17
Texas Chaparrals	30	54	.357	28
Denver Rockets	30	54	.357	28

1971-72

Eastern Division

Kentucky Colonels	68	16	.810	—
Virginia Squires	45	39	.536	23
New York Nets	44	40	.524	24
Floridians	36	48	.429	32
Carolina Cougars	35	49	.417	33
Pittsburgh Condors	25	59	.298	43

Western Division

Utah Stars	60	24	.714	—
Indiana Pacers	47	37	.560	13
Dallas Chaparrals	42	42	.500	18
Denver Rockets	34	50	.405	26
Memphis Pros	26	58	.310	34

1972-73

Eastern Division

Carolina Cougars	57	27	.679	—
Kentucky Colonels	56	28	.667	1
Virginia Squires	42	42	.500	15
New York Nets	30	54	.357	27
Memphis Tams	24	60	.286	33

Western Division

Utah Stars	55	29	.655	—
Indiana Pacers	51	33	.607	4
Denver Rockets	47	37	.560	8
San Diego Conquistadors	30	54	.357	25
Dallas Chaparrals	28	56	.333	27

1973-74

Eastern Division

New York Nets	55	29	.655	—
Kentucky Colonels	53	31	.631	2
Carolina Cougars	47	37	.560	8
Virginia Squires	28	56	.333	27
Memphis Tams	21	63	.250	34

Western Division

Utah Stars	51	33	.607	—
Indiana Pacers	46	38	.548	5
San Antonio Spurs	45	39	.536	6
Denver Rockets	37	47	.440	14
San Diego Conquistadors	37	47	.440	14

1974-75

Eastern Division

*Kentucky Colonels	58	26	.690	—
New York Nets	58	26	.690	—
Spirits of St. Louis	32	52	.381	26
Memphis Sounds	27	57	.321	31
Virginia Squires	15	69	.179	43

Western Division

Denver Nuggets	65	19	.744	—
San Antonio Spurs	51	33	.607	14
Indiana Pacers	45	39	.536	20
Utah Stars	38	46	.452	27
San Diego Conquistadors	31	53	.369	34

1975-76

Eastern Division

Denver	60	24	.714	—
New York	55	29	.665	5
San Antonio	50	34	.595	10
Kentucky	46	38	.548	14
Indiana	39	45	.464	21
St. Louis	35	49	.417	25
Virginia	15	68	.181	44½

---

*Defeated New York in one-game playoff.

All-Time ABA Records

CHAMPIONS

1968	Pittsburgh	1973	Indiana
1969	Oakland	1974	New York
1970	Indiana	1975	Kentucky
1971	Utah	1976	New York
1972	Indiana		

INDIVIDUAL

SINGLE GAME

Most Points	67	Larry Miller, Carolina, vs Memphis at Greensboro, N.C., Mar. 18, 1972
Most 2-Point F. G. Attempted	46	Julius Erving, New York, vs San Diego at San Diego, Feb. 14, 1975 (4 OT)
Most 2-Point F. G. Made	25	Mel Daniels, Indiana, vs New York at Indianapolis, April 18, 1969
	25	Larry Miller, Carolina, vs Memphis at Greensboro, N.C., Mar. 18, 1972
	25	Julius Erving, New York, vs San Diego at San Diego, Feb. 14, 1975 (4 OT)
	25	Marvin Barnes, St. Louis, vs Memphis at St. Louis, Mar. 16, 1975 (OT)
Most 3-Point F. G. Attempted	26	Les Selvage, Anaheim, vs Denver at Denver, Feb. 15, 1968
Most 3-Point F. G. Made	10	Les Selvage, Anaheim, vs Denver at Denver, Feb. 15, 1968
Most F. T. Attempted	30	George Thompson, Memphis, vs San Diego at San Diego, Oct. 14, 1972
Most F. T. Made	24	Tony Jackson, New Jersey, vs Kentucky at Louisville, Nov. 27, 1967
Most Rebounds	40	Artis Gilmore, Kentucky, vs New York at New York, Feb. 3, 1974
Most Assists	23	Larry Brown, Denver, vs Pittsburgh at Denver, Feb. 20, 1972
Most Consecutive F. T.	23	Rick Barry, Oakland, vs Kentucky at Louisville, Feb. 7, 1969

SEASON

Most Points	2,538	Dan Issel, Kentucky, 1971-72
Highest Average	34.58	Charlie Scott, Virginia, 1971-72
Most 2-Point F. G. Attempted	2,082	Charlie Scott, Virginia, 1971-72
Most 2-Point F. G. Made	986	Spencer Haywood, Denver, 1969-70
Highest 2-Point F. G. Percentage	.605	Bobby Jones, Denver, 1974-75
Most 3-Point F. G. Attempted	552	Louie Dampier, Kentucky, 1968-69
Most 3-Point F. G. Made	199	Louie Dampier, Kentucky, 1968-69
Highest 3-Point F. G. Percentage	.420	Billy Shepherd, Memphis, 1974-75
Most F. T. Attempted	805	Mack Calvin, Floridians, 1970-71
Most F. T. Made	696	Mack Calvin, Floridians, 1970-71

Highest F. T. Percentage	.896	Mack Calvin, Denver, 1974-75
Most Rebounds	1,637	Spencer Haywood, Denver, 1969-70
Most Assists	689	Don Buse, Indiana, 1975-76

CAREER

Most Points Scored	13,726	Louie Dampier, Kentucky, 1968-76
Highest Scoring Average (Minimum 250 Games)	28.7	Julius Erving, Virginia and New York, 1971-76
Most 2-Point F. G. Attempted	9,886	Mel Daniels, Minnesota, Indiana and Memphis, 1967-75
Most 2-Point F. G. Made	4,692	Mel Daniels, Minnesota, Indiana and Memphis, 1967-75
Most 3-Point F. G. Attempted	2,217	Louie Dampier, Kentucky, 1968-76
Most 3-Point F. G. Made	794	Louie Dampier, Kentucky, 1968-76
Most F. T. Attempted	4,105	Mack Calvin, Los Angeles, Miami, Carolina, Denver and Virginia, 1969-76
Most F. T. Made	3,554	Mack Calvin, Los Angeles, Miami, Carolina, Denver and Virginia, 1969-76
Most Rebounds	9,494	Mel Daniels, Minnesota, Indiana and Memphis, 1967-75
Most Assists	4,084	Louie Dampier, Kentucky, 1968-76
Most Minutes Played	27,770	Louie Dampier, Kentucky, 1968-76
Most Games	728	Louie Dampier, Kentucky, 1968-76

ABA All-Star Teams

1967-68
Connie Hawkins, Pittsburgh
Doug Moe, New Orleans
Mel Daniels, Minnesota
Larry Jones, Denver
Charlie Williams, Pittsburgh

1968-69
Connie Hawkins, Minnesota
Rich Barry, Oakland
Mel Daniels, Indiana
James Jones, New Orleans
Larry Jones, Denver

1969-70
Rick Barry, Washington
Spencer Haywood, Denver
Mel Daniels, Indiana
Bob Verga, Carolina
Larry Jones, Denver

1970-71
Roger Brown, Indiana
Rick Barry, New York
Mel Daniels, Indiana
Mack Calvin, Floridians
Charlie Scott, Virginia

1971-72
Rick Barry, New York
Dan Issel, Kentucky
Artis Gilmore, Kentucky
Don Freeman, Dallas
Bill Melchionni, New York

1972-73
Billy Cunningham, Carolina
Julius Erving, Virginia
Artis Gilmore, Kentucky
James Jones, Utah
Warren Jabali, Denver

1973-74
Julius Erving, New York
George McGinnis, Indiana
Artis Gilmore, Kentucky
James Jones, Utah
Mack Calvin, Carolina

1974-75
Julius Erving, New York
George McGinnis, Indiana
Artis Gilmore, Kentucky
Mack Calvin, Denver
Ron Boone, Utah

1975-76
Julius Erving, New York
Billy Knight, Indiana
Artis Gilmore, Kentucky
James Silas, San Antonio
Ralph Simpson, Denver

ABA Most Valuable Player

1968	Connie Hawkins	Pittsburgh
1969	Mel Daniels	Indiana
1970	Spencer Haywood	Indiana
1971	Mel Daniels	Indiana
1972	Artis Gilmore	Kentucky

1973	Billy Cunningham	Carolina
1974	Julius Erving	New York
1975	Julius Erving	New York
	George McGinnis	Indiana
1976	Julius Erving	New York

ABA Rookie of the Year

1968	Mel Daniels	Minnesota
1969	Warren Armstrong	Oakland
1970	Spencer Haywood	Denver
1971	Charlie Scott	Virginia
	Dan Issel	Kentucky
1972	Artis Gilmore	Kentucky
1973	Brian Taylor	New York
1974	Swen Nater	San Antonio
1975	Marvin Barnes	St. Louis
1976	David Thompson	Denver

ABA Coach of the Year

1967-68	Vince Cazetta	Pittsburgh
1968-69	Alex Hannum	Oakland
1969-70	Bill Sharman	Los Angeles
	Joe Belmont	Denver
1970-71	Al Bianchi	Virginia
1971-72	Tom Nissalke	Dallas
1972-73	Larry Brown	Carolina
1973-74	Babe McCarthy	Kentucky
	Joe Mullaney	Utah
1974-75	Larry Brown	Denver
1975-76	Larry Brown	Denver

N   B   A

Standings

Team	W	L	Pct.	GB

1949-50

Eastern Division

Syracuse Nationals	51	13	.797	—
N.Y. Knickerbockers	40	28	.588	13
Washington Capitols	32	36	.471	21
Philadelphia Warriors	26	42	.382	27
Baltimore Bullets	25	43	.368	28
Boston Celtics	22	46	.324	31

Central Division

Minneapolis Lakers	51	17	.750	—
Rochester Royals	51	17	.750	—
Fort Wayne Zollner Pistons	40	28	.588	11
Chicago Stags	40	28	.588	11
St. Louis Bombers	26	42	.382	25

Western Division

Indianapolis Olympians	39	25	.609	—
Anderson Duffey Packers	37	27	.578	2
Tri-Cities Blackhawks	29	35	.453	10
Sheboygan Redskins	22	40	.355	16
Waterloo Hawks	19	43	.306	19
Denver Nuggets	11	51	.177	27

1950-51

Eastern Division

Philadelphia Warriors	40	26	.606	—
Boston Celtics	39	30	.565	2.5
N.Y. Knickerbockers	36	30	.545	4
Syracuse Nationals	32	34	.485	8
Baltimore Bullets	24	42	.364	16
Washington Capitols	10	25	.286	14.5

Western Division

Minneapolis Lakers	44	24	.647	—
Rochester Royals	41	27	.603	3
Fort Wayne Zollner Pistons	32	36	.471	12
Indianapolis Olympians	31	37	.456	13
Tri-Cities Blackhawks	25	43	.368	19

1951-52

Eastern Division

Syracuse Nationals	40	26	.606	—
Boston Celtics	39	27	.591	1
N.Y. Knickerbockers	37	29	.561	3
Philadelphia Warriors	33	33	.500	7
Baltimore Bullets	20	46	.303	20

Western Division

Rochester Royals	41	25	.621	—
Minneapolis Lakers	40	26	.606	1
Indianapolis Olympians	34	32	.515	7
Fort Wayne Zollner Pistons	29	37	.439	12
Milwaukee Hawks	17	49	.258	24

1952-53

Eastern Division

N.Y. Knickerbockers	47	23	.671	—
Syracuse Nationals	47	24	.662	0.5
Boston Celtics	46	25	.648	1.5
Baltimore Bullets	16	54	.229	31
Philadelphia Warriors	12	57	.174	34.5

Western Division

Minneapolis Lakers	48 22	.686	—
Rochester Royals	44 26	.629	4
Fort Wayne Zollner Pistons	36 33	.522	11.5
Indianapolis Olympians	28 43	.394	20.5
Milwaukee Hawks	27 44	.380	21.5

1953-54

Eastern Division

N.Y. Knickerbockers	44 28	.611	—
Boston Celtics	42 30	.583	2
Syracuse Nationals	42 30	.583	2
Philadelphia Warriors	29 43	.403	15
Baltimore Bullets	16 56	.222	28

Western Division

Minneapolis Lakers	46 26	.639	—
Rochester Royals	44 28	.611	2
Fort Wayne Zollner Pistons	40 32	.556	6
Milwaukee Hawks	21 51	.292	31

1954-55

Eastern Division

Syracuse Nationals	43 29	.597	—
N.Y. Knickerbockers	38 34	.528	5
Boston Celtics	36 36	.500	7
Philadelphia Warriors	33 39	.458	10

Western Division

Fort Wayne Zollner Pistons	43 29	.597	—
Minneapolis Lakers	40 32	.556	3
Rochester Royals	29 43	.403	14
Milwaukee Hawks	26 46	.361	17

1955-56

Eastern Division

Philadelphia Warriors	45 27	.625	—
Boston Celtics	39 33	.542	6
Syracuse Nationals	35 37	.486	10
N.Y. Knickerbockers	35 37	.486	10

Western Division

Fort Wayne Zollner Pistons	37 35	.514	—
Minneapolis Lakers	33 39	.458	4
St. Louis Hawks	33 39	.458	4
Rochester Royals	31 41	.431	6

1956-57

Eastern Division

Boston Celtics	44 28	.611	—
Syracuse Nationals	38 34	.528	6
Philadelphia Warriors	37 35	.514	7
N.Y. Knickerbockers	36 36	.500	8

Western Division

St. Louis Hawks	34 38	.472	—
Minneapolis Lakers	34 38	.472	—
Fort Wayne Pistons	34 38	.472	—
Rochester Royals	31 41	.431	3

1957-58

Eastern Division

Boston Celtics	49 23	.681	—
Syracuse Nationals	41 31	.569	8
Philadelphia Warriors	37 35	.514	12
N.Y. Knickerbockers	35 37	.486	14

Western Division

St. Louis Hawks	41 31	.569	—
Detroit Pistons	33 39	.458	8
Cincinnati Royals	33 39	.458	8
Minneapolis Lakers	19 53	.264	22

1958-59

Eastern Division

Boston Celtics	52 20	.722	—
N.Y. Knickerbockers	40 32	.556	12
Syracuse Nationals	35 37	.486	17
Philadelphia Warriors	32 40	.444	20

Western Division

St. Louis Hawks	49 23	.681	—
Minneapolis-Lakers	33 39	.458	16
Detroit Pistons	28 44	.389	21
Cincinnati Royals	19 53	.264	30

1959-60

Eastern Division

Boston Celtics	59	16	.787	—
Philadelphia Warriors	49	26	.653	10
Syracuse Nationals	45	30	.600	14
N.Y. Knickerbockers	27	48	.360	32

Western Division

St. Louis Hawks	46	29	.613	—
Detroit Pistons	30	45	.400	16
Minneapolis Lakers	25	50	.333	21
Cincinnati Royals	19	56	.253	27

1960-61

Eastern Division

Boston Celtics	57	22	.722	—
Philadelphia Warriors	46	33	.582	11
Syracuse Nationals	38	41	.481	19
N.Y. Knickerbockers	21	58	.266	36

Western Division

St. Louis Hawks	51	28	.646	—
Los Angeles Lakers	36	43	.456	15
Detroit Pistons	34	45	.430	17
Cincinnati Royals	33	46	.418	18

1961-62

Eastern Division

Boston Celtics	60	20	.750	—
Philadelphia Warriors	49	31	.613	11
Syracuse Nationals	41	39	.513	19
N.Y. Knickerbockers	29	51	.363	31

Western Division

Los Angeles Lakers	54	26	.675	—
Cincinnati Royals	43	37	.538	11
Detroit Pistons	37	43	.463	17
St. Louis Hawks	29	51	.363	25
Chicago Packers	18	62	.225	36

1962-63

Eastern Division

Boston Celtics	58	22	.725	—
Syracuse Nationals	48	32	.600	10
Cincinnati Royals	42	38	.525	16
N.Y. Knickerbockers	21	59	.356	37

Western Division

Los Angeles Lakers	53	27	.663	—
St. Louis Hawks	48	32	.600	5
Detroit Pistons	34	46	.425	19
San Fran. Warriors	31	49	.388	22
Chicago Zephyrs	25	55	.313	28

1963-64

Eastern Division

Boston Celtics	59	21	.738	—
Cincinnati Royals	55	25	.688	4
Philadelphia 76ers	34	46	.425	25
N.Y. Knickerbockers	22	58	.275	37

Western Division

San Fran. Warriors	48	32	.600	—
St. Louis Hawks	46	34	.575	2
Los Angeles Lakers	42	38	.525	6
Baltimore Bullets	31	49	.388	17
Detroit Pistons	23	57	.288	25

1964-65

Eastern Division

Boston Celtics	62	18	.775	—
Cincinnati Royals	48	32	.600	14
Philadelphia 76ers	40	40	.500	22
N.Y. Knickerbockers	31	49	.388	31

Western Division

Los Angeles Lakers	49	31	.613	—
St. Louis Hawks	45	35	.563	4
Baltimore Bullets	37	43	.463	12
Detroit Pistons	31	49	.388	18
San Fran. Warriors	17	63	.213	32

1965-66

Eastern Division

Philadelphia 76ers	55	25	.688	—
Boston Celtics	54	26	.675	1
Cincinnati Royals	45	35	.563	10
N.Y. Knickerbockers	30	50	.375	25

Western Division

Los Angeles Lakers	45 35	.563	—
Baltimore Bullets	38 42	.475	7
St. Louis Hawks	36 44	.450	9
San Fran. Warriors	35 45	.438	10
Detroit Pistons	22 58	.275	23

1966-67

Eastern Division

Philadelphia 76ers	68 13	.840	—
Boston Celtics	60 21	.741	8
Cincinnati Royals	39 42	.481	29
N.Y. Knickerbockers	36 45	.444	32
Baltimore Bullets	20 61	.241	48

Western Division

San Fran. Warriors	44 37	.543	—
St. Louis Hawks	39 42	.481	5
Los Angeles Lakers	36 45	.444	8
Chicago Bulls	33 48	.407	11
Detroit Pistons	30 51	.370	14

1967-68

Eastern Division

Philadelphia 76ers	62 20	.756	—
Boston Celtics	54 28	.659	8
N.Y. Knickerbockers	43 39	.524	19
Detroit Pistons	40 42	.488	22
Cincinnati Royals	39 43	.476	23
Baltimore Bullets	36 46	.439	26

Western Division

St. Louis Hawks	56 26	.683	—
Los Angeles Lakers	52 30	.634	4
San Fran. Warriors	43 39	.524	13
Chicago Bulls	29 53	.354	27
Seattle Supersonics	23 59	.280	33
San Diego Rockets	15 67	.183	41

1968-69

Eastern Division

Baltimore Bullets	57 25	.695	—
Philadelphia 76ers	55 27	.671	2
N.Y. Knickerbockers	54 28	.659	3
Boston Celtics	48 34	.585	9
Cincinnati Royals	41 41	.500	16
Detroit Pistons	32 50	.390	25
MIlwaukee Bucks	27 55	.329	30

Western Division

Los Angeles Lakers	55 27	.671	—
Atlanta Hawks	48 34	.585	7
San Fran. Warriors	41 41	.500	14
San Diego Rockets	37 45	.451	18
Chicago Bulls	33 49	.402	22
Seattle Supersonics	30 52	.366	25
Phoenix Suns	16 66	.195	39

1969-70

Eastern Division

N.Y. Knickerbockers	60 22	.732	—
Milwaukee Bucks	56 26	.683	4
Baltimore Bullets	50 32	.610	10
Philadelphia 76ers	42 40	.512	18
Cincinnati Royals	36 46	.439	24
Boston Celtics	34 48	.415	26
Detroit Pistons	31 51	.378	29

Western Division

Atlanta Hawks	48 34	.585	—
Los Angeles Lakers	46 36	.561	2
Chicago Bulls	39 43	.476	9
Phoenix Suns	39 43	.476	9
Seattle Supersonics	36 46	.439	12
San Fran. Warriors	30 52	.366	18
San Diego Rockets	27 55	.329	21

1970-71

Atlantic Division

N.Y. Knickerbockers	52	30	.634	—
Philadelphia 76ers	47	35	.573	5
Boston Celtics	44	38	.537	8
Buffalo Braves	22	60	.268	30

Central Division

Baltimore Bullets	42	40	.512	—
Atlanta Hawks	36	46	.439	6
Cincinnati Royals	33	49	.402	9
Cleveland Cavaliers	15	67	.183	27

Midwest Division

Milwaukee Bucks	66	16	.805	—
Chicago Bulls	51	31	.622	15
Phoenix Suns	48	34	.585	18
Detroit Pistons	45	37	.549	21

Pacific Division

Los Angeles Lakers	48	34	.585	—
San Fran. Warriors	41	41	.500	7
San Diego Rockets	40	42	.488	8
Seattle Supersonics	38	44	.463	10
Portland Trail Blazers	29	53	.354	19

1971-72

Atlantic Division

Boston Celtics	56	26	.683	—
N.Y. Knickerbockers	48	34	.585	8
Philadelphia 76ers	30	52	.366	26
Buffalo Braves	22	60	.268	34

Central Division

Baltimore Bullets	38	44	.463	—
Atlanta Hawks	36	46	.439	2
Cincinnati Royals	30	52	.366	8
Cleveland Cavaliers	23	59	.280	15

Midwest Division

Milwaukee Bucks	63	19	.768	—
Chicago Bulls	57	25	.695	6
Phoenix Suns	49	33	.598	14
Detroit Pistons	26	56	.317	37

Pacific Division

Los Angeles Lakers	69	13	.841	—
Golden State Warriors	51	31	.622	18
Seattle Supersonics	47	35	.573	22
Houston Rockets	34	48	.415	35
Portland Trail Blazers	18	64	.220	51

1972-73

Atlantic Division

Boston Celtics	68	14	.829	—
N.Y. Knickerbockers	57	25	.695	11
Buffalo Braves	21	61	.256	47
Philadelphia 76ers	9	73	.110	59

Central Division

Baltimore Bullets	52	30	.634	—
Atlanta Hawks	46	36	.561	6
Houston Rockets	33	49	.402	19
Cleveland Cavaliers	32	50	.390	20

Midwest Division

Milwaukee Bucks	60	22	.732	—
Chicago Bulls	51	31	.622	9
Detroit Pistons	40	42	.488	20
Kansas City– Omaha Kings	36	46	.439	24

Pacific Division

Los Angeles Lakers	60	22	.732	—
Golden State Warriors	47	35	.573	13
Phoenix Suns	38	44	.463	22
Seattle Supersonics	26	56	.317	34
Portland Trail Blazers	21	61	.256	39

1973-74

Atlantic Division

Boston Celtics	56	26	.683	—
N.Y. Knickerbockers	49	33	.598	7
Buffalo Braves	42	40	.512	14
Philadelphia 76ers	25	57	.305	31

Central Division

Capital Bullets	47	35	.573	—
Atlanta Hawks	35	47	.427	12
Houston Rockets	32	50	.390	15
Cleveland Cavaliers	29	53	.354	18

Midwest Division

Milwaukee Bucks	59	23	.270 —
Chicago Bulls	54	28	.629 5
Detroit Pistons	52	30	.634 7
Kansas City-Omaha Kings	33	49	.402 26

Pacific Division

Los Angeles Lakers	47	35	.573 —
Golden State Warriors	44	38	.537 3
Seattle Supersonics	36	46	.439 11
Phoenix Suns	30	52	.366 17
Portland Trail Blazers	27	55	.329 20

1974-75

Atlantic Division

Boston Celtics	60	22	.732 —
Buffalo Braves	49	33	.598 11
N.Y. Knickerbockers	40	42	.488 20
Philadelphia 76ers	34	48	.415 26

Central Division

Washington Bullets	60	22	.732 —
Houston Rockets	41	41	.500 19
Cleveland Cavaliers	40	42	.488 20
Atlanta Hawks	31	51	.378 29
New Orleans Jazz	23	59	.280 37

Midwest Division

Chicago Bulls	47	35	.573 —
Kansas City-Omaha Kings	44	38	.537 3
Detroit Pistons	40	42	.488 7
Milwaukee Bucks	38	44	.463 9

Pacific Division

Golden State Warriors	48	34	.585 —
Seattle Supersonics	43	39	.524 5
Portland Trail Blazers	38	44	.463 10
Phoenix Suns	32	50	.390 16
Los Angeles Lakers	30	52	.366 18

1975-76

Atlantic Division

Boston	54	28	.659 —
Buffalo	46	36	.561 8
Philadelphia	46	36	.561 8
New York	38	44	.463 16

Central Division

Cleveland	49	33	.598 —
Washington	48	34	.585 1
Houston	40	42	.488 9
New Orleans	38	44	.463 11
Atlanta	29	53	.354 20

Midwest Division

Milwaukee	38	44	.463 —
Detroit	36	46	.439 2
Kansas City	31	51	.378 7
Chicago	24	58	.293 14

Pacific Division

Golden State	59	23	.720 —
Seattle	43	39	.524 16
Phoenix	42	40	.512 17
Los Angeles	40	42	.488 19
Portland	37	45	.451 22

1976-77

Atlantic Division

Philadelphia	50	32	.610 —
Boston	44	38	.537 6
N.Y. Knicks	40	42	.488 10
Buffalo	30	52	.366 20
N.Y. Nets	22	60	.268 28

Central Division

Houston	49	33	.598 —
Washington	48	34	.585 1
San Antonio	44	38	.537 5
Cleveland	43	39	.524 6
New Orleans	35	47	.427 14
Atlanta	31	51	.378 18

Midwest Division

Denver	50	32	.610 —
Detroit	44	38	.537 6
Chicago	44	38	.537 6
Kansas City	40	42	.488 10
Indiana	36	46	.439 14
Milwaukee	30	52	.366 20

Pacific Division

Los Angeles	53	29	.646 —
Portland	49	33	.598 4
Golden State	46	36	.561 7
Seattle	40	42	.488 13
Phoenix	34	48	.415 19

1977-78

Atlantic Division

Philadelphia	55	27	.671	—
New York	43	39	.524	12
Boston	32	50	.390	23
Buffalo	27	55	.329	28
New Jersey	24	58	.293	31

Central Division

San Antonio	52	30	.634	—
Washington	44	38	.537	8
Cleveland	43	39	.524	9
Atlanta	41	41	.500	11
New Orleans	39	43	.476	13
Houston	28	54	.341	24

Midwest Division

Denver	48	34	.585	—
Milwaukee	44	38	.537	4
Chicago	40	42	.488	8
Detroit	38	44	.463	10
Indiana	31	51	.378	17
Kansas City	31	51	.378	17

Pacific Division

Portland	58	24	.707	—
Phoenix	49	33	.598	9
Seattle	47	35	.573	11
Los Angeles	45	37	.549	13
Golden State	43	39	.524	15

1978-79

Atlantic Division

Washington	54	28	.659	—
Philadelphia	47	35	.573	7
New Jersey	37	45	.451	17
New York	31	51	.378	23
Boston	29	53	.354	25

Central Division

San Antonio	48	34	.585	—
Houston	47	35	.573	1
Atlanta	46	36	.551	2
Cleveland	30	52	.366	18
Detroit	30	52	.366	18
New Orleans	26	56	.317	22

Midwest Division

Kansas City	48	34	.585	—
Denver	47	35	.573	1
Indiana	38	44	.463	10
Milwaukee	38	44	.463	10
Chicago	31	51	.378	17

Pacific Division

Seattle	52	30	.634	—
Phoenix	50	32	.610	2
Los Angeles	47	35	.573	5
Portland	45	37	.549	7
San Diego	43	39	.524	9
Golden State	38	44	.463	14

1979-80

Atlantic Division

Boston	61	21	.744	—
Philadelphia	59	23	.720	2
Washington	39	43	.476	22
New York	39	43	.476	22
New Jersey	34	48	.415	27

Central Division

Atlanta	50	32	.610	—
Houston	41	41	.500	9
San Antonio	41	41	.500	9
Indiana	37	45	.451	13
Cleveland	37	45	.451	13
Detroit	16	66	.195	34

Midwest Division

Milwaukee	49	33	.598	—
Kansas City	47	35	.573	2
Denver	30	52	.366	19
Chicago	30	52	.366	19
Utah	24	58	.293	25

Pacific Division

Los Angeles	60	22	.732	—
Seattle	56	26	.683	4
Phoenix	55	27	.671	5
Portland	38	44	.463	22
San Diego	35	47	.427	25
Golden State	24	58	.293	36

Reggie Theus became the prototype of the big guard who dominated the NBA by the start of the 1980s. *(Chicago Bulls)*

1980-81

Atlantic Division

Boston	62	20	.756	—
Philadelphia	62	20	.756	—
New York	50	32	.610	12
Washington	39	43	.476	23
New Jersey	24	58	.293	38

Central Division

Milwaukee	60	22	.732	—
Chicago	45	37	.549	15
Indiana	44	38	.537	16
Atlanta	31	51	.378	29
Cleveland	28	54	.341	32
Detroit	21	61	.256	39

Midwest Division

San Antonio	52	30	.634	—
Kansas City	40	42	.488	12
Houston	40	42	.488	12
Denver	37	45	.451	15
Utah	28	54	.341	24
Dallas	15	67	.183	37

Pacific Division

Phoenix	57	25	.695	—
Los Angeles	54	28	.659	3
Portland	45	37	.549	12
Golden State	39	43	.476	18
San Diego	36	46	.439	21
Seattle	34	48	.415	23

(left) Gus Williams played a key role as the Seattle SuperSonics won one NBA title and were runners-up in another. *(Seattle SuperSonics)*

(right) Phil Chenier's jump shooting was an important part of the Washington Bullets' offense as the Bullets drove to an NBA title. *(Washington Bullets)*

NBA Champions

Season	Champion	Eastern Division			Western Division		
		W.	L.		W.	L.	
1946-47	Philadelphia	49	11	Washington	39	22	Chicago
1947-48	Baltimore	27	21	Philadelphia	29	19	St. Louis
1948-49	Minneapolis	38	22	Washington	45	15	Rochester
1949-50	Minneapolis	51	13	Syracuse	39	25	Indianapolis*
1950-51	Rochester	40	26	Philadelphia	44	24	Minneapolis
1951-52	Minneapolis	40	26	Syracuse	41	25	Rochester
1952-53	Minneapolis	47	23	New York	48	22	Minneapolis
1953-54	Minneapolis	44	28	New York	46	26	Minneapolis
1954-55	Syracuse	43	29	Syracuse	43	29	Ft. Wayne
1955-56	Philadelphia	45	27	Philadelphia	37	35	Ft. Wayne
1956-57	Boston	44	28	Boston	34	38	StL-Mpl-FtW
1957-58	St. Louis	49	23	Boston	41	31	St. Louis
1958-59	Boston	52	20	Boston	49	23	St. Louis
1959-60	Boston	59	16	Boston	46	29	St. Louis
1960-61	Boston	57	22	Boston	51	28	St. Louis
1961-62	Boston	60	20	Boston	54	26	Los Angeles
1962-63	Boston	58	22	Boston	53	27	Los Angeles
1963-64	Boston	59	21	Boston	48	32	San Fran.
1964-65	Boston	62	18	Boston	49	31	Los Angeles
1965-66	Boston	55	25	Philadelphia	45	35	Los Angeles
1966-67	Philadelphia	68	13	Philadelphia	44	37	San Fran.
1967-68	Boston	62	20	Philadelphia	56	26	St. Louis
1968-69	Boston	57	25	Baltimore	55	27	Los Angeles
1969-70	New York	60	22	New York	48	34	Atlanta
1970-71	Milwaukee	42	40	Baltimore	66	16	Milwaukee
1971-72	Los Angeles	48	34	New York	69	13	Los Angeles
1972-73	New York	57	25	New York	60	22	Los Angeles
1973-74	Boston	56	26	Boston	59	23	Milwaukee
1974-75	Golden State	60	22	Washington	48	34	Golden State
1975-76	Boston	54	28	Boston	42	40	Phoenix
1976-77	Portland	50	32	Philadelphia	49	33	Portland
1977-78	Washington	44	38	Washington	47	35	Seattle
1978-79	Seattle	54	28	Washington	52	30	Seattle
1979-80	Los Angeles	59	23	Philadelphia	60	22	Los Angeles
1980-81	Boston	62	20	Boston	40	42	Houston

*1949-50 Central Division Champ: Minneapolis and Rochester tied 51-17.

Record of NBA Teams

ANDERSON PACKERS

Season	Coach	Reg. Sea'n W.	Reg. Sea'n L.	Playoffs W.	Playoffs L.
1949-50	Howard Schultz, 21-14	—	—	—	—
	Ike Duffey, 1-2	—	—	—	—
	Doxie Moore, 15-11	37	27	4	4

ATLANTA HAWKS

Season	Coach	Reg. Sea'n W.	Reg. Sea'n L.	Playoffs W.	Playoffs L.
1949-50	Roger Potter, 1-6	—	—	—	—
	Arnold A'rbach, 28-29	29	35	1	2
1950-51	Dave McMillan, 9-14	—	—	—	—
	John Logan 2-1	—	—	—	—
	Marko Todorovich, 14-28	25	43	—	—
1951-52*	Doxie Moore	17	49	—	—
1952-53	Andrew Levane	27	44	—	—
1953-54	Andrew Levane, 11-35	—	—	—	—
	Red Holzman, 10-16	21	51	—	—
1954-55	Red Holzman	26	46	—	—
1955-56†	Red Holzman	33	39	4	4
1956-57	Red Holzman, 14-19	—	—	—	—
	Slater Martin, 5-3	—	—	—	—
	Alex Hannum, 15-16	34	38	6	4
1957-58	Alex Hannum	41	31	8	3
1958-59	Andy Phillips, 6-4	—	—	—	—
	Ed Macauley, 43-19	49	23	2	4
1959-60	Ed Macauley	46	29	7	7
1960-61	Paul Seymour	51	28	5	7
1961-62	Paul Seymour, 5-9	—	—	—	—
	Andrew Levane, 20-40	—	—	—	—
	Bob Pettit, 4-2	29	51	—	—
1962-63	Harry Gallatin	48	32	6	5
1963-64	Harry Gallatin	46	34	6	6
1964-65	Harry Gallatin, 17-16	—	—	—	—
	Richie Guerin, 28-19	45	35	1	3
1965-66	Richie Guerin	36	44	6	4
1966-67	Richie Guerin	39	42	5	4

Season	Coach	Reg. Sea'n		Playoffs	
		W.	L.	W.	L.
1967-68	Richie Guerin	56	26	2	4
1968-69‡	Richie Guerin	48	34	5	6
1969-70	Richie Guerin	48	34	4	5
1970-71	Richie Guerin	36	46	1	4
1971-72	Richie Guerin	36	46	2	4
1972-73	Cotton Fitzsimmons	46	36	2	4
1973-74	Cotton Fitzsimmons	35	47	—	—
1974-75	Cotton Fitzsimmons	31	51	—	—
1975-76	Cotton Fitzsimmons, 28-46	—	—	—	—
	Gene Tormohlen, 1-7	29	53	—	—
1976-77	Hubie Brown	31	51	—	—
1977-78	Hubie Brown	41	41	0	2
1978-79	Hubie Brown	46	36	5	4
1979-80	Hubie Brown	50	32	1	4
1980-81	Hubie Brown, 31-48	—	—	—	—
	Michael Fratello, 0-3	31	51	—	—
Totals		1206	1278	79	90

*Team moved from Tri-Cities to Milwaukee.
†Team moved from Milwaukee to St. Louis.
‡Team moved from St. Louis to Atlanta.

BALTIMORE BULLETS

Season	Coach	Reg. Sea'n		Playoffs	
		W.	L.	W.	L.
1947-48	Buddy Jeannette	28	20	8	3
1948-49	Buddy Jeannette	29	31	1	2
1949-50	Buddy Jeannette	25	43	—	—
1950-51	Buddy Jeannette, 14-23	—	—	—	—
	Walter Budko, 10-19	24	42	—	—
1951-52	Fred Scolari, 12-27	—	—	—	—
	John Reiser, 8-19	20	46	—	—
1952-53	John Reiser, 0-3	—	—	—	—
	Clair Bee, 16-51	16	54	0	2
1953-54	Clair Bee	16	56	—	—
1954-55	Claire Bee, 2-9	—	—	—	—
	*Al Barthelme, 1-2	3	11	—	—
Totals		161	303	9	7

*Team disbanded November 27.

BOSTON CELTICS

Season	Coach	Reg. Sea'n		Playoffs	
		W.	L.	W.	L.
1946-47	John Russell	22	38	—	—
1947-48	John Russell	20	28	1	2
1948-49	Alvin Julian	25	35	—	—
1949-50	Alvin Julian	22	46	—	—
1950-51	Arnold Auerbach	39	30	0	2
1951-52	Arnold Auerbach	39	27	1	2
1952-53	Arnold Auerbach	46	25	3	3
1953-54	Arnold Auerbach	42	30	2	4
1954-55	Arnold Auerbach	36	36	3	4
1955-56	Arnold Auerbach	39	33	1	2
1956-57	Arnold Auerbach	44	28	7	3
1957-58	Arnold Auerbach	49	23	6	5
1958-59	Arnold Auerbach	52	20	8	3
1959-60	Arnold Auerbach	59	16	8	5
1960-61	Arnold Auerbach	57	22	8	2
1961-62	Arnold Auerbach	60	20	8	6
1962-63	Arnold Auerbach	58	22	8	5
1963-64	Arnold Auerbach	59	21	8	2
1964-65	Arnold Auerbach	62	18	8	4
1965-66	Arnold Auerbach	54	26	11	6
1966-67	Bill Russell	60	21	4	5
1967-68	Bill Russell	54	28	12	7
1968-69	Bill Russell	48	34	12	6
1969-70	Tom Heinsohn	34	48	—	—
1970-71	Tom Heinsohn	44	38	—	—
1971-72	Tom Heinsohn	56	26	5	6
1972-73	Tom Heinsohn	68	14	7	6
1973-74	Tom Heinsohn	56	26	12	6
1974-75	Tom Heinsohn	60	22	6	5
1975-76	Tom Heinsohn	54	28	12	6
1976-77	Tom Heinsohn	44	38	5	4
1977-78	Tom Heinsohn, 11-23	—	—	—	—
	Tom Sanders, 21-27	32	50	—	—
1978-79	Tom Sanders, 2-12	—	—	—	—
	Dave Cowens, 27-41	29	53	—	—
1979-80	Bill Fitch	61	21	5	4
1980-81	Bill Fitch	62	20	12	5
Totals		1646	1011	183	120

The kind of flashy play that has become the trademark of the NBA is shown in this behind-the-back pass by Ricky Sobers of the Chicago Bulls. *(Chicago Bulls)*

CHICAGO BULLS

Season	Coach	Reg. Sea'n		Playoffs	
		W.	L.	W.	L.
1966-67	John Kerr	33	48	0	3
1967-68	John Kerr	29	53	1	4
1968-69	Dick Motta	33	49	—	—
1969-70	Dick Motta	39	43	1	4
1970-71	Dick Motta	51	31	3	4
1971-72	Dick Motta	57	25	0	4
1972-73	Dick Motta	51	31	3	4
1973-74	Dick Motta	54	28	4	7
1974-75	Dick Motta	47	35	7	6
1975-76	Dick Motta	24	58	—	—
1976-77	Ed Badger	44	38	1	2
1977-78	Ed Badger	40	42	—	—
1978-79	Larry Costello, 20-36	—	—	—	—
	Scotty Robertson, 11-15	31	51	—	—
1979-80	Jerry Sloan	30	52	—	—
1980-81	Jerry Sloan	45	37	2	4
Totals		608	621	22	42

CHICAGO STAGS

Season	Coach	Reg. Sea'n		Playoffs	
		W.	L.	W.	L.
1946-47	Harold Olsen	39	22	5	6

Season	Coach	Reg. Sea'n		Playoffs	
		W.	L.	W.	L.
1947-48	Harold Olsen	28	20	2	3
1948-49	Harold Olsen, 28-21	38	22	0	2
	*Philip Brownstein, 10-1	—	—	—	—
1949-50	Philip Brownstein	40	28	0	2
Totals		145	92	7	13

*Substituted during Olsen's illness.

Matt Mitchell was the lone bright spot in the Cleveland Cavalier picture. *(David Liam Kyle)*

CLEVELAND CAVALIERS

Season	Coach	Reg. Sea'n		Playoffs	
		W.	L.	W.	L.
1970-71	Bill Fitch	15	67	—	—
1971-72	Bill Fitch	23	59	—	—
1972-73	Bill Fitch	32	50	—	—
1973-74	Bill Fitch	29	53	—	—
1974-75	Bill Fitch	40	42	—	—
1975-76	Bill Fitch	49	33	6	7
1976-77	Bill Fitch	43	39	1	2
1977-78	Bill Fitch	43	39	0	2
1978-79	Bill Fitch	30	52	—	—
1979-80	Stan Albeck	37	45	—	—
1980-81	Bill Musselman, 25-46	—	—	—	—
	Don Delaney, 3-8	28	54	—	—
Totals		369	533	7	11

CLEVELAND REBELS

		Reg. Sea'n		Playoffs	
Season	*Coach*	*W.*	*L.*	*W.*	*L.*
1946-47	Dutch Dehnert, 17-20	—	—	—	—
	Roy Clifford, 13-10	30	30	1	2

DENVER NUGGETS

		Reg. Sea'n		Playoffs	
Season	*Coach*	*W.*	*L.*	*W.*	*L.*
1949-50	James Darden	11	51	—	—

DALLAS MAVERICKS

		Reg. Sea'n		Playoffs	
Season	*Coach*	*W.*	*L.*	*W.*	*L.*
1980-81	Dick Motta	15	67	—	—

DENVER NUGGETS

		Reg. Sea'n		Playoffs	
Season	*Coach*	*W.*	*L.*	*W.*	*L.*
1976-77	Larry Brown	50	32	2	4
1977-78	Larry Brown	48	34	6	7
1978-79	Larry Brown, 28-25	—	—	—	—
	Donnie Walsh, 19-10	47	35	1	2
1979-80	Donnie Walsh	30	52	—	—
1980-81	Donnie Walsh, 11-20	—	—	—	—
	Doug Moe, 26-25	37	45	—	—
Totals		212	198	9	13

DETROIT FALCONS

		Reg. Sea'n		Playoffs	
Season	*Coach*	*W.*	*L.*	*W.*	*L.*
1946-47	Glenn Curtis, 12-22	—	—	—	—
	Philip Sachs, 8-18	20	40	—	—

DETROIT PISTONS

		Reg. Sea'n		Playoffs	
Season	*Coach*	*W.*	*L.*	*W.*	*L.*
1948-49	Carl Bennett, 0-6	—	—	—	—
	Paul Armstrong, 22-32	22	38	—	—

Season	Coach	Reg. Sea'n W.	L.	Playoffs W.	L.
1949-50	Murray Mendenhall	40	28	2	2
1950-51	Murray Mendenhall	32	36	1	2
1951-52	Paul Birch	29	37	0	2
1952-53	Paul Birch	36	33	4	4
1953-54	Paul Birch	40	32	0	4
1954-55	Charles Eckman	43	29	6	5
1955-56	Charles Eckman	37	35	4	6
1956-57	Charles Eckman	34	38	0	2
1957-58*	Charles Eckman, 9-16	—	—	—	—
	Ephraim Rocha, 24-23	33	39	3	4
1958-59	Ephraim Rocha	28	44	1	4
1959-60	Ephraim Rocha, 13-21	—	—	—	—
	Dick McGuire, 17-24	30	45	0	2
1960-61	Dick McGuire	34	45	2	3
1961-62	Dick McGuire	37	43	5	5
1962-63	Dick McGuire	34	46	1	3
1963-64	Charles Wolf	23	57	—	—
1964-65	Charles Wolf, 2-9	—	—	—	—
	D. DeBusschere, 29-40	31	49	—	—
1965-66	Dave DeBusschere	22	58	—	—
1966-67	D. DeBusschere, 28-45	—	—	—	—
	Donnis Butcher, 2-6	30	51	—	—
1967-68	Donnis Butcher	40	42	2	4
1968-69	D. Butcher, 10-12	—	—	—	—
	Paul Seymour, 22-38	32	50	—	—
1969-70	Bill van Breda Kolff	31	51	—	—
1970-71	Bill van Breda Kolff	45	37	—	—
1971-72	B. van Breda Kolff, 6-6	—	—	—	—
	Earl Lloyd, 20-50	26	56	—	—
1972-73	Earl Lloyd, 2-5	—	—	—	—
	Ray Scott, 38-37	40	42	—	—
1973-74	Ray Scott	52	30	3	4
1974-75	Ray Scott	40	42	1	2
1975-76	Ray Scott, 17-25	—	—	—	—
	Herb Brown, 19-21	36	46	4	5
1976-77	Herb Brown	44	38	1	2
1977-78	Herb Brown, 9-16	—	—	—	—
	Bob Kauffman, 29-29	38	44	—	—

Season	Coach	Reg. Sea'n		Playoffs	
		W.	L.	W.	L.
1978-79	Dick Vitale	30	52	—	—
1979-80	Dick Vitale, 4-8	—	—	—	—
	Richie Adubato, 12-58	16	66	—	—
1980-81	Scotty Robertson	21	61	—	—
Totals		1106	1440	40	63

*Team moved from Ft. Wayne to Detroit.

GOLDEN STATE WARRIORS

Season	Coach	Reg. Sea'n		Playoffs	
		W.	L.	W.	L.
1946-47	Edward Gottlieb	35	25	8	2
1947-48	Edward Gottlieb	27	21	6	7
1948-49	Edward Gottlieb	28	32	0	2
1949-50	Edward Gottlieb	26	42	0	2
1950-51	Edward Gottlieb	40	26	0	2
1951-52	Edward Gottlieb	33	33	1	2
1952-53	Edward Gottlieb	12	57	—	—
1953-54	Edward Gottlieb	29	43	—	—
1954-55	Edward Gottlieb	33	39	—	—
1955-56	George Senesky	45	27	7	3
1956-57	George Senesky	37	35	0	2
1957-58	George Senesky	37	35	3	5
1958-59	Al Cervi	32	40	—	—
1959-60	Neil Johnston	49	26	4	5
1960-61	Neil Johnston	46	33	0	3
1961-62	Frank McGuire	49	31	6	6
1962-63*	Bob Feerick	31	49	—	—
1963-64	Alex Hannum	48	32	5	7
1964-65	Alex Hannum	17	63	—	—
1965-66	Alex Hannum	35	45	—	—
1966-67	Bill Sharman	44	37	9	6
1967-68	Bill Sharman	43	39	4	6
1968-69	George Lee	41	41	2	4
1969-70	George Lee, 22-30	—	—	—	—
	Al Attles, 8-22	30	52	—	—
1970-71	Al Attles	41	41	1	4
1971-72	Al Attles	51	31	1	4

(right) Houston's Rudy Tomjanovich came back — after suffering a broken jaw and shattered cheek from a punch by Kermit Washington — to resume shooting one of the most accurate jump shots in the league, as shown in this action against Seattle. *(Houston Rockets)*

(left) After admitting to a problem with alcohol, Bernard King reverted back to his earlier form with a great season with the Golden State Warriors in 1981. *(Golden State Warriors)*

Season	Coach	Reg. Sea'n		Playoffs	
		W.	L.	W.	L.
1972-73	Al Attles	47	35	5	6
1973-74	Al Attles	44	38	—	—
1974-75	Al Attles	48	34	12	5
1975-76	Al Attles	59	23	7	6
1976-77	Al Attles	46	36	5	5
1977-78	Al Attles	43	39	—	—
1978-79	Al Attles	38	44	—	—
1979-80	Al Attles, 18-43	—	—	—	—
	John Bach, 6-15	24	58	—	—
1980-81	Al Attles	39	43	—	—
Totals		1327	1325	86	94

*Team moved from Philadelphia to San Francisco.

HOUSTON ROCKETS

Season	Coach	Reg. Sea'n		Playoffs	
		W.	L.	W.	L.
1967-68	Jack McMahon	15	67	—	—
1968-69	Jack McMahon	37	45	2	4
1969-70	Jack McMahon, 9-17	—	—	—	—
	Alex Hannum, 18-38	27	55	—	—
1970-71	Alex Hannum	40	42	—	—
1971-72*	Tex Winter	34	48	—	—
1972-73	Tex Winter, 17-30	—	—	—	—
	John Egan, 16-19	33	49	—	—
1973-74	John Egan	32	50	—	—
1974-75	John Egan	41	41	3	5
1975-76	John Egan	40	42	—	—
1976-77	Tom Nissalke	49	33	6	6
1977-78	Tom Nissalke	28	54	—	—
1978-79	Tom Nissalke	47	35	0	2
1979-80	Del Harris	41	41	2	5
1980-81	Del Harris	40	42	12	9
Totals		504	644	25	31

*Team moved from San Diego to Houston.

INDIANA PACERS

Season	Coach	Reg. Sea'n		Playoffs	
		W.	L.	W.	L.
1976-77	Bob Leonard	36	46	—	—

Season	Coach	Reg. Sea'n		Playoffs	
		W.	L.	W.	L.
1977-78	Bob Leonard	31	51	—	—
1978-79	Bob Leonard	38	44	—	—
1979-80	Bob Leonard	37	45	—	—
1980-81	Jack McKinney	44	38	—	2
Totals		186	224	0	2

INDIANAPOLIS JETS

Season	Coach	Reg. Sea'n		Playoffs	
		W.	L.	W.	L.
1948-49	Bruce Hale, 4-13	—	—	—	—
	Burl Friddle, 14-29	18	42	—	—

INDIANAPOLIS OLYMPIANS

Season	Coach	Reg. Sea'n		Playoffs	
		W.	L.	W.	L.
1949-50	Clifford Barker	39	25	3	3
1950-51	Clifford Barker	24	32	—	—
	Wallace Jones	7	5	1	2
1951-52	Herman Schaefer	34	32	0	2
1952-53	Herman Schaefer	28	43	0	2
Totals		132	137	4	9

KANSAS CITY KINGS

Season	Coach	Reg. Sea'n		Playoffs	
		W.	L.	W.	L.
1948-49	Les Harrison	45	15	2	2
1949-50	Les Harrison	51	17	0	2
1950-51	Les Harrison	41	27	9	5
1951-52	Les Harrison	41	25	3	3
1952-53	Les Harrison	44	26	1	2
1953-54	Les Harrison	44	28	3	3
1954-55	Les Harrison	29	43	1	2
1955-56	Bob Wanzer	31	41	—	—
1956-57	Bob Wanzer	31	41	—	—
1957-58*	Bob Wanzer	33	39	0	2
1958-59	Bob Wanzer, 3-15	—	—	—	—
	Tom Marshall, 16-38	19	53	—	—
1959-60	Tom Marshall	19	56	—	—

*Team moved from Rochester to Cincinnati.

Season	Coach	Reg. Sea'n		Playoffs	
		W.	L.	W.	L.
1960-61	Charles Wolf	33	46	—	—
1961-62	Charles Wolf	43	37	1	3
1962-63	Charles Wolf	42	38	6	6
1963-64	Jack McMahon	55	25	4	6
1964-65	Jack McMahon	48	32	1	3
1965-66	Jack McMahon	45	35	2	3
1966-67	Jack McMahon	39	42	1	3
1967-68	Ed Jucker	39	43	—	—
1968-69	Ed Jucker	41	41	—	—
1969-70	Bob Cousy	36	46	—	—
1970-71	Bob Cousy	33	49	—	—
1971-72	Bob Cousy	30	52	—	—
1972-73†	Bob Cousy	36	46	—	—
1973-74	Bob Cousy, 6-16	—	—	—	—
	Draff Young, 0-3	—	—	—	—
	Phil Johnson, 27-30	33	49	—	—
1974-75	Phil Johnson	44	38	2	4
1975-76	Phil Johnson	31	51	—	—
1976-77	Phil Johnson	40	42	—	—
1977-78	Phil Johnson, 13-24	—	—	—	—
	Larry Staverman, 18-27	31	51	—	—
1978-79	Cotton Fitzsimmons	48	34	1	4
1979-80	Cotton Fitzsimmons	47	35	1	2
1980-81	Cotton Fitzsimmons	40	42	7	8
Totals		1262	1285	45	63

†Team moved from Cincinnati to Kansas City-Omaha.

LOS ANGELES LAKERS

Season	Coach	Reg. Sea'n		Playoffs	
		W.	L.	W.	L.
1948-49	John Kundla	44	16	8	2
1949-50	John Kundla	51	17	10	2
1950-51	John Kundla	44	24	3	4
1951-52	John Kundla	40	26	9	4
1952-53	John Kundla	48	22	9	3
1953-54	John Kundla	46	26	9	4
1954-55	John Kundla	40	32	3	4
1955-56	John Kundla	33	39	1	2
1956-57	John Kundla	34	38	2	3

Season	Coach	Reg. Sea'n		Playoffs	
		W.	L.	W.	L.
1957-58	George Mikan, 9-30	—	—	—	—
	John Kundla, 10-23	19	53	—	—
1958-59	John Kundla	33	39	6	7
1959-60	John Castellani, 11-25	—	—	—	—
	Jim Pollard, 14-25	25	50	5	4
1960-61*	Fred Schaus	36	43	6	6
1961-62	Fred Schaus	54	26	7	6
1962-63	Fred Schaus	53	27	6	7
1963-64	Fred Schaus	42	38	2	3
1964-65	Fred Schaus	49	31	5	6
1965-66	Fred Schaus	45	35	7	7
1966-67	Fred Schaus	36	45	0	3
1967-68	Bill van Breda Kolff	52	30	10	5
1968-69	Bill van Breda Kolff	55	27	11	7
1969-70	Joe Mullaney	46	36	11	7
1970-71	Joe Mullaney	48	34	5	7
1971-72	Bill Sharman	69	13	12	3
1972-73	Bill Sharman	60	22	9	8

Bob Lanier, showing his stuff with a shot rejection and a hook, made the Milwaukee Bucks a big winner when he was traded from Detroit, where he had played most of his career. (*Detroit Pistons*)

Season	Coach	Reg. Sea'n		Playoffs	
		W.	L.	W.	L.
1973-74	Bill Sharman	47	35	1	4
1974-75	Bill Sharman	30	52	—	—
1975-76	Bill Sharman	40	42	—	—
1976-77	Jerry West	53	29	4	7
1977-78	Jerry West	45	37	1	2
1978-79	Jerry West	47	35	3	5
1979-80	Jack McKinney, 10-4	—	—	—	—
	Paul Westhead, 50-18	60	22	12	4
1980-81	Paul Westhead	54	28	1	2
Totals		1478	1069	178	138

*Team moved from Minneapolis to Los Angeles.

MILWAUKEE BUCKS

Season	Coach	Reg. Sea'n		Playoffs	
		W.	L.	W.	L.
1968-69	Larry Costello	27	55	—	—
1969-70	Larry Costello	56	26	5	5
1970-71	Larry Costello	66	16	12	2
1971-72	Larry Costello	63	19	6	5
1972-73	Larry Costello	60	22	2	4
1973-74	Larry Costello	59	23	11	5
1974-75	Larry Costello	38	44	—	—
1975-76	Larry Costello	38	44	1	2
1976-77	Larry Costello, 3-15	—	—	—	—
	Don Nelson, 27-37	30	52	—	—
1977-78	Don Nelson	44	38	5	4
1978-79	Don Nelson	38	44	—	—
1979-80	Don Nelson	49	33	3	4
1980-81	Don Nelson	60	22	3	4
Totals		628	438	48	35

NEW JERSEY NETS

Season	Coach	Reg. Sea'n		Playoffs	
		W.	L.	W.	L.
1976-77	Kevin Loughery	22	60	—	—
1977-78*	Kevin Loughery	24	58	—	—
1978-79	Kevin Loughery	37	45	0	2

*Team moved from New York to New Jersey.

Season	Coach	Reg. Sea'n W.	Reg. Sea'n L.	Playoffs W.	Playoffs L.
1979-80	Kevin Loughery	34	48	—	—
1980-81	Kevin Loughery, 12-23	—	—	—	—
	Bob MacKinnon, 12-35	24	58	—	—
Totals		141	269	0	2

NEW YORK KNICKERBOCKERS

Season	Coach	Reg. Sea'n W.	Reg. Sea'n L.	Playoffs W.	Playoffs L.
1946-47	Neil Cohalan	33	27	2	3
1947-48	Joe Lapchick	26	22	1	2
1948-49	Joe Lapchick	32	28	3	3
1949-50	Joe Lapchick	40	28	3	2
1950-51	Joe Lapchick	36	30	8	6
1951-52	Joe Lapchick	37	29	8	6
1952-53	Joe Lapchick	47	23	6	5
1953-54	Joe Lapchick	44	28	0	4
1954-55	Joe Lapchick	38	34	1	2
1955-56	Joe Lapchick, 26-25	—	—	—	—
	Vince Boryla, 9-12	35	37	—	—
1956-57	Vince Boryla	36	36	—	—
1957-58	Vince Boryla	35	37	—	—
1958-59	Andrew Levane	40	32	0	2
1959-60	Andrew Levane, 8-19	—	—	—	—
	Carl Braun, 19-29	27	48	—	—
1960-61	Carl Braun	21	58	—	—
1961-62	Eddie Donovan	29	51	—	—
1962-63	Eddie Donovan	22	58	—	—
1963-64	Eddie Donovan	22	58	—	—
1964-65	Eddie Donovan	—	—	—	—
	Harry Gallatin, 19-23	31	49	—	—
1965-66	Harry Gallatin, 6-15	—	—	—	—
	Dick McGuire, 24-35	30	50	—	—
1966-67	Dick McGuire	36	45	1	3
1967-68	Dick McGuire, 15-22	—	—	—	—
	Red Holzman, 28-17	43	39	2	4
1968-69	Red Holzman	54	28	6	4
1969-70	Red Holzman	60	22	12	7
1970-71	Red Holzman	52	30	7	5

Season	Coach	Reg. Sea'n		Playoffs	
		W.	L.	W.	L.
1971-72	Red Holzman	48	34	9	7
1972-73	Red Holzman	57	25	12	5
1973-74	Red Holzman	49	33	5	7
1974-75	Red Holzman	40	42	1	2
1975-76	Red Holzman	38	44	—	—
1976-77	Red Holzman	40	42	—	—
1977-78	Willis Reed	43	39	2	4
1978-79	Willis Reed, 6-8	—	—	—	—
	Red Holzman, 25-43	31	51	—	—
1979-80	Red Holzman	39	43	—	—
1980-81	Red Holzman	50	32	0	2
Totals		1340	1313	89	85

PHILADELPHIA 76ERS

Season	Coach	Reg. Sea'n		Playoffs	
		W.	L.	W.	L.
1949-50	Al Cervi	51	13	6	5
1950-51	Al Cervi	32	34	4	3
1951-52	Al Cervi	40	26	3	4
1952-53	Al Cervi	47	2	0	2
1953-54	Al Cervi	42	30	9	4
1954-55	Al Cervi	43	29	7	4
1955-56	Al Cervi	35	37	4	4
1956-57	Al Cervi, 4-8	—	—	—	—
	Paul Seymour, 34-26	38	34	2	3
1957-58	Paul Seymour	41	31	1	2
1958-59	Paul Seymour	35	37	5	4
1959-60	Paul Seymour	45	30	1	2
1960-61	Alex Hannum	38	41	4	4
1961-62	Alex Hannum	41	39	2	3
1962-63	Alex Hannum	48	32	2	3
1963-64*	Dolph Schayes	34	46	2	3
1964-65	Dolph Schayes	40	40	6	5
1965-66	Dolph Schayes	55	25	1	4
1966-67	Alex Hannum	68	13	11	4
1967-68	Alex Hannum	62	20	7	6
1968-69	Jack Ramsay	55	27	1	4

| Season | Coach | Reg. Sea'n | | Playoffs | |
		W.	L.	W.	L.
1969-70	Jack Ramsay	42	40	1	4
1970-71	Jack Ramsay	47	35	3	4
1971-72	Jack Ramsay	30	52	—	—
1972-73	Roy Rubin, 4-47	—	—	—	—
	Kevin Loughery, 5-26	9	73	—	—
1973-74	Gene Shue	25	57	—	—
1974-75	Gene Shue	34	48	—	—
1975-76	Gene Shue	46	36	1	2
1976-77	Gene Shue	50	32	10	9
1977-78	Gene Shue, 2-4	—	—	—	—
	Billy Cunningham, 53-23	55	27	6	4
1978-79	Billy Cunningham	47	35	5	4
1979-80	Billy Cunningham	59	23	12	6
1980-81	Billy Cunningham	62	20	9	7
	Totals	1396	1086	125	113

*Team moved from Syracuse to Philadelphia.

Len (Truck) Robinson formed an important part of an overpowering Phoenix front line — and he could shoot, too. (Phoenix Suns)

PHOENIX SUNS

Season	Coach	Reg. Sea'n		Playoffs	
		W.	L.	W.	L.
1968-69	Johnny Kerr	16	66	—	—
1969-70	Johnny Kerr, 15-23	—	—	—	—
	Jerry Colangelo, 24-20	39	43	3	4
1970-71	Cotton Fitzsimmons	48	34	—	—
1971-72	Cotton Fitzsimmons	49	33	—	—
1972-73	B. van Breda Kolff 3-5	—	—	—	—
	Jerry Colangelo, 35-39	38	44	—	—
1973-74	John MacLeod	30	52	—	—
1974-75	John MacLeod	32	50	—	—
1975-76	John MacLeod	42	40	10	9
1976-77	John MacLeod	34	48	—	—
1977-78	John MacLeod	49	33	0	2
1978-79	John MacLeod	50	32	9	6
1979-80	John MacLeod	55	27	3	5
1980-81	John MacLeod	57	25	3	4
Totals		539	527	28	30

PITTSBURGH IRONMEN

Season	Coach	Reg. Sea'n		Playoffs	
		W.	L.	W.	L.
1946-47	Paul Birch	15	45	—	—

PORTLAND TRAIL BLAZERS

Season	Coach	Reg. Sea'n		Playoffs	
		W.	L.	W.	L.
1970-71	Rolland Todd	29	53	—	—
1971-72	Rolland Todd, 12-44	—	—	—	—
	Stu Inman, 6-20	18	64	—	—
1972-73	Jack McCloskey	21	61	—	—
1973-74	Jack McCloskey	27	55	—	—
1974-75	Len Wilkens	38	44	—	—
1975-76	Len Wilkens	37	45	—	—
1976-77	Jack Ramsay	49	33	14	5
1977-78	Jack Ramsay	58	24	2	4
1978-79	Jack Ramsay	45	37	1	2
1979-80	Jack Ramsay	38	44	1	2
1980-81	Jack Ramsay	45	37	1	2
Totals		405	497	19	15

PROVIDENCE STEAMROLLERS

Season	Coach	Reg. Sea'n		Playoffs	
		W.	L.	W.	L.
1946-47	Robert Morris	28	32	—	—
1947-48	Albert Soar, 2-17	—	—	—	—
	Nat Hickey, 4-25	6	42	—	—
1948-49	Ken Loeffler	12	48	—	—
Totals		46	122	—	—

ST. LOUIS BOMBERS

Season	Coach	Reg. Sea'n		Playoffs	
		W.	L.	W.	L.
1946-47	Ken Loeffler	38	23	1	2
1947-48	Ken Loeffler	29	19	3	4
1948-49	Grady Lewis	29	31	0	2
1949-50	Grady Lewis	26	42	—	—
Totals		122	115	4	8

SAN ANTONIO SPURS

Season	Coach	Reg. Sea'n		Playoffs	
		W.	L.	W.	L.
1976-77	Doug Moe	44	38	0	2
1977-78	Doug Moe	52	30	2	4
1978-79	Doug Moe	48	34	7	7
1979-80	Doug Moe, 32-33	—	—	—	—
	Bob Bass, 8-8	41	41	1	2
1980-81	Stan Albeck	52	30	3	4
Totals		237	173	13	19

SAN DIEGO CLIPPERS

Season	Coach	Reg. Sea'n		Playoffs	
		W.	L.	W.	L.
1970-71	Dolph Schayes	22	60	—	—
1971-72	Dolph Schayes, 0-1	—	—	—	—
	John McCarthy, 22-59	22	60	—	—
1972-73	Jack Ramsay	21	61	—	—
1973-74	Jack Ramsay	42	40	2	4
1974-75	Jack Ramsay	49	33	3	4
1975-76	Jack Ramsay	46	36	4	5
1976-77	Tates Locke, 16-30	—	—	—	—

Season	Coach	Reg. Sea'n		Playoffs	
		W.	L.	W.	L.
	Bob MacKinnon, 3-4	—	—	—	—
	Joe Mullaney, 11-18	30	52	—	—
1977-78	Cotton Fitzsimmons	27	55	—	—
1978-79*	Gene Shue	43	39	—	—
1979-80	Gene Shue	35	47	—	—
1980-81	Paul Silas	36	46	—	—
Totals		376	526	9	13

*Team moved from Buffalo to San Diego.

SEATTLE SUPERSONICS

Season	Coach	Reg. Sea'n		Playoffs	
		W.	L.	W.	L.
1967-68	Al Bianchi	23	59	—	—
1968-69	Al Bianchi	30	52	—	—
1969-70	Len Wilkens	36	46	—	—
1970-71	Len Wilkens	38	44	—	—
1971-72	Len Wilkens	47	35	—	—
1972-73	Tom Nissalke, 13-32	—	—	—	—
	B. Buckwalter, 13-24	26	56	—	—
1973-74	Bill Russell	36	46	—	—
1974-75	Bill Russell	43	39	4	5
1975-76	Bill Russell	43	39	2	4
1976-77	Bill Russell	40	42	—	—
1977-78	Bob Hopkins, 5-17	—	—	—	—
	Len Wilkens, 42-18	47	35	13	9
1978-79	Len Wilkens	52	30	12	5
1979-80	Len Wilkens	56	26	7	8
1980-81	Len Wilkens	34	48	—	—
Totals		551	597	38	31

SHEBOYGAN REDSKINS

Season	Coach	Reg. Sea'n		Playoffs	
		W.	L.	W.	L.
1949-50	Ken Suesens	22	40	1	2

TORONTO HUSKIES

Season	Coach	Reg. Sea'n		Playoffs	
		W.	L.	W.	L.
1946-47	Ed Sadowski, 3-9	—	—	—	—
	Lew Hayman, 0-1	—	—	—	—
	Dick Fitzgerald, 2-1	—	—	—	—
	Robert Rolfe, 17-27	22	38	—	—

Darrell Griffith electrified fans of the Utah Jazz with his spectacular jumpers and dunks as a rookie in 1981. *(Utah Jazz)*

UTAH JAZZ

Season	Coach	Reg. Sea'n		Playoffs	
1974-75	Scotty Robertson, 1-14	—	—	—	—
	Elgin Baylor, 0-1	—	—	—	—
	B. van Breda Kolff, 22-44	23	59	—	—
1975-76	B. van Breda Kolff	38	44	—	—
1976-77	B. van Breda Kolff, 14-22	—	—	—	—
	Elgin Baylor, 21-35	35	47	—	—
1977-78	Elgin Baylor	39	43	—	—
1978-79	Elgin Baylor	26	56	—	—
1979-80*	Tom Nissalke	28	58	—	—
1980-81	Tom Nissalke	24	54	—	—
Totals		213	361	—	—

*Team moved from New Orleans to Utah.

WASHINGTON BULLETS

Season	Coach	Reg. Sea'n		Playoffs	
		W.	L.	W.	L.
1961-62*	Jim Pollard	18	62	—	—
1962-63†	Jack McMahon, 12-26	—	—	—	—

Season	Coach	Reg. Sea'n		Playoffs	
		W.	L.	W.	L.
	Bob Leonard, 13-29	25	55	—	—
1963-64‡	Bob Leonard	31	49	—	—
1964-65	Buddy Jeannette	37	43	5	5
1965-66	Paul Seymour	38	42	0	3
1966-67	Mike Farmer, 1-8	—	—	—	—
	Buddy Jeannette, 3-13	—	—	—	—
	Gene Shue, 16-40	20	61	—	—
1967-68	Gene Shue	36	46	—	—
1968-69	Gene Shue	57	25	0	4
1969-70	Gene Shue	50	32	3	4
1970-71	Gene Shue	42	40	8	10
1971-72	Gene Shue	38	44	2	4
1972-73	Gene Shue	52	30	1	4
1973-74**	K. C. Jones	47	35	3	4
1974-75	K. C. Jones	60	22	8	9
1975-76	K. C. Jones	48	34	3	4
1976-77	Dick Motta	48	34	4	5
1977-78	Dick Motta	44	38	14	7
1978-79	Dick Motta	54	28	9	10
1979-80	Dick Motta	39	43	0	2
1980-81	Gene Shue	39	43	—	—
Totals		823	806	60	75

*Known as Chicago Packers.
†Name changed to Chicago Zephyrs.
‡Moved to Baltimore: new name Bullets.
**Known as Capital Bullets.

WASHINGTON CAPITOLS

Season	Coach	Reg. Sea'n		Playoffs	
		W.	L.	W.	L.
1946-47	Arnold Auerbach	49	11	2	4
1947-48	Arnold Auerbach	28	20	—	—
1948-49	Arnold Auerbach	38	22	6	5
1949-50	Robert Feerick	32	36	0	2
1950-51*	Horace McKinney	10	25	—	—
Totals		157	114	8	11

*Team disbanded January 9.

WATERLOO HAWKS

Season	Coach	Reg. Sea'n W.	L.	Playoffs W.	L.
1949-50	Charles Shipp	8	27	—	—
	Jack Smiley	11	16	—	—
Totals		19	43	—	—

All-Time Winningest NBA Coaches

Coach	W-L	Pct.	Coach	W-L	Pct.
Red Auerbach	938-479	.662	BILLY CUNNINGHAM	219-103	.680
RED HOLZMAN	663-555	.544	DON NELSON	218-174	.556
JACK RAMSAY	567-499	.549	HUBIE BROWN	199-208	.491
GENE SHUE	565-563	.501	Dick McGuire	197-260	.431
DICK MOTTA	556-516	.522	TOM NISSALKE	189-266	.415
Alex Hannum	471-412	.533	Bob Leonard	186-264	.413
AL ATTLES	482-429	.529	Doug Moe	177-135	.567
Larry Costello	430-300	.589	Phil Johnson	155-185	.456
Tom Heinsohn	427-263	.619	K. C. Jones	155-91	.630
BILL FITCH	427-475	.473	Dolph Schayes	151-172	.467
John Kundla	423-302	.583	Ray Scott	147-134	.523
COTTON FITZSIMMONS	399-413	.491	Jerry West	145-101	.589
LEN WILKENS	380-336	.531	Charles Wolf	143-187	.433
JOHN MacLEOD	349-307	.532	Bob Cousy	141-209	.403
Bill Sharman	333-240	.581	Harry Gallatin	136-120	.531
Richie Guerin	327-291	.529	Buddy Jeannette	136-173	.440
Al Cervi	326-241	.575	KEVIN LOUGHERY	134-260	.340
Joe Lapchick	326-247	.569	Johnny Egan	129-152	.459
Bill Russell	324-249	.565	Larry Brown	126-91	.581
Fred Schaus	315-245	.563	Charlie Eckman	123-118	.510
Les Harrison	295-181	.620	Paul Birch	120-147	.449
Paul Seymour	271-241	.529	George Senesky	119-97	.551
Bill van Breda Kolff	266-256	.510	Fuzzy Levane	107-70	.384
Eddie Gottlieb	263-318	.453	Joe Mullaney	105-88	.544
Jack McMahon	260-289	.474			

Active head coaches in capital letters.

N B A
Records

INDIVIDUAL CAREER

MOST GAMES: John Havlicek, Boston, 1270

MOST FIELD GOALS ATTEMPTED: John Havlicek, Boston, 23,900

MOST FIELD GOALS MADE: Wilt Chamberlain, Philadelphia-San Francisco-Los Angeles, 12,681

HIGHEST SCORING AVERAGE (minimum 400 games): Wilt Chamberlain, Philadelphia-San Francisco-Los Angeles, 30.1

HIGHEST FIELD GOAL PERCENTAGE (minimum 2000 FG): Artis Gilmore, Chicago, .559

HIGHEST FREE THROW PERCENTAGE (minimum 1200 FT): Rick Barry, Golden State-Houston, .900

MOST FREE THROWS ATTEMPTED: Wilt Chamberlain, Philadelphia-San Francisco-Los Angeles, 11,862

MOST FREE THROWS MADE: Oscar Robertson, Cincinnati-Milwaukee, 7694

MOST REBOUNDS: Wilt Chamberlain, Philadelphia-San Francisco-Los Angeles, 23,924

MOST ASSISTS: Oscar Robertson, Cincinnati-Milwaukee, 9887

INDIVIDUAL SEASON

MOST FIELD GOALS ATTEMPTED: Wilt Chamberlain, Philadelphia, 1961-62, 3159

MOST FIELD GOALS MADE: Wilt Chamberlain, Philadelphia, 1961-62, 1597

HIGHEST SCORING AVERAGE: Wilt Chamberlain, Philadelphia, 1961-62, 50.4

HIGHEST FIELD GOAL PERCENTAGE: Wilt Chamberlain, Los Angeles, 1972-73, .727

HIGHEST FREE THROW PERCENTAGE: Rick Barry, Houston, 1978-79, .947

MOST FREE THROWS ATTEMPTED: Wilt Chamberlain, Philadelphia, 1961-62, 1363

MOST FREE THROWS MADE: Jerry West, Los Angeles, 1965-66, 840

MOST REBOUNDS: Wilt Chamberlain, Philadelphia, 1960-61, 2149

MOST ASSISTS: Kevin Porter, Detroit, 1978-79, 1099

INDIVIDUAL GAME

MOST POINTS: Wilt Chamberlain, Philadelphia vs. New York, March 2, 1962, 100

MOST FIELD GOALS ATTEMPTED: Wilt Chamberlain, Philadelphia vs. New York, March 2, 1962, 63

MOST FIELD GOALS MADE: Wilt Chamberlain, Philadelphia vs. New York, March 2, 1962, 36

MOST FREE THROWS ATTEMPTED: Wilt Chamberlain, Philadelphia vs. St. Louis, February 22, 1962, 34

MOST FREE THROWS MADE: Wilt Chamberlain, Philadelphia vs. New York, March 2, 1962, 28

MOST REBOUNDS: Wilt Chamberlain, Philadelphia vs. Boston, Nov. 24, 1960, 55

MOST ASSISTS: Kevin Porter, New Jersey vs. Houston, Feb. 24, 1978, 29

MOST POINTS SCORED IN ONE GAME
(IN REGULAR SEASON PLAY)

	FG	F	Pts.
Wilt Chamberlain, Philadelphia vs. New York at Hershey, Pa., March 2, 1962	36	28	100
Wilt Chamberlain, Philadelphia vs. Los Angeles at Philadelphia, December 8, 1961	***31	16	78
Wilt Chamberlain, Philadelphia vs. Chicago at Philadelphia, January 13, 1962	29	15	73
Wilt Chamberlain, San Francisco at New York, November 16, 1962	29	15	73
David Thompson, Denver at Detroit, April 9, 1978	28	17	73
Wilt Chamberlain, San Francisco at Los Angeles, November 3, 1962	29	14	72
Elgin Baylor, Los Angeles at New York, November 15, 1960	28	15	71
Wilt Chamberlain, San Francisco at Syracuse, March 10, 1963	27	16	70
Wilt Chamberlain, Philadelphia at Chicago, December 16, 1967	30	8	68
Pete Maravich, New Orleans vs. Knicks, February 25, 1977	26	16	68
Wilt Chamberlain, Philadelphia vs. New York at Philadelphia, March 9, 1961	27	13	67
Wilt Chamberlain, Philadelphia at St. Louis, February 17, 1962	26	15	67
Wilt Chamberlain, Philadelphia vs. New York at Philadelphia, February 26, 1962	25	17	67
Wilt Chamberlain, San Francisco vs. Los Angeles at San Francisco, January 17, 1963	28	11	67
Wilt Chamberlain, Los Angeles at Phoenix, February 9, 1969	29	8	66

Wilt Chamberlain, Philadelphia at Cincinnati, February 13, 1962	24	17	65
Wilt Chamberlain, Philadelphia at St. Louis, February 27, 1962	25	15	65
Wilt Chamberlain, Philadelphia vs. Los Angeles at Philadelphia, February 7, 1966	28	9	65
Elgin Baylor, Minneapolis vs. Boston at Minneapolis, November 8, 1959	25	14	64
Rick Barry, Golden State vs. Portland at Oakland, March 26, 1974	30	4	64
Joe Fulks, Philadelphia vs. Indianapolis at Philadelphia, February 10, 1949	27	9	63
Elgin Baylor, Los Angeles at Philadelphia, December 8, 1961	***23	17	63
Jerry West, Los Angeles vs. New York at Los Angeles, January 17, 1962	22	19	63
Wilt Chamberlain, San Francisco vs. Los Angeles at San Francisco, December 14, 1963	24	15	63
Wilt Chamberlain, San Francisco at Philadelphia, November 26, 1964	27	9	63
George Gervin, San Antonio at New Orleans, April 9, 1978	23	17	63
Wilt Chamberlain, Philadelphia at Boston, January 14, 1962	27	8	62
Wilt Chamberlain, Philadelphia vs. St. Louis at Detroit, January 17, 1962	*24	14	62
Wilt Chamberlain, Philadelphia vs. Syracuse at Utica, New York, January 21, 1962	*25	12	62
Wilt Chamberlain, San Francisco at New York, January 29, 1963	27	8	62
Wilt Chamberlain, San Francisco at Cincinnati, November 15, 1964	26	10	62
Wilt Chamberlain, Philadelphia vs. San Francisco at Philadelphia, March 3, 1966	26	10	62
George Mikan, Minneapolis vs. Rochester at Minneapolis, January 20, 1952	**22	17	61
Wilt Chamberlain, Philadelphia vs. Chicago at Philadelphia, December 9, 1961	28	5	61
Wilt Chamberlain, Philadelphia vs. St. Louis at Philadelphia, February 22, 1962	21	19	61
Wilt Chamberlain, Philadelphia at Chicago, February 28, 1962	24	13	61
Wilt Chamberlain, San Francisco vs. Cincinnati at San Francisco, November 21, 1962	27	7	61
Wilt Chamberlain, San Francisco vs. Syracuse at San Francisco, December 11, 1962	25	11	61
Wilt Chamberlain, San Francisco vs. St. Louis at San Francisco, December 18, 1962	26	9	61
Wilt Chamberlain, Philadelphia at Los Angeles, December 1, 1961	22	16	60
Wilt Chamberlain, Philadelphia vs. Los Angeles at Hershey, Pa., December 29, 1961	24	12	60

Wilt Chamberlain, Los Angeles vs. Cincinnati at Cleveland, January 26, 1969	22	16	60
Jack Twyman, Cincinnati vs. Minneapolis at Cincinnati, January 15, 1960	21	17	59
Wilt Chamberlain, Philadelphia at New York, December 25, 1961	**23	13	59
Wilt Chamberlain, Philadelphia vs. New York at Syracuse, February 8, 1962	23	13	59
Wilt Chamberlain, San Francisco vs. New York at San Francisco, October 30, 1962	24	11	59
Wilt Chamberlain, San Francisco at Cincinnati, November 18, 1962	24	11	59
Wilt Chamberlain, San Francisco vs. St. Louis at San Francisco, December 2, 1962	25	9	59
Wilt Chamberlain, San Francisco vs. Los Angeles at San Francisco, December 6, 1963	22	15	59
Wilt Chamberlain, San Francisco at Philadelphia, January 28, 1964	24	11	59
Wilt Chamberlain, San Francisco at Detroit, February 11, 1964	*25	9	59
Wilt Chamberlain, Philadelphia vs. Detroit at Bethlehem, Pa., January 25, 1960	24	10	58
Wilt Chamberlain, Philadelphia at New York, February 21, 1960	26	6	58
Wilt Chamberlain, Philadelphia at Cincinnati, February 25, 1961	25	8	58
Wilt Chamberlain, Philadelphia vs. Detroit at Philadelphia, November 4, 1961	24	10	58
Wilt Chamberlain, Philadelphia at Detroit, November 8, 1961	23	12	58
Wilt Chamberlain, Philadelphia at New York, March 4, 1962	24	10	58
Wilt Chamberlain, San Francisco vs. Detroit at Bakersfield, Calif., January 24, 1963	25	8	58
Wilt Chamberlain, San Francisco at New York, December 15, 1964	*25	8	58
Wilt Chamberlain, Philadelphia vs. Cincinnati at Philadelphia, February 13, 1967	26	6	58
Fred Brown, Seattle at Golden State, March 23, 1974	24	10	58

*Denotes each overtime period played.

(left) Pete Maravich was a high-scoring, spectacular-passing guard who was often surrounded by controversy during his career. (*Utah Jazz*)

NBA Hall of Famers

CONTRIBUTORS

Name	Year Elected
BEE, CLAIR F.	1967
*BROWN, WALTER A.	1965
*GOTTLIEB, EDWARD	1971
HARRISON, LESTER	1979
IRISH, NED	1964
KENNEDY, J. WALTER	1980
*MOKRAY, WM. G. (BILL)	1965
NEWELL, PETER F.	1978
*OLSEN, HAROLD G.	1959
PODOLOFF, MAURICE	1973

PLAYERS

ARIZIN, PAUL J.	1977
BAYLOR, ELGIN	1976
CHAMBERLAIN, WILT	1978
COUSY, ROBERT J.	1970
DAVIES, ROBERT E. (BOB)	1969
*DEHNERT, H. G. (DUTCH)	1968
*FULKS, JOSEPH F. (JOE)	1977
GOLA, TOM	1975
HAGAN, CLIFFORD O.	1977
*LAPCHICK, JOE	1966
LUCAS, JERRY	1979
MACAULEY, C. EDWARD	1960

MIKAN, GEORGE L.	1959
PETTIT, ROBERT L.	1970
PHILLIP, ANDY	1961
POLLARD, JAMES C. (JIM)	1977
ROBERTSON, OSCAR	1979
*RUSSELL, JOHN (HONEY)	1964
RUSSELL, WILLIAM (BILL)	1974
SCHAYES, ADOLPH	1972
SHARMAN, BILL	1975
WEST, JERRY	1979

COACHES

AUERBACH, A. J. (RED)	1968
*JULIAN, ALVIN F. (DOGGIE)	1967
*LOEFFLER, KENNETH D.	1964
MCGUIRE, FRANK	1976

REFEREES

*KENNEDY, MATTHEW P.	1959
NUCATOLA, JOHN P.	1977

TEAMS (NOT NBA)

Original Celtics	1959
Buffalo Germans	1961
Renaissance	1963

*Deceased.

NBA All-Star Teams

SELECTED BY WRITERS AND BROADCASTERS

1946-47
Joe Fulks (Philadelphia)
Bob Feerick (Washington)
Stan Miasek (Detroit)
Bones McKinney (Washington)
Max Zaslofsky (Chicago)

1947-48
Joe Fulks (Philadelphia)
Max Zaslofsky (Chicago)
Ed Sadowski (Boston)
Howie Dallmar (Philadelphia)
Bob Feerick (Washington)

1948-49
George Mikan (Minneapolis)
Joe Fulks (Philadelphia)
Bob Davies (Rochester)
Max Zaslofsky (Chicago)
Jim Pollard (Minneapolis)

1949-50
George Mikan (Minneapolis)
Jim Pollard (Minneapolis)
Alex Groza (Indianapolis)
Bob Davies (Rochester)
Max Zaslofsky (Chicago)

1950-51
George Mikan (Minneapolis)
Alex Groza (Indianapolis)
Ed Macauley (Boston)
Bob Davies (Rochester)
Ralph Beard (Indianapolis)

1951-52
George Mikan (Minneapolis)
Ed Macauley (Boston)
Paul Arizin (Philadelphia)
Bob Cousy (Boston)
Bob Davies (Rochester)
Dolph Schayes (Syracuse)

1952-53
George Mikan (Minneapolis)
Bob Cousy (Boston)
Neil Johnston (Philadelphia)
Ed Macauley (Boston)
Dolph Schayes (Syracuse)

1953-54
Bob Cousy (Boston)
Neil Johnston (Philadelphia)
George Mikan (Minneapolis)
Dolph Schayes (Syracuse)
Harry Gallatin (New York)

1954-55
Neil Johnston (Philadelphia)
Bob Cousy (Boston)
Dolph Schayes (Syracuse)
Bob Pettit (Milwaukee)
Larry Foust (Fort Wayne)

1955-56
Bob Pettit (St. Louis)
Paul Arizin (Philadelphia)
Neil Johnston (Philadelphia)
Bob Cousy (Boston)
Bill Sharman (Boston)

1956-57
Paul Arizin (Philadelphia)
Dolph Schayes (Syracuse)
Bob Pettit (St. Louis)
Bob Cousy (Boston)
Bill Sharman (Boston)

1957-58
Dolph Schayes (Syracuse)
George Yardley (Detroit)
Bob Pettit (St. Louis)
Bob Cousy (Boston)
Bill Sharman (Boston)

1958-59
Bob Pettit (St. Louis)
Elgin Baylor (Minneapolis)
Bill Russell (Boston)
Bob Cousy (Boston)
Bill Sharman (Boston)

1959-60
Bob Pettit (St. Louis)
Elgin Baylor (Minneapolis)
Wilt Chamberlain (Philadelphia)
Bob Cousy (Boston)
Gene Shue (Detroit)

1960-61
Elgin Baylor (Los Angeles)
Bob Pettit (St. Louis)
Wilt Chamberlain (Philadelphia)
Bob Cousy (Boston)
Oscar Robertson (Cincinnati)

1961-62
Bob Pettit (St. Louis)
Elgin Baylor (Los Angeles)
Wilt Chamberlain (Philadelphia)
Jerry West (Los Angeles)
Oscar Robertson (Cincinnati)

1962-63
Elgin Baylor (Los Angeles)
Bob Pettit (St. Louis)
Bill Russell (Boston)
Oscar Robertson (Cincinnati)
Jerry West (Los Angeles)

1963-64
Bob Pettit (St. Louis)
Elgin Baylor (Los Angeles)
Wilt Chamberlain (San Francisco)
Oscar Robertson (Cincinnati)
Jerry West (Los Angeles)

1964-65
Elgin Baylor (Los Angeles)
Jerry Lucas (Cincinnati)
Bill Russell (Boston)
Oscar Robertson (Cincinnati)
Jerry West (Los Angeles)

1965-66
Rick Barry (San Francisco)
Jerry Lucas (Cincinnati)
Wilt Chamberlain (Philadelphia)
Oscar Robertson (Cincinnati)
Jerry West (Los Angeles)

1966-67
Rick Barry (San Francisco)
Elgin Baylor (Los Angeles)
Wilt Chamberlain (Philadelphia)
Jerry West (Los Angeles)
Oscar Robertson (Cincinnati)

1967-68
Elgin Baylor (Los Angeles)
Jerry Lucas (Cincinnati)
Wilt Chamberlain (Philadelphia)
Dave Bing (Detroit)
Oscar Robertson (Cincinnati)

1968-69
Billy Cunningham (Philadelphia)
Elgin Baylor (Los Angeles)
Wes Unseld (Baltimore)
Earl Monroe (Baltimore)
Oscar Robertson (Cincinnati)

1969-70
Billy Cunningham (Philadelphia)
Connie Hawkins (Phoenix)
Willis Reed (New York)
Jerry West (Los Angeles)
Walt Frazier (New York)

1970-71
John Havlicek (Boston)
Billy Cunningham (Philadelphia)
Lew Alcindor (Milwaukee)
Jerry West (Los Angeles)
Dave Bing (Detroit)

1971-72
John Havlicek (Boston)
Spencer Haywood (Seattle)
Kareem Abdul-Jabbar (Milwaukee)
Jerry West (Los Angeles)
Walt Frazier (New York)

1972-73
John Havlicek (Boston)
Spencer Haywood (Seattle)
Kareem Abdul-Jabbar (Milwaukee)
Nate Archibald (Kansas City-Omaha)
Jerry West (Los Angeles)

1973-74
John Havlicek (Boston)
Rick Barry (Golden State)
Kareem Abdul-Jabbar (Milwaukee)
Walt Frazier (New York)
Gail Goodrich (Los Angeles)

1974-75
Rick Barry (Golden State)
Elvin Hayes (Washington)
Bob McAdoo (Buffalo)
Nate Archibald (Kansas City-Omaha)
Walt Frazier (New York)

1975-76
Rick Barry (Golden State)
George McGinnis (Philadelphia)
Kareem Abdul-Jabbar (Los Angeles)
Nate Archibald (Kansas City)
Pete Maravich (New Orleans)

1976-77
Elvin Hayes (Washington)
David Thompson (Denver)
Kareem Abdul-Jabbar (Los Angeles)
Pete Maravich (New Orleans)
Paul Westphal (Phoenix)

1977-78
Leonard Robinson (New Orleans)
Julius Erving (Philadelphia)
Bill Walton (Portland)
George Gervin (San Antonio)
David Thompson (Denver)

1978-79
Marques Johnson (Milwaukee)
Elvin Hayes (Washington)
Moses Malone (Houston)
George Gervin (San Antonio)
Paul Westphal (Phoenix)

1979-80
Julius Erving ((Philadelphia)
Larry Bird (Boston)
Kareem Abdul-Jabbar (Los Angeles)
George Gervin (San Antonio)
Paul Westphal (Phoenix)

(left) Paul Westphal, getting off a jump shot against the Lakers' Michael Cooper, was one of the best offensive guards in the NBA. *(Seattle SuperSonics)*

1980-81
Julius Erving (Philadelphia)
Larry Bird (Boston)

Kareem Abdul-Jabbar (Los Angeles)
George Gervin (San Antonio)
Dennis Johnson (Phoenix)

N B A

Post-Season Awards

MOST VALUABLE PLAYER (MAURICE PODOLOFF TROPHY)

By Vote of NBA Players

1955-56—Bob Pettit, St. Louis
1956-57—Bob Cousy, Boston
1957-58—Bill Russell, Boston
1958-59—Bob Pettit, St. Louis
1959-60—Wilt Chamberlain, Phila.
1960-61—Bill Russell, Boston
1961-62—Bill Russell, Boston
1962-63—Bill Russell, Boston
1963-64—Oscar Robertson, Cincinnati
1964-65—Bill Russell, Boston
1965-66—Wilt Chamberlain, Phila.
1966-67—Wilt Chamberlain, Phila.
1967-68—Wilt Chamberlain, Phila.

1968-69—West Unseld, Baltimore
1969-70—Willis Reed, New York
1970-71—Lew Alcindor, Milwaukee
1971-72—Kareem Abdul-Jabbar, Milw.
1972-73—Dave Cowens, Boston
1973-74—Kareem Abdul-Jabbar, Milw.
1974-75—Bob McAdoo, Buffalo
1975-76—Kareem Abdul-Jabbar, L.A.
1976-77—Kareem Abdul-Jabbar, L.A.
1977-78—Bill Walton, Portland
1978-79—Moses Malone, Houston
1979-80—Kareem Abdul-Jabbar, L.A.
1980-81—Julius Erving, Phila.

EXECUTIVE OF THE YEAR

Selected by The Sporting News

1972-73—Joe Axelson, Kansas City-
　　　　　Omaha
1973-74—Eddie Donovan, Buffalo
1974-75—Dick Vertlieb, Golden State
1975-76—Jerry Colangelo, Phoenix

1976-77—Ray Patterson, Houston
1977-78—Angelo Drossos, San Antonio
1978-79—Bob Ferry, Washington
1979-80—Red Auerbach, Boston
1980-81—Jerry Colangelo, Phoenix

COACH OF THE YEAR

Selected by Writers and Broadcasters

1962-63—Harry Gallatin, St. Louis
1963-64—Alex Hannum, San Francisco
1964-65—Red Auerbach, Boston
1965-66—Dolph Schayes, Philadelphia
1966-67—Johnny Kerr, Chicago
1967-68—Richie Guerin, St. Louis
1968-69—Gene Shue, Baltimore
1969-70—Red Holzman, New York
1970-71—Dick Motta, Chicago
1971-72—Bill Sharman, Los Angeles
1972-73—Tom Heinsohn, Boston

1973-74—Ray Scott, Detroit
1974-75—Phil Johnson, Kansas City-Omaha
1975-76—Bill Fitch, Cleveland
1976-77—Tom Nissalke, Houston
1977-78—Hubie Brown, Atlanta
1978-79—Cotton Fitzsimmons, Kansas City
1979-80—Bill Fitch, Boston
1980-81—Jack McKinney, Indiana

ROOKIE OF THE YEAR (EDDIE GOTTLIEB TROPHY)

Selected by Writers and Broadcasters

1952-53—Don Meineke, Fort Wayne
1953-54—Ray Felix, Baltimore
1954-55—Bob Pettit, Milwaukee
1955-56—Maurice Stokes, Rochester
1956-57—Tom Heinsohn, Boston
1957-58—Woody Sauldsberry, Phila.
1958-59—Elgin Baylor, Minneapolis
1959-60—Wilt Chamberlain, Phila.
1960-61—Oscar Robertson, Cincinnati
1961-62—Walt Bellamy, Chicago
1962-63—Terry Dischinger, Chicago
1963-64—Jerry Lucas, Cincinnati
1964-65—Willis Reed, New York
1965-66—Rick Barry, San Francisco
1966-67—Dave Bing, Detroit

1967-68—Earl Monroe, Baltimore
1968-69—Wes Unseld, Baltimore
1969-70—Lew Alcindor, Milwaukee
1970-71—Dave Cowens, Boston and Geoff Petrie, Portland
1971-72—Sidney Wicks, Portland
1972-73—Bob McAdoo, Buffalo
1973-74—Ernie DiGregorio, Buffalo
1974-75—Keith Wilkes, Golden State
1975-76—Alvan Adams, Phoenix
1976-77—Adrian Dantley, Buffalo
1977-78—Walter Davis, Phoenix
1978-79—Phil Ford, Kansas City
1979-80—Larry Bird, Boston
1980-81—Darrell Griffith, Utah

Alvan Adams was a quick, sharp-passing and good-shooting center for Phoenix. Though sometimes overpowered by bigger centers, he gave opposing centers fits with his quickness. *(Phoenix Suns)*

Neither Bobby Jones (*left*) **nor Darryl Dawkins seems able to stop the determined Wes Unseld as he drives for the basket.** (*Washington Bullets; Gary N. Fine*)

Leaders

YEARLY INDIVIDUAL LEADERS—REGULAR SEASON

Year	League	POINTS PER GAME			FIELD GOAL PERCENTAGE			FREE THROW PERCENTAGE		
		Name	Team	PPG	Name	Team	FG%	Name	Team	FT%
1937-38	NBA	Leroy Edwards	Osh	16.2						
1938-39	NBL	Leroy Edwards	Osh	11.9						
1939-40	NBL	Leroy Edwards	Osh	12.9						
1940-41	NBL	Ben Stephens	AG	11.0						
1941-42	NBL	Chuck Chuckovits	Tol	18.5						
1942-43	NBL	Bobby McDermott	FtW	13.7						
1943-44	NBL	Mel Riebe	Cle	17.9						
1944-45	NBL	Mel Riebe	Cle	20.2						
1945-46	NBL	Bob Carpenter	Osh	13.9				Herm Feutsch	Cle	.813
1946-47	NBL	George Mikan	Chi	16.5				Bruce Hale	Chi	.823
1946-47	BAA	Joe Fulks	Phi	23.2	Bob Feerick	Was	.401	Freddie Scolari	Was	.811
1947-48	NBL	George Mikan	Min	21.3				Hal Tidrick	Tol	.778
1947-48	BAA	Joe Fulks	Phi	22.1	Buddy Jeannette	Bal	.349	Stan Stutz	NY	.837
1948-49	NBL	Don Otten	TC	14.0				Frankie Brian	And	.785
1948-49	BAA	George Mikan	Min	28.3	Arnie Risen	Roch	.423	Bob Feerick	Was	.859
1949-50	NBA	George Mikan	Min	27.4	Alex Groza	Ind	.478	Max Zaslofsky	Chi	.843
1950-51	NBA	George Mikan	Min	28.4	Alex Groza	Ind	.470	Joe Fulks	Phi	.855
1951-52	NBA	Paul Arizin	Phi	25.4	Paul Arizin	Phi	.448	Bobby Wanzer	Roch	.904
1952-53	NBA	Neil Johnston	Phi	22.3	Neil Johnston	Phi	.452	Bill Sharman	Bos	.850
1953-54	NBA	Neil Johnston	Phi	24.4	Ed Macauley	Bos	.486	Bill Sharman	Bos	.844
1954-55	NBA	Neil Johnston	Phi	22.7	Larry Foust	FtW	.487	Bill Sharman	Bos	.897
1955-56	NBA	Bob Pettit	StL	25.7	Neil Johnston	Phi	.457	Bill Sharman	Bos	.867
1956-57	NBA	Paul Arizin	Phi	25.6	Neil Johnston	Phi	.447	Bill Sharman	Bos	.905
1957-58	NBA	George Yardley	Det	27.8	Jack Twyman	Cin	.452	Dolph Schayes	Syr	.904
1958-59	NBA	Bob Pettit	StL	29.2	Kenny Sears	NY	.490	Bill Sharman	Bos	.932
1959-60	NBA	Wilt Chamberlain	Phi	37.6	Kenny Sears	NY	.477	Dolph Schayes	Syr	.893
1960-61	NBA	Wilt Chamberlain	Phi	38.4	Wilt Chamberlain	Phi	.509	Bill Sharman	Bos	.921

Year	League	POINTS PER GAME Name	Team	PPG	FIELD GOAL PERCENTAGE Name	Team	FG%	FREE THROW PERCENTAGE Name	Team	FT%
1961-62	NBA	Wilt Chamberlain	Phi	50.4	Walt Bellamy	Chi	.519	Dolph Schayes	Syr	.896
1962-63	NBA	Wilt Chamberlain	SF	44.8	Wilt Chamberlain	SF	.528	Larry Costello	Syr	.881
1963-64	NBA	Wilt Chamberlain	SF	36.9	Jerry Lucas	Cin	.527	Oscar Robertson	Cin	.853
1964-65	NBA	Wilt Chamberlain	SF-Phi	34.7	Wilt Chamberlain	SF-Phi	.510	Larry Costello	Phi	.877
1965-66	NBA	Wilt Chamberlain	Phi	33.5	Wilt Chamberlain	Phi	.540	Larry Siegfried	Bos	.881
1966-67	NBA	Rick Barry	SF	35.6	Wilt Chamberlain	Phi	.683	Adrian Smith	Cin	.903
1967-68	NBA	Dave Bing	Det	27.1	Wilt Chamberlain	Phi	.595	Oscar Robertson	Cin	.873
1967-68	ABA	Connie Hawkins	Pit	26.8	Trooper Washington	Pit	.523	Charlie Beasley	Dal	.872
1968-69	NBA	Elvin Hayes	SD	28.4	Wilt Chamberlain	LA	.583	Larry Siegfried	Bos	.864
1968-69	ABA	Larry Jones	Den	28.4	Bill McGill	Den	.552	Rick Barry	Oak	.888
1969-70	NBA	Jerry West	LA	31.2	Johnny Green	Cin	.559	Flynn Robinson	Mil	.898
1969-70	ABA	Spencer Haywood	Den	30.0	Frank Card	Den	.527	Darel Carrier	Ky	.892
1970-71	NBA	Lew Alcindor (Jabbar)	Mil	31.7	Johnny Green	Cin	.587	Chet Walker	Chi	.859
1970-71	ABA	Dan Issel	KY	29.9	Zelmo Beaty	Utah	.555	Rick Barry	NY	.890
1971-72	NBA	Kareem Abdul-Jabbar	Mil	34.8	Wilt Chamberlain	LA	.649	Jack Marin	Bal	.894
1971-72	ABA	Charlie Scott	Va	34.6	Artis Gilmore	Ky	.598	Rick Barry	NY	.878
1972-73	NBA	Nate Archibald	KCO	34.9	Wilt Chamberlain	LA	.727	Rick Barry	GS	.902
1972-73	ABA	Julius Erving	Va	31.9	Artis Gilmore	Ky	.550	Bill Keller	Ind	.870
1973-74	NBA	Bob McAdoo	Buf	30.6	Bob McAdoo	Buf	.547	Ernie DiGregorio	Buf	.902
1973-74	ABA	Julius Erving	NY	27.4	Swen Nater	Va-SA	.552	Jimmy Jones	Utah	.884
1974-75	NBA	Bob McAdoo	Buf	34.5	Don Nelson	Bos	.539	Rick Barry	GS	.904
1974-75	ABA	George McGinnis	Ind	29.8	Bobby Jones	Den	.604	Mack Calvin	Den	.896
1975-76	NBA	Bob McAdoo	Buf	31.1	Wes Unseld	Was	.561	Rick Barry	GS	.923
1975-76	ABA	Julius Erving	NY	29.3						
1976-77	NBA	P. Maravich	NO	31.1	K. Abdul-Jabbar	LA	.579	E. DiGregorio	Buf	.945
1977-78	NBA	G. Gervin	SA	27.2	Bobby Jones	Den	.578	Rick Barry	GS	.924
1978-79	NBA	G. Gervin	SA	29.6	C. Maxwell	Bos	.584	Rick Barry	Hou	.947
1979-80	NBA	G. Gervin	SA	33.1	C. Maxwell	Bos	.609	Rick Barry	Hou	.935
1980-81	NBA	Adrian Dantley	Utah	30.7	Artis Gilmore	Chi	.670	Calvin Murphy	Hou	.958

Yearly Individual Leaders—Regular Season

The Warriors traded for the right to pick J.B. Carroll, here operating during a 46-point night against Swen Nater of San Diego, and made him the No. 1 pick before the **1980-81 season.** (*Golden State Warriors*)

REBOUNDS PER GAME

Year	League	Name	Team	Reb/G
1950-51	NBA	Dolph Schayes	Syr	16.4
1951-52	NBA	George Mikan	Min	13.5
1952-53	NBA	George Mikan	Min	14.4
1953-54	NBA	Harry Gallatin	NY	15.3
1954-55	NBA	Neil Johnston	Phi	15.1
1955-56	NBA	Maurice Stokes	Roch	16.3
1956-57	NBA	Bill Russell	Bos	19.6
1957-58	NBA	Bill Russell	Bos	22.7
1958-59	NBA	Bill Russell	Bos	23.0
1959-60	NBA	Wilt Chamberlain	Phi	27.0
1960-61	NBA	Wilt Chamberlain	Phi	27.2
1961-62	NBA	Wilt Chamberlain	Phi	25.7
1962-63	NBA	Wilt Chamberlain	SF	24.3
1963-64	NBA	Bill Russell	Bos	24.7
1964-65	NBA	Bill Russell	Bos	24.1
1965-66	NBA	Wilt Chamberlain	Phi	24.6

Year	League	Name	Team	Reb/G
1966-67	NBA	Wilt Chamberlain	Phi	24.2
1967-68	NBA	Wilt Chamberlain	Phi	23.8
1967-68	ABA	Mel Daniels	Min	15.6
1968-69	NBA	Wilt Chamberlain	LA	21.1
1968-69	ABA	Mel Daniels	Ind	16.5
1969-70	NBA	Elvin Hayes	SD	16.9
1969-70	ABA	Spencer Haywood	Den	19.5
1970-71	NBA	Wilt Chamberlain	LA	18.2
1970-71	ABA	Mel Daniels	Ind	18.0
1971-72	NBA	Wilt Chamberlain	LA	19.2
1971-72	ABA	Artis Gilmore	Ky	17.8
1972-73	NBA	Wilt Chamberlain	LA	18.6
1972-73	ABA	Artis Gilmore	Ky	17.5
1973-74	NBA	Elvin Hayes	Cap	18.1
1973-74	ABA	Artis Gilmore	Ky	18.3
1974-75	NBA	Wes Unseld	Was	14.8
1974-75	ABA	Swen Nater	SA	16.4
1975-76	ABA	Artis Gilmore	Ky	15.5
1975-76	NBA	K. Abdul-Jabbar	LA	16.9
1976-77	NBA	Bill Walton	Port	14.4
1977-78	NBA	Len Robinson	NO	15.7
1978-79	NBA	Moses Malone	Hous	17.6
1979-80	NBA	Sven Nater	SD	15.0
1980-81	NBA	Moses Malone	Hou	14.8

Blocked Shots

Year	League	Name	Team	Reb/G
1972-73	ABA	Artis Gilmore	Chi	3.2
1973-74	NBA	Elmore Smith	LA	4.9
1973-74	ABA	Caldwell Jones	SD	4.0
1974-75	NBA	K. Abdul-Jabbar	LA	3.3
1974-75	ABA	Artis Gilmore	Ky	3.2
1975-76	NBA	K. Abdul-Jabbar	LA	4.1
1976-77	NBA	Bill Walton	Port	3.3
1977-78	NBA	George Johnson	NJ	3.4
1978-79	NBA	K. Abdul-Jabbar	LA	4.0
1979-80	NBA	K. Abdul-Jabbar	LA	3.4
1980-81	NBA	George Johnson	SA	3.4

Yearly Individual Leaders—Regular Season

ASSISTS PER GAME

Year	League	Name	Team	Ass./G
1946-47	BAA	Ernie Calverly	Prov	3.4
1947-48	BAA	Ernie Calverly	Prov	2.5
1948-49	BAA	Bob Davies	Roch	5.4
1949-50	NBA	Andy Phillip	Chi	5.8
1950-51	NBA	Andy Phillip	Phi	6.3
1951-52	NBA	Andy Phillip	Phi	8.2
1952-53	NBA	Bob Cousy	Bos	7.7
1953-54	NBA	Bob Cousy	Bos	7.2
1954-55	NBA	Bob Cousy	Bos	7.8
1955-56	NBA	Bob Cousy	Bos	8.9
1956-57	NBA	Bob Cousy	Bos	7.5
1957-58	NBA	Bob Cousy	Bos	7.1
1958-59	NBA	Bob Cousy	Bos	8.6
1959-60	NBA	Bob Cousy	Bos	9.5
1960-61	NBA	Oscar Robertson	Cin	9.7
1961-62	NBA	Oscar Robertson	Cin	11.4
1962-63	NBA	Guy Rodgers	SF	10.4
1963-64	NBA	Oscar Robertson	Cin	11.0
1964-65	NBA	Oscar Robertson	Cin	11.5
1965-66	NBA	Oscar Robertson	Cin	11.1
1966-67	NBA	Guy Rodgers	Chi	11.2
1967-68	NBA	Wilt Chamberlain	Phi	8.6
1967-68	ABA	Larry Brown	NO	6.5
1968-69	NBA	Oscar Robertson	Cin	9.8
1968-69	ABA	Larry Brown	Oak	7.1
1969-70	NBA	Lenny Wilkens	Sea	9.1
1969-70	ABA	Larry Brown	Was	7.1
1970-71	NBA	Norm Van Lier	Cin	10.1
1970-71	ABA	Bill Melchionni	NY	8.3
1971-72	NBA	Jerry West	LA	9.7
1971-72	ABA	Bill Melchionni	NY	8.4
1972-73	NBA	Nate Archibald	KCO	11.4
1972-73	ABA	Bill Melchionni	NY	7.5
1973-74	NBA	Ernie DiGregorio	Buf	8.2
1973-74	ABA	Al Smith	Den	8.2
1974-75	NBA	Kevin Porter	Was	8.0

Year	League	Name	Team	Ass./G
1974-75	ABA	Mack Calvin	Den	7.7
1975-76	NBA	Don Buse	Ind	8.2
1975-76	NBA	Donn Watts	Sea	8.1
1976-77	NBA	Don Buse	Ind	8.2
1977-78	NBA	Kevin Porter	Det-NJ	10.2
1978-79	NBA	Kevin Porter	Det	13.4
1979-80	NBA	M. Richardson	NY	10.1
1980-81	NBA	Kevin Porter	Wash	9.1

Norm Van Lier, whose hustle sparked the Chicago Bulls in the '70s, drives for the basket against the Knicks. (*Chicago Bulls*)

		3-POINT FIELD GOALS			3-POINT FIELD GOAL PERCENTAGE		
Year	League	Name	Team	3-Pt. FG	Name	Team	%
1967-68	ABA	Les Selvage	Ana	147	Darel Carrier	Ky	.357
1968-69	ABA	Louie Dampier	Ky	199	Darel Carrier	Ky	.379
1969-70	ABA	Louie Dampier	Ky	198	Darel Carrier	Ky	.375
1970-71	ABA	George Lehmann	Car	154	George Lehmann	Car	.403
1971-72	ABA	Glen Combs	Utah	103	Glen Combs	Utah	.406
1972-73	ABA	Bill Keller	Ind	71	Glen Combs	Utah	.381
1973-74	NBA						
1973-74	ABA	Bo Lamar	SD	69	Louie Dampier	Ky	.387
1974-75	NBA						
1974-75	ABA	Bill Keller	Ind	80	Billy Shepherd	Mem	.420
1975-76							
1976-77							
1977-78							
1978-79							
1979-80	NBA	Brian Taylor	SD	90	Fred Brown	Sea	.443
1980-81	NBA	Mike Bratz	Cleve	51	Brian Taylor	SD	.383

Steals

Year	League	Name	Team	Per Game
1972-73	ABA	Billy Cunningham	Car	2.6
1973-74	NBA	Larry Steele	Port	2.7
1973-74	ABA	Ted McClain	Car	3.0
1974-75	NBA	Rick Barry	GS	2.9
1974-75	ABA	Brian Taylor	NY	2.8
1975-76	NBA	Don Watts	Sea	3.2
1976-77	NBA	Don Buse	Ind	3.5
1977-78	NBA	Ron Lee	Phoenix	2.7
1978-79	NBA	M. L. Carr	Detroit	2.5
1979-80	NBA	M. Richardson	NY	3.2
1980-81	NBA	Magic Johnson	LA	3.4

Bibliography

Axthelm, Pete. *The City Game.* Harper & Row, 1970.

Barry, Rick (with Bill Libby). *Confessions of a Basketball Gypsy.* Prentice-Hall, 1972.

Bradley, Bill. *Life on the Run.* Quadrangle, 1976.

Cohen, Richard M., Deutsch, Jordan A., Neft, David S., and Johnson, Roland T., editors. *The Sports Encyclopedia: Pro Basketball.* Grosset & Dunlap, 1975.

Cohen, Stanley. *The Game They Played.* Farrar, Straus and Giroux, 1977.

Harris, Merv. *The Lonely Heroes: Pro Basketball's Great Centers.* Viking Press, 1975.

Hollander, Zander, editor. *The Modern Encyclopedia of Basketball.* Doubleday, 1979.

_____. *The Pro Basketball Encyclopedia.* Doubleday, 1979.

Holzman, Red (with Leonard Lewin). *A View from the Bench.* Norton, 1980.

Koppett, Leonard. *24 Seconds to Shoot: An Informal History of the NBA.* Macmillan, 1971.

_____. *The Essence of the Game Is Deception.* Little, Brown, 1971.

Liss, Howard. *The Pocket Book of Pro Basketball, '80-'81.* Pocket Books, 1980.

Libby, Bill. *Goliath: The Wilt Chamberlain Story.* Dodd, Mead, 1977.

McCallum, John D. *College Basketball USA: Since 1892.* Stein and Day, 1978, updated 1980.

Rosen, Charles. *God, Man and Basketball Jones: The Thinking Fan's Guide to Professional Basketball.* Holt, Rinehart & Winston, 1979.

_____. *Scandals of '51.* Holt, Rinehart & Winston, 1978.

Rudman, Daniel, editor. *Take It to the Hoop: A Basketball Anthology.* North Atlantic Books, 1980.

Russell, Bill (with Taylor Branch). *Second Wind: The Memoirs of an Opinionated Man.* Random House, 1979.

Winick, Matt, editor. *Official 1980-81 NBA Guide.* Sporting News Publishing Co., 1980.

Index